Projecting Morphology

Stanford Studies in Morphology and the Lexicon

A series edited by
Farrel Ackerman
Beth Levin
Andrew Spencer
Arnold Zwicky

The goal of this series is to provide linguists and researchers in related areas with thoeretically informed works that focus on morphology as an independent subdiscipline, as well as on the interface of morphology with the lexicon, syntax, and semantics.

Projecting Morphology

edited by

Louisa Sadler
Andrew Spencer

CSLI
PUBLICATIONS
Center for the Study of
Language and Information
Stanford, California

Center for the Study of Language and Information
Leland Stanford Junior University
Printed in the United States
08 07 06 05 04 1 2 3 4 5

Library of Congress Cataloging-in-Publication Data

Projecting morphology /
by Louisa Sadler and Andrew Spencer (eds.).

p. cm. – (Stanford studies in morphology and the lexicon)

Includes bibliographical references and indexes.

ISBN 1-57586-470-3 (pbk. : alk. paper)
ISBN 1-57586-469-X (cloth : alk. paper)

1. Grammar, Comparative and general – Morphology. 2. Grammar, Comparative and general – Syntax. 3. Lexical-functional grammar. I. Sadler, Louisa. II. Spencer, Andrew. III. Series.

P241.P76 2004
415′.9–dc22 2004022190
CIP

∞ The acid-free paper used in this book meets the minimum requirements of the American National Standard for Information Sciences—Permanence of Paper for Printed Library Materials, ANSI Z39.48-1984.

CSLI was founded in 1983 by researchers from Stanford University, SRI International, and Xerox PARC to further the research and development of integrated theories of language, information, and computation. CSLI headquarters and CSLI Publications are located on the campus of Stanford University.

CSLI Publications reports new developments in the study of language, information, and computation. Please visit our web site at
http://cslipublications.stanford.edu/
for comments on this and other titles, as well as for changes and corrections by the author and publisher.

Contents

Contributors

FARRELL ACKERMAN: Department of Linguistics, University of California, San Diego, 9500 Gilman Drive, #0108 La Jolla, CA 92093-0108, USA
ackerman@ling.ucsd.edu

MIRIAM BUTT: Fachbreich Sprachwissenschaft, Universität Konstanz, Fach 184, 78457 Konstanz, Germany
miriam.butt@uni-konstanz.de

ANETTE FRANK: DFKI GmbH, Stuhlsatzenhausweg 3, D-66123 Saarbrücken, Germany
frank@dfki.de

MARÍA-EUGENIA NIÑO: CCS 11348, PO Box 025323, Miami, FL 33102-5323, USA
menino@cantv.net

RACHEL NORDLINGER: Department of Linguistics and Applied Linguistics, University of Melbourne, VIC 3010, Australia
racheln@unimelb.edu.au

LOUISA SADLER: Department of Language and Linguistics, University of Essex, Wivenhoe Park, Colchester, CO4 3SQ, Essex, UK
louisa@essex.ac.uk

FRÉDÉRIQUE SEGOND: Xerox Research Centre Europe, 6, chemin de Maupertuis, 38240 Meylan, France
frederique.segond@xrce.xerox.com

PETER SELLS: Department of Linguistics, Stanford University, Stanford, CA 94305-2150, USA
sells@stanford.edu

ANDREW SPENCER: Department of Language and Linguistics, University of Essex, Wivenhoe Park, Colchester, CO4 3SQ, Essex, UK
spena@essex.ac.uk

GREGORY STUMP: Department of English, University of Kentucky, 1215 Patterson Office Tower, Lexington, KY 40506-0027, USA
gstump@uky.edu

ANNIE ZAENEN: Palo Alto Research Center, QSC/ISTL, 3333 Coyote Hill Road, Palo Alto, CA 94304, USA
zaenen@parc.com

Preface and Acknowledgements

This volume brings together a number of papers which examine problems and issues in the interface between (mainly inflectional) morphology and the syntax, within the architecture of Lexical Functional Grammar (LFG). The idea for this volume grew out of some lively debate at the morphology workshop at the LFG 2000 conference at the University of California, Berkeley, and the present collection contains both new work addressing the morphology-syntax interface and two important, previously published papers on this issue.

We would like to thank all of our contributors for their cooperation, patience and general collegiality in the preparation of this volume. What seemed at first to be a simple task has, inevitably, involved a number of complexities and delays.

We have received help from a number of sources in preparing this volume.

We gratefully acknowledge the time and effort of the anonymous reviewers, who have done much to improve the quality of the volume, the publishers Niemeyer and Mouton de Gruyter for granting us permission to reprint, and of course Dikran Karagueuzian and his team at CSLI Publications.

Finally, we are extremely grateful for the invaluable and extensive assistance in editing, indexing and typesetting this volume provided by Ryo Otoguro, and to the Department of Language and Linguistics at the University of Essex for financially supporting Ryo's work as editorial assistant.

1

Introduction

LOUISA SADLER AND ANDREW SPENCER

This volume brings together papers exploring the interface between morphology and syntax within the architecture of Lexical Functional Grammar (LFG) (Bresnan 2001). Several of the papers are based on talks presented at the Workshop on Morphology in LFG at the LFG2000 Conference, University of California at Berkeley. The clear separation between the morphological and syntactic components of the grammar is reflected in LFG by the centrality of the principle of lexical integrity, which holds that the leaves of c-structure are complete, fully inflected words. In addition the recognition of the key, independent contribution of morphology to relational structure, and the importance placed on the description and analysis of morphologically rich languages, have been central to the development of LFG since its inception. It is hoped that the present volume will make some further contribution to our understanding of the interplay between morphology and syntax.

An important aspect of the LFG model is that the separation of the levels of constituent structure (c-structure) and functional structure (f-structure) makes it possible to represent the fact that different languages may express essentially the same grammatical properties in very different ways. Put in another way, external differences in expression structure such as differences in word order or in the use of morphological means of expression, do not necessarily equate to differences in internal or relational (syntactic) structure. For instance, we might find that three languages express the grammaticalized property 'Future Tense' by purely morphological means (synthetic realization), by purely syntactic means (analytic realization) or by some combination of the

Projecting Morphology.
Louisa Sadler and Andrew Spencer (Eds.).

two (for instance by means of a periphrastic construction which uses dedicated morphological forms). In principle at least, it seems that the LFG architecture is ideally suited to capturing what is common to the languages, in the form of an attribute TENSE FUTURE in f-structure, as well as what is different, at the level of c-structure.

In fact, early analyses treated auxiliary verbs as PRED bearing elements under a raising analysis (Bresnan 1982; Falk 1984). On this approach, the English auxiliary *have* subcategorises for an XCOMP headed by a past participle (e.g by placing the constraint ($\uparrow$ XCOMP PART) $=_c$ PASTP). On this view, however, the f-structures associated with sentences with synthetically expressed tense/aspects differ radically from those associated with sentences with analytically or periphrastically expressed tense/aspects, running counter to the intuition that there are very significant functional similarities between them. Some later work, on the other hand, treats auxiliary verbs as contributing only grammatical information to the f-structure projected by the main verb, that is, as non-PRED bearing elements (Bresnan 2001; King 1995).

These considerations form the starting point for the first paper in our collection, which is concerned with the treatment of periphrastic verbal constructions within the context of the parallel grammar development project PARGRAM, and specifically in response to the question of how to translate between languages with different modes of expression for temporal and aspectual attributes. The paper by Butt, Niño and Segond, first appeared in conference proceedings from 1996 (Butt et al. 1996) and by reprinting it here we hope to make more widely available some of the discussion of grammar parallelism and the factorisation of information across levels which is involved when implemented LFG grammars are developed. Taking as their point of departure (key differences in) the expression of temporal and aspectual information in French, German and English, Butt et al. propose a very flat f-structure approach in which temporal and aspectual auxiliaries contribute grammatical feature information (for example, in *The driver will have turned the lever*, the string *will have* corresponds to the f-structure attribute (TENSE) = FUTPERF), but do not themselves have PRED values. The leading idea here is to maximise the extent to which f-structures are crosslinguistically similar. In order to capture the morphosyntactic selectional requirements imposed by auxiliary verbs, Butt et al. posit a further projection, the μ projection, which permits these purely parochial, language specific constraints to be captured at m-structure (itself, an attribute-value structure). In the architecture which Butt et al. introduce, the μ projection places nodes of c-structure and m-structure in correspondence.

The following paper, which is also being reprinted, takes up and explores further the idea of a specifically morphological or morphosyntactic projection, the m-structure (Frank and Zaenen 2002). Frank and Zaenen explore further the consequences of the architectural assumptions made by Butt et al. under which the m-structure is projected from nodes of the c-structure. They note that the specific architectural proposal of Butt et al., which projects the m-structure from the c-structure encounters some quite severe difficulties in relation to certain long-distance agreement phenomena (on the assumption that agreement features such as NUM, GEND, and so on, belong in the m-structure). The data at issue involve long-distance past participle agreement in French as illustrated in (1) (Frank and Zaenen this volume: 30):

(1) Les enfants adorent les histoires qu'on sait bien qu'on leur a déjà raconté*(es) mille fois.
Children are fond of the stories that one knows perfectly (that) one has told them already a thousand times

The relative pronoun is assigned the OBJ function by means of a functional uncertainty equation at f-structure, and a past participle must agree if it is preceded by the OBJ which it subcategorises, as in (1). But if agreement features properly belong to m-structure, then on the model of Butt et al. it is necessary both to replicate much of the structure of f-structure at this level, and permit functional uncertainty equations over m-structures. Frank and Zaenen propose instead that m-structure is projected off f-structure. In this sequenced architecture, morphological constraints on syntax can be defined locally, as morphological information is directly associated with the f-structure that it relates to, without structural duplication in the m-structure. Accompanying the proposal for a sequenced architecture in which m-structure is projected from f-structure, Frank and Zaenen provide a detailed analysis of French auxiliary constructions within this architecture. A consequence of the sequenced architecture is that since the f-structure is flat, the hierarchical morphological structure of complex auxiliary constructions can only be defined in the lexicon, with the result that some verb forms are lexically associated with complex m-structure equations, as opposed to m-structure annotations in the phrase structure rules.

These two reprinted papers neatly set the scene for the rest of the collection, an examination of the morphology-syntax interface. The last three papers all presuppose a model of morphology that departs in important respects from the morpheme-based model inherited from American Structuralism. For a great many purposes in syntax (and indeed in morphology) little harm is done by assuming that words are inflected by means of affixal morphemes which have a set meaning or feature content and which can thus be thought of as lexical entries. However, this classical model runs into difficulties when we start looking for a general theory of inflection, as is widely recognized in morphological circles. As Spencer points out in his chapter 'Morphology - an overview of central concepts', many morphologists reject the view of morphemes as lexical entries, at least for inflection. Thus, rather than saying that the *-s* of *cats* is an object which contributes the meaning 'Plural' to the word *cat*, many morphologists argue for a realizational theory, under which there is some process or set of processes which can act on the root of a lexeme (*cat*, *man*, *sheep*) to deliver the appropriate plural form. On this conception the *-s* of *cats* is simply a marker indicating, or helping to indicate, the value of the [Number] attribute.

The realizational approach[1] has been adopted in some form or other by all the most influential approaches to inflectional morphology. Having summarized the morpheme-based and lexeme-based approaches, Spencer surveys a number of widely-acknowledged difficulties with the classical morpheme doctrine. For example, we may have meaningless morphs or zero (morph-less) realizations of feature values. In addition, a morph may realize two or more features simultaneously (cumulation), and a single feature value may spread over several distinct morphs (multiple exponence). The conclusion is that we must separate form from function (the Separation Hypothesis, (Beard 1995)): morphs are not Saussurean signs. In effect, all inflectional affix strings constitute 'constructional idioms', whose overall meaning may very well be non-compositional. Spencer then summarizes the most carefully worked out of current realizational, paradigm-based approaches, Stump's theory of Paradigm Function Morphology (Stump 2001). The one:one mapping of form and function in classical morpheme theory can be thought of as a limiting case of the many:many mappings found in realizational models, so that merely pointing to instances in which a unique feature value is expressed by a unique affix cannot by itself adjudicate between the two models. The conclusion to Spencer's chapter contributes to the debate over morphemes by asking under what conditions we might be tempted to prefer a morpheme-based analysis. He argues that such a situation might conceivably arise given a suitable set of coincidences, though advocates of morphemes seem not to have looked for such cases.

In recent years a number of researchers have pursued the question of periphrastic constructions in LFG. Ackerman and Webelhuth (1998)

[1]This is often, but perhaps somewhat misleadingly, known as the WORD-AND-PARADIGM approach.

discuss auxiliary + participle constructions such as the English perfect *has walked* and observe that it is generally difficult or entirely arbitrary to associate a particular meaning or feature value with an auxiliary or participial form. Rather, the construction as a whole expresses feature values such as ASPECT PERFECT or VOICE PASSIVE. This leads them to analyse such periphrastic constructions in the same way that morphologists analyse inflected word forms in realizational frameworks. The auxiliary and the participial morphology do not themselves constitute 'lexical entries', but rather serve as realizations of (an ensemble of) feature values (what Blevins (2001) has called 'Realizational Lexicalism'). Much of Ackerman and Webelhuth's empirical justification came from a study of the German passive construction. However, a particularly interesting set of facts is revealed in the way that Latin expresses the passive voice. Imperfective verbs form a synthetic passive, but the perfective forms are synthetic only in the active voice. The passive of perfectives is expressed by means of the copular verb and a perfective passive participle. A simple way of looking at this would be to say that the conjugation system lacks the perfective passive subparadigm as such and the meaning that such a subparadigm would express is given by a syntactic copula + participle construction which happens to have essentially the same meaning (by virtue of the 'perfective passive' meaning of the participle). However, as pointed out by Börjars, Vincent and Chapman (1997) this can't be the right solution. Latin has deponent verbs, which are passive in form but active in meaning. Such verbs form their perfective tense series analytically, just as though they were passive in meaning. But the 'perfective passive' participle can't have a passive meaning in deponents, and this undercuts the analysis of ordinary perfective passives as purely syntactic constructions. Sadler and Spencer (2001) argued that these facts provide motivation for the approach to proposed in Ackerman and Webelhuth (1998).

One of the claims made by Sadler and Spencer (2001) is that the Latin data motivate a systematic distinction between grammatical properties which are essentially syntactic, such as the f-structure attributes ('s-features') and features which regulate morphological form ('m-features'). In many cases there is a straightforward mapping between the two sets, as when a verb form realizing the morphological feature [Tense: Past] contributes the f-structure information TENSE PAST. However, there are numerous cases of mismatches. Schwarze (1996) drew attention to the fact that a present tense form auxiliary + perfect participle often realizes what is effectively a simple past tense form, paradigmatically opposed to synthetic tense/aspect/mood (TAM) forms such as present, imperfective past and future. For instance, in

Spoken French the construction *a vu* 'have-PRES see-PERF PART' means not just 'has seen' but also the simple past 'saw'. Similar facts motivate the proposals of Butt et al. and Frank and Zaenen and indeed the previous work on the m-structure f-structure distinction is also clearly relevant to Sadler and Spencer's distinction between two sets of features. Spencer (2001) demonstrates that this phenomenon is particularly widespread in the Slavic languages. For instance, in Czech there is no present perfect construction and the simple past is expressed by means of a present tense form auxiliary ('be') and a participle. The only conclusion that can be drawn is that a simplex f-structure TAM is expressed by a periphrastic construction. Spencer (2003b) shows that in Bulgarian whole clauses are used to express TAM attributes such as 'negative future'.

In effect, what Ackerman and Webelhuth (1998), Börjars et al. (1997), Sadler and Spencer (2001), Spencer (2001), Spencer (2003b) and others are claiming is that certain syntactic constructions (‘') behave as though they were part of the inflectional paradigm of the lexeme. This raises a number of issues, the most central of which is 'how do we distinguish from ordinary syntactic constructions?'[2] For example, what is to stop us from saying that *Mary wants to leave* represents the desiderative mood of the verb lexeme LEAVE, expressed periphrastically (see also Blevins (2001)).

This is the question addressed in the chapter by Ackerman and Stump. Following Ackerman and Webelhuth (1998) they argue for an inferential-realizational model of verbal , on a par with the WORD-&-PARADIGM models of word inflection. Syntactic constructions are allowed to be part of the definition of the paradigm of a lexeme (part of its PARADIGM FUNCTION in Stump's (2001) terms). In order to achieve this interleaving Ackerman and Stump adopt a particular version of the separation between syntactic and morphological properties. For any given lexeme they distinguish a content paradigm and a form paradigm. The content paradigm expresses the semantically interpretable properties, corresponding to Sadler and Spencer's (2001) 'syntactic features'. The form paradigm regulates the way inflected word forms are constructed (cf. 'm-features'). In the absence of periphrasis or other mismatches there is a more-or-less trivial mapping between the two paradigms ('default paradigm linkage') but in the case of periphrasis we find deviations from this default, as when a cell in the morphological paradigm is filled by a periphrastic construction.

[2]Many of these issues are explored in the collected papers in Ackerman, Blevins and Stump (eds.) (to appear).

Ackerman and Stump describe three sufficient criteria for periphrastic constructions, and illustrate these with a remarkable array of data, principally from the Uralic language family. The first criterion is that of 'feature intersectivity'. A simple example is provided by Japanese conjugation (Spencer 2003a). Japanese verbs are inflected for tense ({present, past}), status ({plain, polite}) and polarity ({affirmative, negative}). However, at most two of the marked features can be expressed synthetically on a Japanese verb: *tabemasen* 'eat-NEG-POLITE', *tabemasita* 'eat-PAST-POLITE', *tabenakatta* 'eat-PAST-NEG'. However, to express all three marked values on one verb we need to use a periphrastic construction with the copula: *tabemasen desita* 'eat-NEG-POLITE COP-PAST-POLITE'. The logic of the verb paradigm leads us to expect a cell labelled 'past, polite, negative', but that cell can't be filled because of the constraint that only two marked suffixes are allowed on one verb root, so that the has to occupy that cell.

The second criterion is that of non-compositionality: one conclusion to be drawn from cases such as Spoken French *a vu* and their kin is that we are dealing with a kind of idiomatic construction. Ackerman and Stump claim that idiomaticity of this sort is a sufficient criterion for a periphrastic construction. In some respects, this is the central criterion. The recognition that non-compositional constructions ('idioms') are used to express inflectional properties can be thought of as an extension of the Separation Hypothesis, thus establishing an important parallel between periphrastic expressions and affixation.

The third criterion is more subtle: 'distributed exponence'. Ackerman and Stump argue that it is characteristic for syntactic constructions to express one and the same attribute value in more than one location (this is essentially what agreement is). They then describe the negative future construction in the Uralic language Udmurt. In this language (as is very common cross-linguistically) person-number features are cumulated on a single affix in most finite verb forms (and possessed noun forms). The negative future is expressed by a negation auxiliary and the lexical verb, in which the person features are realized on the auxiliary, while the lexical verb form expresses singular/plural number. Such a split of person from number is very uncharacteristic of Udmurt, or indeed of Uralic languages generally. Moreover, such behaviour is not what would be expected of a purely syntactic construction. It would be surprising, for instance, to find a language with a Uralic (or Indo-European) person-number system which expressed a sentence such as *Mary wants to leave* by realizing '3rd person' on WANT and 'singular' on LEAVE. Ackerman and Stump therefore conclude that such deviations from the expected pattern are indicative of a periphrastic construction.

The paper by Sadler and Nordlinger is essentially focussed on the interface between inflectional morphology and f-structure, and has as its empirical domain the phenomenon of case stacking, in which a word may bear multiple case markers, each one relating to a successively higher f-structure relationship. A simple example of case stacking is shown in (2), from Guugu Yalanji. Here the nominal *Dick-ndamun-du* is specified for genitive case, signalling its (possessor) role in relation to the f-structure head *kaya-* 'dog', and also bears ergative case in agreement with the head.

(2) Dicki-ndamun-du kaya-ngka
Dick-GEN-ERG dog-ERG
Dick's dog (Plank 1995: 65)

The paper takes as its starting point the analysis of case stacking developed in Nordlinger (1998) and known as the constructive case model. Nordlinger's theory involves essentially two ideas: the use of inside-out constraints associated with words (or 'parts' of words) to enable nominal constituents to define the f-structure context within which they appear; and a principle specifying how the discrete pieces of f-structure information contributed word-internally must combine together, the Principle of Morphological Composition. In its original formulation, the principle appealed to operations which did not fall within the LFG formalism. The paper in this volume extends the previous work by Nordlinger (1998) by showing how the insights of this principle can be incorporated into a model of the morphology/syntax interface which is fully compatible with the LFG formalism. Sadler and Nordlinger take the morphology-syntax interface to associate f-descriptions with morphological descriptions which take the form of pairings of lemmas with sets of morphological tags or features (that is, paradigm cell or the output of morphological analysis). Using a new sort of designator, $\leftarrow_s$, to denote the f-structure of the left sister, they show how the correct interaction of f-structure information associated with different case markers can be captured.

A recurrent theme of the chapter by Ackerman and Stump is that apparently syntactic constructions behave rather as though they were pieces of morphology. The lesson from Frank and Zaenen's chapter (and expanded upon in Sadler and Spencer (2001) and Spencer (2001)) is that in LFG we can profitably treat such constructions as realizations of f-sructure attributes. Sells' chapter takes up these themes against the background of a number of intriguing construction in Swedish morphosyntax, specifically the V2 phenomenon, periphrastic tense/aspect forms, and the multiple realization of tense forms and the 'parasitic supine'.

Sells argues that the V2 construction in Swedish is triggered by an f-structure attribute that is realized as a complex combination of syntactic configuration and morphological forms (specifically, the construction is headed by a finite verb or the adverb *kanske* 'maybe'). Swedish expresses the perfect aspect with an auxiliary, HA 'have', which selects a non-finite verb complement (the 'supine'). This shows some of the by now familiar properties of periphrastic constructions. However, it is also associated with the phenomenon of the 'parasitic supine'. A number of verbs, such as VILJA 'want' select a bare form verb complement. When such a verb is itself in the perfect aspect, and hence in the supine form, it optionally permits its complement verb to appear in the supine form rather than the expected base form: *Han har velat läsa/läst den* 'He has wanted-SUPINE read-BASE/SUPINE it' ('He has wanted to read it'). This is an instance of multiple exponence in the syntax: the property of 'perfect aspect' is expressed on both VILJA and LÄSA (as well as on the auxiliary).

Sells analyses these phenomena within a model of LFG in which f-structure-c-structure relations are captured by means of Optimality Theoretic constraints. He makes the interesting suggestion that multiple (indeed, universal) exponence is the default but that suitably ranked constraints serve to rule out most instances of multiple exponence. Sells' chapter illustrates the point that the program of realizational lexicalism isn't wedded to a particular model of morphology. What is important is the idea that pieces of syntax can serve the needs of morphology and can exhibit the behaviour of typically morphological objects.

Much of the work reported in this volume represents a new departure for LFG morphosyntax, though one informed by a much earlier descriptive tradition. Clearly, none of these papers represents the last word on their subject, but we hope that they will stimulate a fresh way of looking at old problems and that the perspective they introduce will help us to unearth further patterns and regularities that might remain undetected by linguists working from a more conventional viewpoint.

References

Ackerman, Farrell and Gert Webelhuth. 1998. *A Theory of Predicates*. Stanford, CA: CSLI Publications.

Ackerman, Farrell and James P. Blevins and Gregory T. Stump, ed. to appear. *Periphrasis and Paradigms*. Stanford, CA: CSLI Publications.

Beard, Robert. 1995. *Lexeme-Morpheme Base Morphology*. Stony Brook, NY: SUNY Press.

Blevins, James P. 2001. Realisation-based lexicalism (F. Ackerman and G. Webelhuth, A Theory of Predicates). *Journal of Lingustics* 37:355–365.

Börjars, Kersti, Nigel Vincent, and Carol Chapman. 1997. Paradigms, Periphrasis and Pronominal Inflection: a feature-based account. In G. Booij and J. van Marle, eds., *Yearbook of Morphology 1996*, pages 155–180. Kluwer Academic Publishers.

Bresnan, Joan, ed. 1982. *The Mental Representation of Grammatical Relations*. Cambridge, MA: MIT Press.

Bresnan, Joan. 2001. *Lexical Functional Syntax*. Oxford: Blackwell.

Butt, Miriam, María-Eugenia Niño, and Frédérique Segond. 1996. Multilingual Processing of Auxiliaries in LFG. In D. Gibbon, ed., *Natural Language Processing and Speech Technology*, pages 111–122. Berlin: Mouton de Gruyter.

Falk, Yehuda N. 1984. The English Auxiliary System: A Lexical-Functional Analysis. *Language* 60:483–509.

Frank, Anette and Annie Zaenen. 2002. Tense in LFG: Syntax and Morphology. In H. Kamp and U. Reyle, eds., *How we say WHEN it happens*, pages 17–53. Niemeyer.

King, Tracy Holloway. 1995. *Configuring Topic and Focus in Russian*. Stanford, CA: CSLI Publications.

Nordlinger, Rachel. 1998. *Constructive Case: Evidence from Australian Languages*. Stanford, CA: CSLI Publications.

Plank, Frans, ed. 1995. *Double Case: Agreement by Suffixaufnahme*. Oxford: Oxford University Press.

Sadler, Louisa and Andrew Spencer. 2001. Syntax as an exponent of morphological features. In G. Booij and J. van Marle, eds., *Yearbook of Morphology 2000*, pages 71–97. Kluwer Academic Publishers.

Schwarze, Christoph. 1996. The syntax of Romance auxiliaries. In M. Butt and T. H. King, eds., *Proceedings of LFG 1996*. CSLI Publications, Stanford, CA.

Spencer, Andrew. 2001. The Word-and-Paradigm approach to morphosyntax. *Transactions of the Philological Society* 99:279–313.

Spencer, Andrew. 2003a. Paradigm-based lexicalism: Negation in Japanese. Unpublished ms. University of Essex.

Spencer, Andrew. 2003b. Periphrastic Paradigms in Bulgarian. In U. Junghanns and L. Szucsich, eds., *Syntactic Structures and Morphological Information*, pages 249–282. Berlin: Mouton de Gruyter.

Stump, Gregory. 2001. *Inflectional Morphology: A Theory of Paradigm Structure*. Cambridge: Cambridge University Press.

2

Multilingual Processing of Auxiliaries within LFG

MIRIAM BUTT, MARÍA-EUGENIA NIÑO, FRÉDÉRIQUE SEGOND

2.1 Introduction

This paper takes up an old debate and proposes a solution based on an implementation for German (IMS, Stuttgart), French (RANK Xerox, Grenoble), and English (Xerox PARC, Palo Alto) within the cooperative parallel grammar development project PARGRAM: are auxiliaries simply main verbs with special properties (Gazdar et al. (1982), Pullum and Wilson (1977), Ross (1967)), or should they instantiate a special category AUX (Akmajian et al. (1979), Chomsky (1957))?[1] In current lexical approaches, for example, Lexical-Functional-Grammar (LFG) and Head-driven Phrase Structure Grammar (HPSG), auxiliaries (e.g. *have*, *be*) and modals (e.g. *must*, *should*) have traditionally been treated as *raising* verbs, which are marked as special in some way: in HPSG through an [AUX: +] feature (Pollard and Sag 1994),[2] in LFG

This paper originally appeared in *Natural Language Processing and Speech Technology*, ed. Dafydd Gibbon (Berlin: Mouton de Gruyter, 1996), 111–122.

[1]We would like to thank Mark Johnson, Ron Kaplan, and Annie Zaenen for many helpful discussions with regard to auxiliaries and word order. We are also grateful to Judith Berman, Tracy King, John Maxwell, Paula Newman, Christian Rohrer and the anonymous reviewer for further input and discussions.

[2]Newer work in HPSG on French (e.g., Abeillé and Godard (1994)) and Italian (Monachesi (1995)) has moved away from this particular implementation, instead relying on the mechanism of *argument composition* first introduced by Hinrichs and Nakazawa (1990) for German. While these approaches advocate a "flat" represen-

Projecting Morphology.
Louisa Sadler and Andrew Spencer (Eds.).

(Bresnan 1982) by a difference in PRED value. Newer work within LFG (Bresnan (1995), T.H. King (1995)) has been moving away from the raising approach towards an analysis where auxiliaries are elements which contribute to the clause tense/aspect, agreement, or voice information, but not a subcategorization frame.[3] This view is also in line with approaches within GB (Government-Binding), which see auxiliaries simply as possible instantiations of the functional category I (e.g., Roberts 1983, 1985) for some early formulations), and in fact reverts to a traditional view that considers auxiliaries as simple morphological markers.[4]

In LFG, morphology and phrase structure are considered loci of language variation, while information about grammatical functions (f-structure) and semantics (σ-structure) is considered a more crosslinguistic invariant. In order to construct analyses as *parallel* as possible for each of the languages (English, French, German) we adopt and expand on the newer directions within LFG in that we treat auxiliaries as functional elements, not as raising verbs. This allows parallel representations for sentences which would yield varying structures for each of the three languages under the raising analysis (see section 3.1). One very obvious advantage of such parallel analyses lies in the area of machine translation (MT), another in the subsequent construction of semantic representations for tense and aspect (see section 3.2).

The invariant contribution of auxiliaries to (complex) tense is modeled in a crosslinguistically realistic manner at the level of f(unctional)-structure, while language particular, idiosyncratic syntactic properties (e.g. number of auxiliaries involved, VP-deletion, VP-fronting) continue to be handled by phrase structure rules. In addition, morphological wellformedness conditions imposed by an auxiliary on its "dependents" are modeled at a further level of projection *m(orphological)-structure*. Our implementation thus combines the advantages of the older analyses on which LFG (Bresnan 1982, Falk 1984) and HPSG (Pollard and Sag 1994) treatments of auxiliaries are based, while abstracting away from

tation of auxiliaries, they do so at the level of phrase structure. A hierarchical relationship between auxilaries and main verbs (complements) is maintained (COMPS) and arguments from the main verb are inherited by the auxiliaries. This approach must thus be regarded as a variant of the original raising analysis, in contrast to the more radical approach implemented here.

[3]See Falk (1984) for an early LFG treatment of 'do' in line with that proposed here and Niño (1995), Ackerman (1984, 1987) for related argumentation. However, these approaches do not deal with the implementational challenge of formulating morphological wellformedness conditions that arise as a consequence of a non-raising approach (see section 3.2).

[4]See, for instance, Wagner and Pinchon (1991) for French.

the particular realization of tense: whether it be periphrastic (auxiliaries), or morphological, the f-structure representation of tense is parallel.

2.2 The Formalism

We assume here the "traditional" LFG architecture of Bresnan (1982), as well as the newer advances within the theory (Dalrymple et al. (1995)). A grammar is viewed as a set of *correspondences* expressed in terms of *projections* from one level of representation to another. Two fundamental levels of representation within LFG are the c(onstituent)-structure and the f(unctional)-structure. The c-structure encodes idiosyncratic phrase structural properties of a given language, while the more universal f-structure provides a representation of information on grammatical functions (e.g. SUBJect, OBJect) and complementation, and allows the statement of general conditions on tense, binding, etc. The correspondence between c-structure and f-structure is not onto or one-to-one, but many-to-one, allowing an abstraction over idiosyncratic c-structure properties of a language (e.g. discontinuous constituents).

The grammars are implemented using the *Xerox Linguistic Environment* (XLE)[5], which allows the integration of the projection-based architecture of LFG (Dalrymple et al. 1995) and the correspondence-based MT approach of Kaplan et al. (1989).[6]

2.3 Auxiliaries — a flat approach

2.3.1 The Received Wisdom

The traditional treatment of auxiliaries in both HPSG and LFG has its roots in Ross's (1967) proposal to treat auxiliaries and modals on a par with main verbs.[7] In particular, auxiliaries are treated as a subclass of raising verbs (e.g. Pollard and Sag (1994), Falk (1984)). The simple English sentence (1) would correspond to the c-structure and f-structure in (2) and (3), respectively. The level of embedding in the f-structure exactly mirrors the c-structure: each verbal element takes a

[5]See Kaplan and Maxwell (1993) for a description of XLE's predecessor, the *Grammar Writer's Workbench.*

[6]See also Sadler et al. (1990), Sadler and Thompson (1991), Kaplan and Wedekind (1993) for further work on MT within LFG.

[7]The term *auxiliary* has often been taken to subsume both modals and elements such as *have* and *be*. However, the distinction between the two is necessary not only semantically, but also syntactically. In German (and some dialects of) English modals can be stacked, while the distribution of auxiliaries is more restricted. Also, assuming that semantic interpretation is driven primarily off of the f-structure, the relative embedding of modals must be preserved at that level in order to allow an interpretation of their scope and semantic force.

complement. The German representation is similar, but French has one level of embedding less (see (4), (5)). Thus, simple sentences which are predicationally equivalent are represented by diverging f-structures.

(1) The driver will have turned the lever.
Der Fahrer wird den Hebel gedreht haben. (German)
Le conducteur aura tourné le levier. (French)

(2)

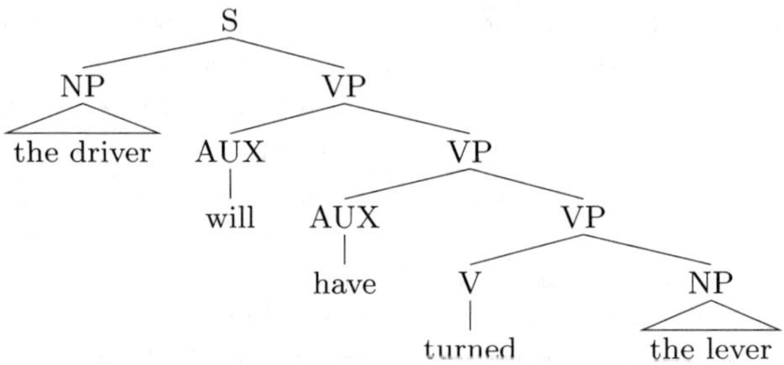

(3)

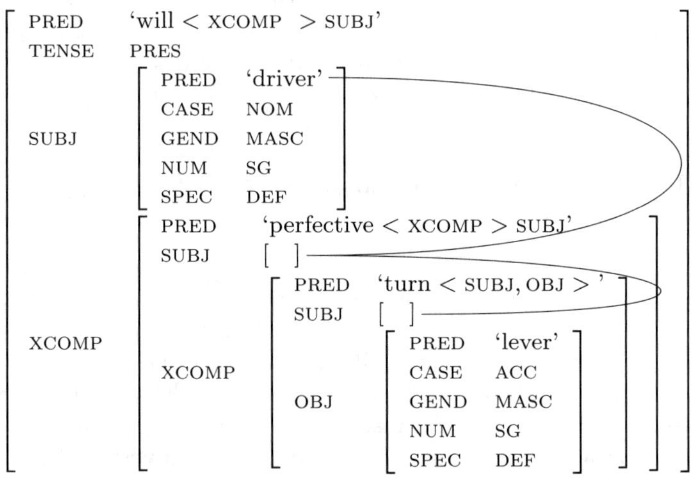

(4)

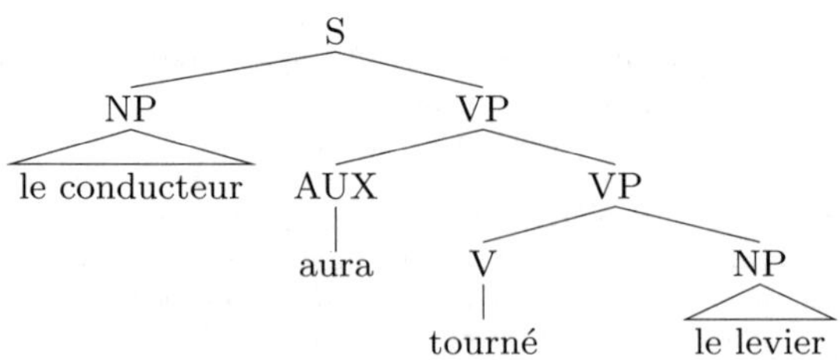

(5)

$$
\left[\begin{array}{ll}
\textsc{pred} & \text{`auxiliary} < \textsc{xcomp} > \textsc{subj'} \\
\textsc{tense} & \textsc{fut} \\
\textsc{subj} & \left[\begin{array}{ll}
\textsc{pred} & \text{`conducteur'} \\
\textsc{pers} & 3 \\
\textsc{gend} & \textsc{masc} \\
\textsc{num} & \textsc{sg} \\
\textsc{spec} & \textsc{def}
\end{array}\right] \\
\textsc{xcomp} & \left[\begin{array}{ll}
\textsc{pred} & \text{`tourner} < \textsc{subj}, \textsc{obj} > \text{'} \\
\textsc{subj} & [\ \ ] \\
\textsc{obj} & \left[\begin{array}{ll}
\textsc{pred} & \text{`levier'} \\
\textsc{pers} & 3 \\
\textsc{gend} & \textsc{masc} \\
\textsc{num} & \textsc{sg} \\
\textsc{spec} & \textsc{def}
\end{array}\right]
\end{array}\right]
\end{array}\right]
$$

The main reasons to treat auxiliaries as complement taking verbs in English are: 1) an account of VP-ellipsis, VP-topicalization, etc. follows immediately; 2) restrictions on the nature of the verbal complement (progressive, past participle, etc.) following the auxiliary can be stated straightforwardly (Pullum and Wilson (1977), Akmajian et al. (1979), Gazdar et al. (1982)). There are also major reasons, however, for not adopting this analysis: 1) linguistic adequacy; 2) unmotivated structural complexity; 3) non-parallel analyses for predicationally equivalent sentences.

As already argued by Akmajian et al. (1979), crosslinguistic evidence indicates that elements bearing only tense/aspect, mood, or voice should belong to a distinct syntactic category. In languages like French the information carried by *will* (future), or *have* (perfect) in (1) is realized morphologically rather than periphrastically. The analyses in (3) and (5) thus effectively claim that there exists a deep difference in the predicational structure of auxiliaries like *will* and *have* and the French *aura*. The f-structures for English and German posit one more XCOMP than the French in the overall subcategorization frame. This is not desirable from a crosslinguistic point of view, nor is it helpful for MT. Finally, for French, there is also language internal evidence based on clitic placement that argues against the treatment of auxiliary elements as raising verbs (Abeillé and Godard (1994)).

2.3.2 Alternative Implementation

The approach adopted here is a *flat* analysis of auxiliaries at f-structure (6).

(6)

$$
\left[\begin{array}{ll}
\text{PRED} & \text{`turn/drehen/tourner} < \text{SUBJ}, \text{OBJ} > \text{'} \\
\text{TENSE} & \text{FUTPERF} \\
\text{SUBJ} & \left[\begin{array}{ll}
\text{PRED} & \text{`driver/Fahrer/conducteur'} \\
\text{CASE} & \text{NOM} \\
\text{GEND} & \text{MASC} \\
\text{NUM} & \text{SG} \\
\text{SPEC} & \text{DEF}
\end{array}\right] \\
\text{OBJ} & \left[\begin{array}{ll}
\text{PRED} & \text{`lever/Hebel/levier'} \\
\text{CASE} & \text{ACC} \\
\text{GEND} & \text{MASC} \\
\text{NUM} & \text{SG} \\
\text{SPEC} & \text{DEF}
\end{array}\right]
\end{array}\right]
$$

The f-structures for French, German, and English here are fully parallel. The language particular differences in the number of auxiliaries are represented at c-structure. The contribution of the auxiliaries to the overall tense is still reflected at f-structure,[8] but they do not subcategorize for complements. Structural phenomena like VP-ellipsis, coordination, or topicalization can, however, still be accounted for by an appropriate embedding at c-structure (cf. (2) and (4)).[9] This adequately models the role of auxiliaries in natural language, in particular with regard to a more realistic treatment of tense (compare (3), (5) and (5)).

However, the flat f-structure in (6) provides no room for a statement of selectional requirements, allowing massive overgeneration (e.g. nothing blocks the presence of two *have* in (2)). Neither can the particular order of auxiliaries be regulated. Our solution takes advantage of LFG's flexible projection-based architecture by implementing a projection which models the hierarchical selectional requirements of auxiliaries, yet does not interfere with the subcategorizational properties of verbs, as would be the case under a raising analysis.

[8] The construction of the value for the composed tenses results from a complex interaction between the lexical entries. Alternatively to this solution of "collapsing" the contribution of syntactically independent auxiliaries, one could envision decomposing the French *aura* into a *will* and *have* and thus telescoping the French f-structure so that it is parallel to that of the English and German. However, this is clearly an undesirable solution. For one there is no solid linguistic motivation for this approach. For another, an ugly computational problem arises in that arguments must then be "filled in" for the newly created layer of f-structure (Maxwell/Newman (p.c.)).

[9] As is well known, English *will* has the syntactic properties of a modal, rather than that of an auxiliary. This fact is reflected in terms of c-structure.

A Projection for Morphological Forms

The view of auxiliaries as raising verbs is particularly costly for German. In LFG, the flexible word order of German is handled via *functional uncertainty*, which characterizes long-distance dependencies without resorting to movement analyses (Netter (1988), Zaenen and Kaplan (1995)). As in (7), which illustrates our alternative solution, functional uncertainty is represented by the Kleene Star (XCOMP*). The annotation on the NPs indicates that they could fulfill the role of any possible grammatical function (GF), e.g. SUBJ or OBJ, and that the level of embedding ranges from zero to infinite. With every auxiliary subcategorizing for an XCOMP, the two NPs could conceivably be arguments of three different verbs: *wird*, *haben*, or *gedreht*. Thus, the greater structural complexity unnecessarily increases the search space for the determination of a verb's arguments.

(7)

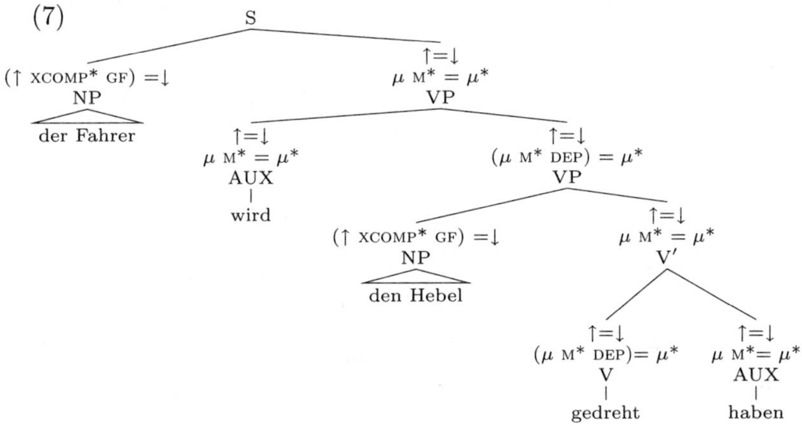

As discussed, we posit no subcategorization frame for auxiliaries, but rather propose projecting a further level of representation from the c-structure, the m-structure (following a suggestion by Kaplan (p.c.)).

Like the f-structure, the m-structure is an attribute-value matrix. It encodes language-specific information about idiosyncratic constraints on morphological forms. In "traditional" LFG this kind of information appears at f-structure, despite being mostly unrelated to the grammatical relations and function-argument structure the f-structure is intended to encode. The annotation μ M* in (7) refers to the m-structure associated with the parent c-structure node, and μ^* refers to the m-structure associated with the child node.[10] The m-structure

[10]The more familiar ↑ and ↓ of LFG are simply shorthand notations of the same idea, but restricted to the projection from c-structure to f-structure: ↑= ϕ M*,

corresponding to the matrix VP in (7) is (8). The desired flat f-structure resulting from the usual $\uparrow$ and $\downarrow$ annotations is as in (6).

(8)

$$m - structure \begin{bmatrix} \text{AUX} & + \\ \text{FIN} & + \\ \text{DEP} & \begin{bmatrix} \text{AUX} & + \\ \text{FIN} & - \\ \text{VFORM} & \text{BASE} \\ \text{DEP} & \begin{bmatrix} \text{FIN} & - \\ \text{VFORM} & \text{PERFP} \end{bmatrix} \end{bmatrix} \end{bmatrix}$$

The m-structure is not derived from the f-structure. Rather, both representations are in simultaneous correspondence with the c-structure. The following (abbreviated) lexical entries exemplify the pieces of information contributed by each verbal element. The disjunctive lexical entry for *wird* 'will' takes the various combinatory possibilities of auxiliaries and main verbs into account, and provides the appropriate tense feature. In (9), the second disjunct for *wird* requires that the embedded VFORM be BASE, that there be no passive involved, and that the next embedded verbal element, the main verb, be a perfect participle. The auxiliary *haben* in turn requires that its dependent be a perfect participle, and that it be unergative (via *constraint equations*: $=c$).[11]

(9) wird AUX ($\uparrow$ SUBJ CASE) = NOM
($\uparrow$ SUBJ NUM) = SG
(μ M* AUX) = +
{ (μ M* DEP VFORM) $=c$ BASE
(μ M* DEP DEP VFORM) $\neq$ PERFP
($\uparrow$ PASSIVE) $\neq$ +
"simple future: wird drehen"
($\uparrow$ TENSE) = FUT
|
(μ M* DEP VFORM) $=c$ BASE
(μ M* DEP DEP VFORM) $=c$ PERFP
($\uparrow$ PASSIVE) $\neq$ +
"future perfect: wird gedreht haben"
($\uparrow$ TENSE) = FUTPERF }

$\downarrow = \phi^*$. Note that the '*' in this notation is not equivalent to the Kleene Star in 'XCOMP*'.

[11] Lexical semantic information such as the unergative nature of a verb does not correlate with its *morphological* form, and is not modeled at m-structure. The distinction between unergative and unaccusative verbs is needed for auxiliary selection in German and French.

(10) haben AUX $(\mu$ M* AUX$) = +$
$(\mu$ M* VFORM$) =$ BASE
$(\mu$ M* FIN$) = -$
$(\mu$ M* DEP VFORM$) =c$ PERFP
$(\uparrow$ VSEM$) =c$ UNERG
$(\uparrow$ PASSIVE$) \neq +$

(11) gedreht V $(\uparrow$ PRED $=)$ 'drehen< SUBJ, OBJ>'
$(\mu$ M* VFORM$) =$ PERFP
$(\mu$ M* FIN$) = -$
$(\uparrow$ VSEM$) =$ UNERG

Statements about "morphological" dependents (DEP) are thus decoupled from functional uncertainty: the relation of NP arguments to their predicator now does not extend through various layers of linguistically artificial structural complexity (XCOMPs). The assumption of an m-structure can also be extended effectively to other parts of the grammar. Language particular morphological wellformedness conditions on adjective inflection or relative pronoun agreement, for example, can now be stated on the m-structure as idiosyncratic, language particular information which can be ignored for purposes of MT or semantic interpretation.

Long Distance Dependencies

Note that functional uncertainty *per se* is not the central problem, nor is it the motivating factor for the adoption of an m-structure. For flexible word order languages like German, the association of NP arguments with their predicators must be resolved within any implementation. Our approach reduces structural complexity at the level of subcategorization frames regardless of the precise framework.

VP-topicalization as in (12) or extraposition, however, still require an unbounded long-distance dependency to be assumed.

(12) [Den Hebel gedreht] wird der Fahrer haben
the.Acc lever turn.PPart will.Pres.Sg the driver have.Inf
'The lever turned, will have the driver.'

The overall gain remains considerable though, as the functional uncertainty is distributed only over the m-structure of the verb complex $((\mu$ M* DEP*$) = \mu$*), and does not involve the resolution of the role of NP arguments in cases like (13) and (1) where there is only one main predicator (for example, no modals).

Morphosyntactic vs. Semantic Tense

Note that this treatment of auxiliaries does not as yet include a fine-grained represention of tense and aspect, but does provide the basis needed for a thorough crosslinguistic analysis of tense and aspect. For example, while the particular morphosyntactic of future perfect may differ from language to language and not always be entirely equivalent in its semantic interpretation, the very fact that the morphosyntactic information has been encoded in a systematic and easily accessible fashion for a particular language opens the door for a subsequent semantic analysis of tense. For example, the German present tense corresponds both to the English present progressive and the English future. The German perfect corresponds to both the English perfect and the English simple past. These correspondences are semantic in nature and require an analysis in terms of, for example, relative relations between *Speech*, *Event* and *Reference* times (Reichenbach (1947)) as discussed, for example, in Kamp and Reyle (1993). Consider the future perfect of (1). The speech time (S) is assigned a given value on a time line. The reference time (R) must follow the speech time (S < R), but the event time (E) must precede the reference time (E < R): S < E < R.

In this case, the semantic evaluation will be parallel in German, French and English. In a case like (13), on the other hand, it is only the semantic interpretation of the entire clause, rather than a simple evaluation of the morphological tense/aspect information which allows a correct semantic interpretation of the English present progressive as a future.

(13) I am flying to Boston tomorrow.

However, collecting and registering the morphosyntactic temporal information of a given language in a simple, standardized encoding in terms of a single feature which is easily accesible provides the necessary basis for the further construction of a deeper semantic representation that can be truly considered to be language universal.

2.4 Conclusion

In the spirit of LFG, our analysis of auxiliaries in English, French, and German factors out language specific information from crosslinguistically general f-structure information through the use of a separate level of representation, the m-structure. Features needed only to ensure language particular wellformedness are no longer unified into the f-structure, cluttering a representation that is meant to be language independent. In our analysis, only features needed for further semantic interpretation, MT, or for the expression of language universal syntactic generalizations are represented at f-structure. For example, morphologically encoded information like case, gender, or agreement is needed for statements as to binding, predicate-argument relations, or the determination of complex clause structures (given that agreement is generally clause-bounded). The solution allows a language universal 'flat' f-structure analysis for auxiliaries and complex tenses, while enforcing idiosyncratic wellformedness conditions at another level of representation. We claim that the rules necessary for semantic interpretation or MT between languages do not need to know whether tense was encoded by an affix or by a full auxiliary. Indeed, the analyses proposed facilitate the task of MT and provide a solid basis for subsequent semantic interpretation.

References

Abeillé, Anne and Danielle Godard. 1994. The complementation of French auxiliaries. In *Proceedings of the Thirteenth West Coast Conference on Formal Linguistics*.

Ackerman, Farrell. 1984. Verbal modifiers as argument taking predicates: Complex verbs as predicate complexes in Hungarian. In *Groningen Working Papers in Linguistics*, pages 23–71. University of Groningen.

Ackerman, Farrell. 1987. *Miscreant morphemes: phrasal predicates in Ugric*. Ph.D. thesis, University of California, Berkeley.

Akmajian, Adrian, Susan Steele, and Thomas Wasow. 1979. The category AUX in Universal Grammar. *Linguistic Inquiry* 10:1–64.

Bresnan, Joan, ed. 1982. *The Mental Representation of Grammatical Relations*. Cambridge, MA: MIT Press.

Bresnan, Joan. 1995. Lexical-functional syntax. Lecture Notes, ESSLI 7, Barcelona.

Chomsky, Noam. 1957. *Syntactic Structures*. The Hague: Mouton.

Dalrymple, Mary, Ronald Kaplan, John T. Maxwell III, and Annie Zaenen, eds. 1995. *Formal Issues in Lexical-Functional Grammar*. Stanford, CA: CSLI Publications.

Falk, Yehuda. 1984. The English auxiliary system: a Lexical-Functional analysis. *Language* 60:483–509.

Gazdar, Gerald, Geoff Pullum, and Ivan Sag. 1982. Auxiliaries and related phenomena in a restrictive theory of grammar. *Language* 58:591–638.

Hinrichs, Erhard and Tsuneko Nakazawa. 1989. Subcategorization and VP structure in German. In *Proceedings of the Third Symposium on Germanic Linguistics*. Amsterdam: Benjamins.

Kamp, Hans and Uwe Reyle. 1993. *From Discourse to Logic*. Dordrecht: Kluwer Academic Publishers.

Kaplan, Ronald and John T. Maxwell III. 1993. Grammar writer's workbench. Manuscript, Xerox.

Kaplan, Ronald, Klaus Netter, Jürgen Wedekind, and Annie Zaenen. 1989. Translation by structural correspondences. In *EACL 4*, pages 272–281. University of Manchester.

Kaplan, Ronald and Jürgen Wedekind. 1993. Restriction and correspondence-based translation. In *Proceedings of the Sixth Meeting of the European Chapter of the Association for Computational Linguistics*. University of Utrecht.

King, Tracy Holloway. 1995. *Configuring Topic and Focus in Russian*. Stanford, CA: CSLI Publications.

Monachesi, Paola. 1995. *A Grammar of Italian Clitics*. Ph.D. thesis, Tilburg University.

Netter, Klaus. 1988. Non-local dependencies and infinitival constructions in German. In U. Reyle and C. Rohrer, eds., *Natural language parsing and linguistics*. Dordrecht: Reidel.

Niño, María-Eugenia. 1995. The multiple expression of inflectional information and grammatical architecture. In *Proceedings of CSSP 95*.

Pollard, Carl and Ivan Sag. 1994. *Head-Driven Phrase Structure Grammar*. Chicago, IL: The University of Chicago Press.

Pullum, Geoff and Deirdre Wilson. 1977. Autonomous syntax and the analysis of auxiliaries. *Language* 53(4):741–788.

Reichenbach, Hans. 1947. *Elements of Symbolic Logic*. London: Macmillan.

Roberts, Ian G. 1983. The syntax of English modals. In *Proceedings of the Second West Coast Conference on Formal Linguistics*, pages 227–246. Stanford.

Roberts, Ian G. 1985. Agreement parameters and the development of English modal auxiliaries. *Natural Language and Linguistic Theory* 3:21–58.

Ross, John. 1967. *Constraints on Variables in Syntax*. Ph.D. thesis, Massachusetts Institute of Technology.

Sadler, Louisa, Ian Crookston, Douglas Arnold, and Andy Way. 1990. LFG and translation. In *Proceedings of the Third International Conference on Theoretical and Methodological Issues in Machine Translation*, pages 11–13. Linguistic Research Center, University of Texas at Austin.

Sadler, Louisa and Henry Thompson. 1991. Structural non-correspondence in translation. In *EACL 5*, pages 293–298. Berlin.

Wagner, Robert Léon and Jacqueline Pinchon. 1991. *Grammaire du Français*. Hachette. First Edition 1962.

Zaenen, Annie and Ronald Kaplan. 1995. Formal devices for linguistic generalizations: West Germanic word order in LFG. In M. Dalrymple, R. Kaplan, J. T. Maxwell III, and A. Zaenen, eds., *Formal Issues in Lexical-Functional Grammar*, pages 215–239. Stanford, CA: CSLI Publications.

3

Tense in LFG: Syntax and Morphology

Anette Frank and Annie Zaenen

3.1 The morphology–syntax interface in LFG

An important tenet of LFG is the lexical integrity principle which says that the leaves of c–structure trees are complete surface words.[1] Given this principle, the morphological component is seen as distinct from the syntax. It can be modelled by sublexical rules as we will illustrate below but the principles that apply to these rules are different from those applying in the syntax (see Bresnan and Mchombo (1995) for discussion). The way LFG is set up allows single words and phrases to contribute the same or similar information to an f–structure. For example a form like *parla*, passé simple of *parler*, contributes information similar to that contributed by *a parlé*, the passé composé of the same verb. The framework allows a similar treatment for the two forms as well as the maintenance of lexical integrity and makes it possible to

This paper originally appeared in *How We Say WHEN It Happens: Contributions to the Theory of Temporal Reference in Natural Language*, ed. Hans Kamp and Uwe Reyle (Tübingen: Max Niemeyer Verlag, 2002), 17–52.

[1] We would like to thank the following people for helpful comments on earlier versions of this article: John Maxwell, who proposed a similar architecture in conversations with the second author, Ron Kaplan, Miriam Butt, Frédérique Segond and Veronika Knüppel. In particular we thank Joan Bresnan for extensive comments and suggestions. The issues she raised could not be discussed in sufficient detail in this short contribution. Needless to say that the commentators do not necessarily share the perspective we are taking here. Special thanks go also to Marc Dymetman for judgements on French data. We alone are responsible for remaining errors.

Projecting Morphology.
Louisa Sadler and Andrew Spencer (Eds.).

avoid word formation rules in the syntax without losing paradigmatic transparency (see Vincent and Börjars (1996) for discussion). These possibilities, however, are not always exploited as well as they could be, and using them transparently is made less easy than it could be by another architectural feature of LFG.

The distinction that the architecture of LFG makes between c–structure and f–structure was meant to embody the insight that word order and other constituent structure differences are not necessarily indicative of profound syntactic differences among languages. LFG follows here the distinction made e.g. in Keenan (1976) between coding properties and genuine syntactic characteristics. The f–structure allows us to abstract away from superficial word order differences to bring out the more fundamental syntactic similarities (or differences) among languages. This abstracting away from certain differences is theoretically important but also practically, e.g. in the context of translation. It makes the f–structure into a structure that comes close to the underspecified representation used in the Core Language Engine (see Genabith and Crouch (1996); (Alshawi (1992), Alshawi and Crouch (1992)), which can be argued to be, from a practical point of view, a good candidate for input and output of transfer rules (see Dorna et al. (1998)). But the traditional architecture gets us only half way: while it abstracts away from c–structure phenomena, it encodes all the morphological information in the f–structure. This information, however, is to a large extent as much encoding information as word order is.

The way things stand in the traditional architecture, it is possible to get all the f–structure relevant information about *parla* and *a parlé* into the right place in the f–structure. But it is not possible for the f–structure to ignore the additional information needed to impose the right verbal form on *parlé* (past participle). In what follows we discuss some proposals made to remedy this and try to improve technically on them. We then use our tools to model the French auxiliary system.

3.1.1 Analyses of auxiliaries

Early analyses in LFG (Falk (1984), Bresnan (1982)) analyzed auxiliaries as raising verbs, assigning them a PRED value, e.g., 'perf' in the case of a temporal auxiliary. Later approaches (Bresnan (1995), King (1995), Schwarze (1996)) treat auxiliaries as non–subcategorizing elements, which contribute tense and aspectual information to the f–structure of the clause. Under this type of analysis, the main verb is the functional head of the clause. Among the arguments that are put forward for an analysis of auxiliaries as non–subcategorizing elements we find the following. Auxiliaries contribute essentially temporal and aspectual information, which indicates that they should belong to a different syntactic category than ordinary predicational verbs (see Butt et al. (1996a)). Even within a single language system – there may be analytic and synthetic tense forms which do not differ substantially in meaning (besides, of course, certain aspectual or temporal differences). If the analytic form is analyzed as contributing a PRED on top of the tense and aspect information whereas the synthetic form doesn't, we of course do not express the functional similarity between the two cases. The auxiliary in the analytic form should therefore not be analyzed as a PRED–bearing element, but only contribute its tense and aspectual information (see King (1995)). Butt et al. (1996a) consider cross–linguistic variation in (analytic vs. synthetic) tense formation as providing support for an analysis of temporal auxiliaries as non–subcategorizing elements. In recent work Bresnan (1995) treats auxiliaries as functional categories in an LFG framework and enforces an analysis in which tense auxiliaries as well as passive ones are non PRED–bearing elements.

3.1.2 The m–structure analysis of auxiliaries

In line with this movement towards a flat f–structure analysis of auxiliary constructions, Butt et al. (1996a) and Butt et al. (1996b) propose a unified analysis of auxiliaries in English, French, and German, with a flat f–structure for all three languages. Their emphasis is on problems of parallel grammar development and machine translation. In particular, one way of looking at their proposal is that – although morphology and c–structure make different contributions to the functional and semantic analysis of a sentence in different languages – the corresponding f–structure representations should not be distinct because their contribution to the meaning of the sentence is the same.
Their analysis differs from the previous ones in providing a clear separation between cross–linguistically invariant f–structure features of temporal constructions, and language specific differences in the way this information is encoded. Such differences are exemplified in (1): while in English and German future tense is formed analytically (*will turn/ wird drehen*), French has a synthetic future tense (*tournera*).

(1) a. The driver will turn the lever.
    b. Der Fahrer wird den Hebel drehen.
    c. Le conducteur tournera le levier.

In this analysis, a new projection is introduced, the morphological structure, or *m–structure*. The m–structure is, just like the f–structure, an attribute–value matrix, but – while f–structure is the level of syntax that encodes grammatical functions, like SUBJ, OBJ, etc., and the PREDicate with its subcategorization requirements – the m–structure is viewed as the level of representation that encodes information about idiosyncratic constraints on morphological forms. Thus, m–structure is the level of representation where the language specific differences in the morpho–syntax of tense formation are represented. In much the same way as the f–structure is defined as the ϕ–projection off the c–structure, Butt et al. (1996a,1996b) define the m–structure as a μ–projection off the c–structure (2).

(2)

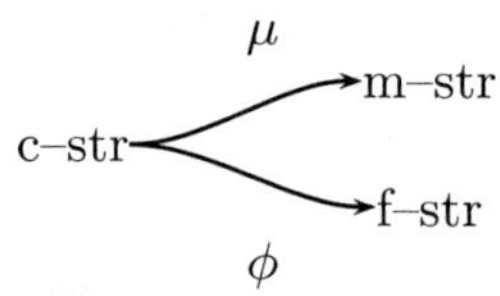

Syntax–morphology interface (Butt et al. (1996a,b))

In this projection architecture, the analyses assigned to the sentences in (3) will be isomorphic at the level of f–structure (4). The associated morphological structures will be distinct for English and German, where the future is an analytic tense form (5a.–b.), as opposed to French (5c), where future tense is formed synthetically by inflectional morphology. The phrase structure rule will of course also encode the differences in word order which are likewise ignored in the f–structure.[2]

(3) a. The driver will have turned the lever.
   b. Der Fahrer wird den Hebel gedreht haben.
   c. Le conducteur aura tourné le levier.

[2] We do not attempt to give semantically motivated features for tense and aspect in this paper. However, it is possible to define minimal semantic temporal conditions triggered by tense forms (like imparfait, passé simple, passé composé, etc.) in a semantic projection σ of ϕ. Kamp and Rohrer (1983) propose that such an encoding be based upon notions like Reichenbach's (1947) *temporal reference point*, etc. Further refinements for a Reichenbachian approach to the French tense system have been proposed by Kamp and Rohrer (1988) and Gosselin (1996). A substantial fragment of English is treated in Kamp and Reyle (1993).

(4) a./b./c.

$$
\phi \left[\begin{array}{ll}
\textsc{pred} & \text{`turn/drehen/tourner } \langle(\uparrow\textsc{subj})(\uparrow\ \textsc{obj})\rangle\text{'} \\
\textsc{tense} & \textsc{futperf} \\
\textsc{subj} & \left[\begin{array}{ll}
\textsc{pred} & \text{`driver/Fahrer/conducteur'} \\
\textsc{case} & \textsc{nom} \\
\textsc{gend} & \textsc{masc} \\
\textsc{num} & \textsc{sg} \\
\textsc{spec} & \textsc{def}
\end{array}\right] \\
\textsc{obj} & \left[\begin{array}{ll}
\textsc{pred} & \text{`lever/Hebel/levier'} \\
\textsc{case} & \textsc{acc} \\
\textsc{gend} & \textsc{masc} \\
\textsc{num} & \textsc{sg} \\
\textsc{spec} & \textsc{def}
\end{array}\right]
\end{array}\right]
$$

Structurally identical f–structures for English, German, French (3)

(5)a.–b.

$$
\mu \left[\begin{array}{ll}
\textsc{fin} & + \\
\textsc{aux} & + \\
\textsc{dep} & \left[\begin{array}{ll}
\textsc{fin} & - \\
\textsc{aux} & + \\
\textsc{vform} & \textsc{base} \\
\textsc{dep} & \left[\begin{array}{ll}
\textsc{fin} & - \\
\textsc{aux} & - \\
\textsc{vform} & \textsc{perfp}
\end{array}\right]
\end{array}\right]
\end{array}\right]
$$

c.

$$
\mu \left[\begin{array}{ll}
\textsc{fin} & + \\
\textsc{aux} & + \\
\textsc{dep} & \left[\begin{array}{ll}
\textsc{fin} & - \\
\textsc{aux} & - \\
\textsc{vform} & \textsc{perfp}
\end{array}\right]
\end{array}\right]
$$

Structurally distinct m–structures for English, German (a./b.) vs. French (c.)

Following the projection architecture displayed in (2), the morphological structures in (5) are defined in terms of c–structure annotations. We will use the notation $\widehat{*}_\mu$ to refer to the m–structure node projected from the mother node $\widehat{*}$ of the actual c–structure node $*$. In the same way, the traditional $\uparrow$ can be expressed by $\widehat{*}_\phi$. We will call such equations morphological equations.[3] (6) illustrates how structurally divergent m– and f–structures are projected from the c–structure: here the

[3]Butt et al. (1996a) misleadingly introduced the notation "$\mu\uparrow$" to refer to the m–structure of the actual node's mother node. This is in fact not the correct notation for the architecture displayed in (2): it defines m–structure to be projected off the f–structure.

VP node of the auxiliary construction defines a hierarchical structure at the level of the μ–projection (($\widehat{*}_\mu$ DEP) = $*_\mu$), whereas the functional equation of this node is a trivial one, $\uparrow=\downarrow$.

(6)

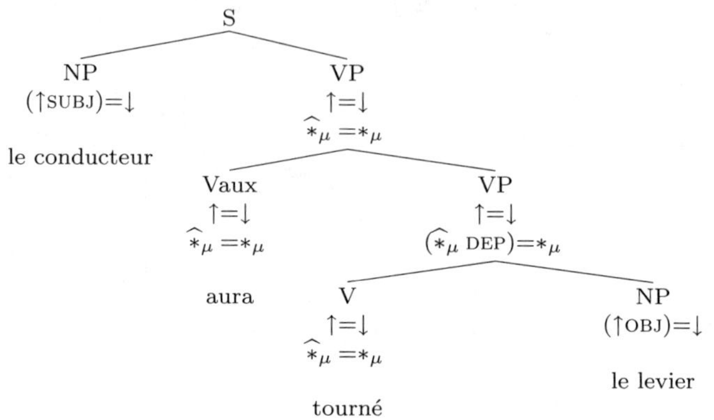

The lexical entries of auxiliary verbs and main verbs come with both functional and morphological equations, which define the language particular properties of morpho–syntactic tense formation, as well as the corresponding tense information, which is encoded in the f–structure. We briefly illustrate this with the two lexical entries used in (6), the future auxiliary *aura* (*will have*), and the participle verb *tourné* (*turned*). The auxiliary is morphologically marked for future tense in French, and is constrained to combine with a past participle verb form, in its m–structure's DEP feature. The TENSE feature in f–structure can therefore be set to the value FUTPERF.[4]

(7)

aura: Vaux
$(\uparrow$ SUBJ NUM$)$ = SG
$(\uparrow$ SUBJ PERS$)$ = 3
$(\uparrow$ TENSE$)$= FUTPERF
$(\widehat{*}_\mu$ FIN$)= +$
$(\widehat{*}_\mu$ AUX$)= +$
$(\widehat{*}_\mu$ DEP VFORM$)=_c$ PERFP.

tourné: V
$(\uparrow$ PRED$)$ = 'tourner$\langle(\uparrow$ SUBJ$)(\uparrow$ OBJ$)\rangle$'
$(\widehat{*}_\mu$ AUX$)= -$
$(\widehat{*}_\mu$ VFORM$)=$ PERFP.

In what follows we take the freedom to rephrase their approach in terms of the notation introduced above, which follows Butt et al. (1997). Alternatively, the annotations could equally well be restated in terms of the notation introduced in Kaplan(1987), where $\mu\mathcal{M}*$ refers to the m–structure node projected from mother node $\mathcal{M}*$.

[4]The main verb *avoir* is assumed to have a different entry and is not discussed in this paper.

3.1.3 Some problems of the current morphology–syntax interface

The syntax–morphology interface described above works very well for verbal morphology and the distinct temporal and aspectual constructions in the diverse languages described in the paper (see Butt et al. (1999)). Yet, one may have noticed that the m–structure (5c) for the sentence displayed in (6) does not contain features like NUM, PERS, GEND, or CASE, which prima facie should also be considered as morphological features. This raises the general question as to the distinction between morphological, functional syntactic, and finally also semantic information, and the distribution of these respective types of features over the various levels of representation assumed in the overall projection architecture of grammar.

If morphological features like number, gender and person are to be represented in m–structure, we cannot simply introduce them by means of trivial morphological equations $\widehat{*}_\mu = *_\mu$. Since the various arguments of the verb may instantiate conflicting values of number, person, and case, the m–structure must specify "blueprints" of the f–structural grammatical functions SUBJ, OBJ, etc., to host the respective morphological features. In the actual LFG grammar implementations of the ParGram project (see Butt et al. (1999) for information) the m–structure is defined to contain an attribute EXT-ARG (external argument), corresponding to the morphological structure of the f–structure's SUBJ, a set–valued feature INT-ARGS (internal arguments) for non–subject arguments (OBJ, OBJ2, OBL, etc.), a feature DEP corresponding to sentential arguments (COMP, XCOMP), and finally a set–valued feature NON-DEP for adjuncts.[5]

Defining subject verb agreement

This "blueprint" of the functional argument structure of a sentence would in fact allow us to move agreement and case features to the mor-

[5]The feature EXT-ARG, e.g., was introduced to account for the morphological selection of infinitival vs. finite sentential adjective SUBJects in cases like (i) and (ii). The verbal inflectional features FIN and INF being stated in m–structure, the morphological form of the sentential adjective SUBJ cannot be constrained in terms of these features without resorting to some EXT-ARG feature in m–structure. The distinction between finite and infinite sentential subjects could, alternatively, only be captured in terms of the f–structure attribute TENSE, which should then not be assigned in structures like (i) and (ii).

(i) Obtenir son accord n'est pas facile.
Getting her/his agreement is not easy.

(ii) Avoir obtenu son accord est une victoire.
Having gotten her/his agreement is a victory.

phological representation level. The subject verb agreement constraints of, e.g., a finite third person singular verb can then be stated in terms of the following morphological equations:

$(\widehat{*}_{\mu}\ \text{EXT-ARG NUM}) = \text{SG}$ and $(\widehat{*}_{\mu}\ \text{EXT-ARG PERS}) = 3$.

With this extension, the m–structure for (6) would spell out as in (8):[6]

(8)
$$\mu \begin{bmatrix} \text{EXT-ARG} & \begin{bmatrix} \text{CASE} & \text{NOM} \\ \text{GEND} & \text{MASC} \\ \text{PERS} & 3 \\ \text{NUM} & \text{SG} \end{bmatrix} \\ \text{FIN} & + \\ \text{AUX} & + \\ \text{DEP} & \begin{bmatrix} \text{FIN} & - \\ \text{AUX} & - \\ \text{VFORM} & \text{PERFP} \end{bmatrix} \\ \text{INT-ARGS} & \begin{bmatrix} \text{CASE} & \text{ACC} \\ \text{GEND} & \text{MASC} \\ \text{NUM} & \text{SG} \end{bmatrix} \end{bmatrix}$$

This, however, starts to look suspicious: the m–structure proposal was originally motivated by the wish to have a clean f–structure representation of what matters to semantic interpretation. But now we start to get an m–structure representation that repeats most of the information pertaining to f–structure. The morphological representation level now contains subcategorization information, which is functional in nature. It is becoming a complete "blueprint" for the functional structure. Besides this conceptual issue, it turns out that this approach is confronted with rather severe problems in the analysis of long–distance phenomena that involve morphological constraints.

The problem of long–distance dependencies

A typical example for a long–distance phenomenon in the morphology–syntax interface is past participle agreement in French. In object relative clauses (9) the past participle must agree, in number and gender, with the embedding head noun, as opposed to cases where the OBJ is realized in VP position, and where past participle agreement is illicit.

(9) a. Les enfants adorent les histoires qu'on leur a déjà raconté*(*es*) mille fois.
'Children are found of the stories that one has told them already a thousand times.'

[6] For ease of exposition INT-ARGS is not represented as a set-valued feature here.

b. Les enfants adorent les histoires qu'on sait bien qu'on leur a déjà raconté*(*es*) mille fois.
'Children are fond of the stories that one knows perfectly (that) one has told them already a thousand times.'

The grammar assigns the relative pronoun the OBJect function, but can do so only in terms of a functional uncertainty equation, since relative clause constructions are unbounded in French (see (9b)). In order to trigger past participle agreement of the verb that subcategorizes for the object introduced by the relative pronoun, the morphological features of number and gender must be stated in the position of the relative pronoun,[7] yet have to be "transmitted" to the level of the subcategorizing past participle. In the architecture depicted in (2), this will only be possible if these morphological features are defined in terms of a functional uncertainty equation over the "f–structure blueprint" that is encoded in the morphological structure, in particular functional uncertainty over the DEP attribute (see (10) below).[8]
For concreteness, we add morphological equations to the annotations of the category PRONrel (for relative pronouns) in (10) that enforce the choice of the inflected participle form *racontées* (see (11)), which agrees with the head noun *histoires* in number and gender. The lexicon entry (11)[9] constrains this inflected form to syntactic contexts in which the OBJ *head-precedes* the verb:[10] $(\uparrow \text{OBJ}) <_h \uparrow$.[11] . This constraint is fulfilled in (10), with the functional uncertainty $\{\text{COMP}|\text{XCOMP}\}^*$ resolved to ϵ.
The agreement constraints in (11) are stated via the "m–structure blueprint" of the OBJ function, INT-ARG. The corresponding morpho-

[7]The relative pronoun is defined to agree in number and gender with the relative clause's head noun.

[8]Cf. Kaplan and Zaenen (1989) for functional uncertainty.

[9]The lexicon entry (11) is oversimplified: it doesn't account for passive voice, and more refined constraints for past participle agreement are necessary. Also, we display a full form lexicon entry instead of sublexical rules in conjunction with a stem lexicon. sublexical rules will be introduced in section 3.2.3.

[10]In French, object agreement only occurs in constructions where the object is realized in a preverbal position (as a clitic, or as a relative or interrogative phrase).

[11]*head precedence*, as implemented in the XLE system, is defined as follows (cf. XLE Documentation):

$f_1 <_h f_2$ is true iff f_1 and f_2 have heads and the head of f_1 precedes the head of f_2 in the c–structure.

For the purpose of this definition, the "head" of an f–structure is the constituent where the f–structure's PRED semantic form was instantiated if the constituent also maps via the ϕ–projection to the same f–structure. Alternatively, the precedence constraint could be stated in terms of *f–precedence*, following Zaenen and Kaplan (1995).

logical features are defined in the position of the relative pronoun, where the object function is realized (cf. (10)). As the relative clause construction can be nonlocal, the morphological equation ($\widehat{*}_\mu$ DEP* INT-ARG)= $*_\mu$ must involve the path definition DEP*.

(10)

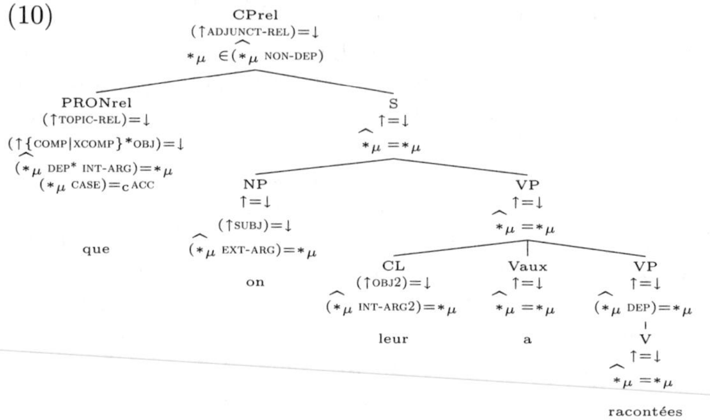

(11) racontées: V (↑ PRED) = 'raconter⟨(↑ SUBJ)(↑ OBJ2)(↑ OBJ)⟩'
($\widehat{*}_\mu$ VFORM)= PERFP
($\widehat{*}_\mu$ OBJ) $<_h$ ↑
($\widehat{*}_\mu$ INT-ARG NUM)$=_c$ PL
($\widehat{*}_\mu$ INT-ARG GEND)$=_c$ FEM.

In the local construction (10), with the m–structure path DEP* resolved to DEP, the morphological features NUM and GEND are appropriately instantiated to satisfy the local morphological constraints of the past participle (11).

However, in a construction like (12), which does not involve a past participle, the m–structure path DEP* in the annotation of PRONrel will not be uniquely resolved by the grammar. Since the m–structure argument features that correspond to grammatical functions in f–structure are not subject to coherence and completeness constraints, the morphological features of the head noun can be introduced as values of the feature INT-ARG at every possible level of embedding along the path DEP*. As a result, in cases like (12) we get multiple unwarranted ambiguities, with in fact inappropriate analyses.[12]

[12]We could try to solve this problem by restricting the morphological equation ($\widehat{*}_\mu$ DEP* INT-ARG)= $*_\mu$ to those constructions where the subcategorizing verb is a past participle. I.e., we could replace the annotations of PRONrel in (10) by the

(12) Les enfants adorent des histoires qu'on ne veut pas vraiment leur raconter.
'Children love stories that one doesn't really want to tell them.'

To summarize, the morphology–syntax projection architecture (2) not only leads to an account where more and more information which is functional in nature has to be reproduced in m–structure; moreover, it is confronted with serious problems in the analysis of long–distance phenomena that involve morphological constraints.[13]
The principal problem is that the "blueprint" of f–structure grammatical functions that is reproduced at the level of m–structure is not controlled by completeness and coherence constraints. While in f–structure the functional uncertainty {COMP|XCOMP}* will be uniquely resolved in terms of completeness and coherence constraints, the same will not be true for the corresponding uncertainty path over DEP in m–structure. And, since the μ–projection is not directly related to the ϕ–projection, it is not possible to state the morphological constraints relative to the (resolved) f–structure without requiring the inverse function $\phi^{-1} \circ \mu$. Importing the notion of completeness and coherence into the m–structure would of course make it even more f–structure-like and undermine the motivation for a separate projection further. In what follows we will try to solve the problem by proposing a leaner m–structure instead of a more complex one.

3.1.4 Moving towards a sequenced architecture

In the following we propose a projection architecture for the morphology–syntax interface that diverges from the proposal in Butt et al. (1996a,b) in that the μ– and ϕ–projections are not independent, parallel projec-

following ones (where we use the variable %PATH-M to express constraints on the morphological uncertainty path):

PRONrel
(↑ {COMP|XCOMP}* OBJ)= ↓
(↑ TOPIC REL)= ↓
%PATH-M = $(\widehat{*_\mu}$ DEP*)
{ (%PATH-M VFORM)$=_c$ PERFP
(%PATH-M INT-ARG)= $*_\mu$
| (%PATH-M VFORM)$\neq$ PERFP}

But this will not solve the problem. Note that in a case like (12) the second disjunct will be satisfied for every possible choice of %PATH-M. This is again a consequence of the fact that the m–structure argument feature DEP that corresponds to the f–structure functions COMP or XCOMP is not subject to completeness and coherence constraints. The grammar will therefore yield a two–ways spurious ambiguity for (12).

[13] Similar problems have been noted, in the context of the ParGram project, by Tracy King for English interrogative clauses, and by Jonas Kuhn for extraposition of *zu*–infinitives in German.

tions off the c–structure, but sequenced, in the way outlined in (13):

(13) $$\text{c–str} \xrightarrow{\phi} \text{f–str} \xrightarrow{\mu} \text{m–str}$$

Syntax–morphology interface (sequenced architecture)

This picture is, at first sight, quite surprising, in that the m–structure is projected off the f–structure. Given that we tend to think of functional structure as being build *on the basis of* morphological information, we would expect the ϕ–projection to be projected off the m–structure, rather than the other way round.
Yet, the projection mechanism of LFG allows us to state the "dependency" of functional information on morphological information in a natural way in the architecture displayed in (13). For example the fact that in a language like German nominative case is indicative of the subject function can be expressed in terms of the equation, $((\uparrow \text{SUBJ})_\mu$ CASE$)=$ NOM, or the pair of equations $(\uparrow \text{SUBJ}) = \downarrow$ and $(\downarrow_\mu$ CASE$)=$ NOM if they are annotations of the subject NP.[14]

The advantage of the projection architecture (13) for the morphology–syntax interface is that morphological constraints on syntax can be defined locally. The morphological information is closely tied to the partial f–structure that it contributes to identify. This can be clearly seen in (14), which displays the f–structure and its dependent μ–projections for the sentence (3c). The uppermost m–structure corresponds to the morphological information that is contributed by the verbal projection, and is referenced by the equation $\uparrow_\mu$, pointing to the verbal head's f–structure's μ–projection. Similarly, the morphological features contributed by the subject NP are identified in terms of the equation $(\uparrow$ SUBJ$)_\mu$, referring to the f–structure's SUBJect's μ–projection.

(14)

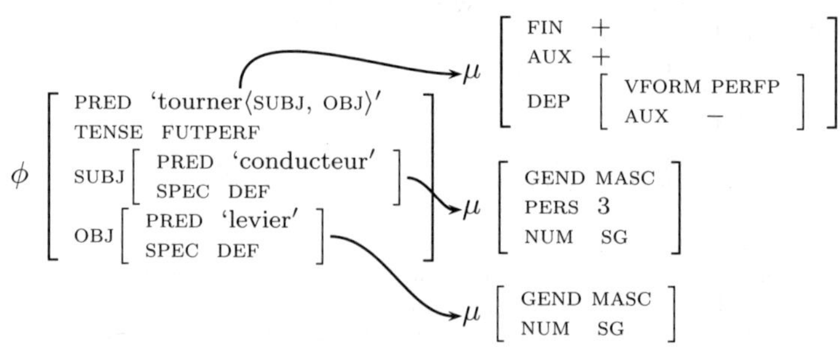

[14]We use the notation $(\uparrow$ SUBJ$)_\mu$ to refer to the m–structure projected from the f–structure's SUBJ value, and $\uparrow_\mu$ to refer to the m–structure projected from the f–structure referred to by $\uparrow$. Alternatively, we could refer to the m–structure projected from the mother node's f–structure by use of $\widehat{*}_{\phi\mu}$, and to the m–structure of the SUBJ by $(\widehat{*}_\phi$ SUBJ$)_\mu$ (cf. fn. 3 section 3.1.2).

We will first illustrate how this analysis accounts for the basic types of agreement phenomena that have to be accounted for in the interface between morphology and syntax: local subject verb agreement, and past participle agreement in long–distance relative clause constructions. In Section 3.2.3 we will then build on this new architecture for the morphology–syntax interface, to investigate in more detail the analysis of auxiliary constructions and cliticization in French.

Defining subject verb agreement

The advantage of the sequenced architecture (13) is that both local and nonlocal agreement phenomena can be stated in terms of "morphological equations" which do not necessitate any duplication of essentially functional information in the m–structure. This is first illustrated for the simple example of subject verb agreement.

The lexical entry of a finite third person singular verb like *tournera* in (15) specifies morphological equations which define a μ–projection off the ϕ–projection. The m–structure is defined to carry the feature FIN + by the equation $(\uparrow_\mu \text{ FIN}) = +$. For finite verbs we require subject verb agreement, here in terms of the equations $((\uparrow \text{ SUBJ})_\mu \text{ NUM}) = \text{SG}$ and $((\uparrow \text{ SUBJ})_\mu \text{ PERS}) = 3$. Thus, the subject's m–structure is directly defined to carry the appropriate morphological features NUM= SG and PERS= 3.[15]

(15) tournera: V

$$
\begin{array}{l}
(\uparrow \text{ PRED}) = \text{`tourner}\langle(\uparrow \text{ SUBJ})(\uparrow \text{ OBJ})\rangle\text{'} \\
(\uparrow_\mu \text{ AUX}) = - \\
(\uparrow_\mu \text{ FIN}) = + \\
(\uparrow \text{ TENSE}) = \text{FUTURE} \\
((\uparrow \text{ SUBJ})_\mu \text{ NUM}) = \text{SG} \\
((\uparrow \text{ SUBJ})_\mu \text{ PERS}) = 3.
\end{array}
$$

The result of these annotations is illustrated in (16), the f–structure and projected m–structures for sentence (1c). The local m–structures contain only morphological features, and do not duplicate any genuinely functional notions, like grammatical functions.

[15] Sections 3.2.3 and 3.2.3 will introduce the device of *sublexical rules*, which allows us to define morphological phenomena like subject verb agreement in a more general way.

(16)

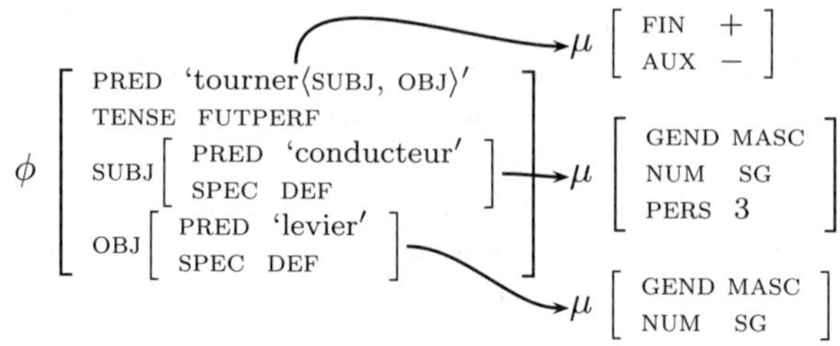

Defining long–distance constraints with local m–structures

The advantage of defining morphological constraints as "dependent" on functional structure becomes even more compelling if we reconsider the problem of stating morphological constraints in long–distance constructions. As we argued in Section 3.1.3, the basic problem of the "parallel architecture" of Butt et al. (1996a) is the fact that morphological constraints in long–distance constructions have to make use of uncertainty equations, which operate not on the functional structure, where the uncertainty is constrained by completeness and coherence conditions, but on a "blueprint" of f–structure information in m–structure. Since m–structure is not subject to coherence and completeness constraints, these uncertainty equations can in many cases not be uniquely resolved, leading to spurious ambiguities or inappropriate analyses.

To illustrate how long–distance phenomena can be treated in the "sequenced architecture" of the morphology–syntax interface, we take up our previous example, past participle agreement in French object relative clauses. In the sequenced architecture we can assign an analysis to object relative clauses as illustrated in (17). Morphological equations define the case feature of the relative pronoun, as well as the morphological features NUM and GEND, which are unified with the head noun's morphological features. With the uncertainty {COMP|XCOMP}* resolved by f–structure constraints on completeness and coherence, the morphological features in the μ–projection of the OBJect relative pronoun will be defined at the appropriate level of embedding, where we find the OBJect subcategorizing verb. If the verb is a participle, it must satisfy the morphological constraints on gender and number agreement that are now stated as in (18).

(17) (Les enfants adorent les histoires) qu'on leur a (déjà) racontées (mille fois).

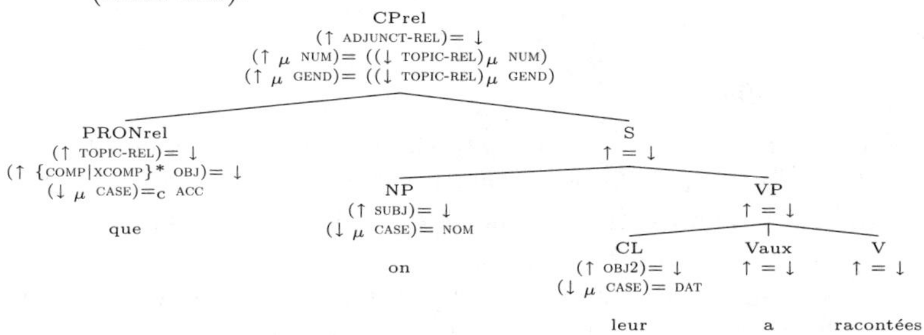

(18) racontées: V $(\uparrow \text{PRED}) = \text{`raconter}\langle(\uparrow \text{SUBJ})(\uparrow \text{OBJ2})(\uparrow \text{OBJ})\rangle\text{'}$
$(\uparrow_{\mu} \text{AUX}) = -$
$(\uparrow_{\mu} \text{DEP}^{*} \text{ VFORM}) = \text{PERFP}$
$(\uparrow \text{OBJ}) <_{h} \uparrow$
$((\uparrow \text{OBJ})_{\mu} \text{ NUM}) =_{c} \text{PL}$
$((\uparrow \text{OBJ})_{\mu} \text{ GEND}) =_{c} \text{FEM}.$

3.2 The morphosyntax of auxiliaries in French

Before proceeding to the formalization of auxiliary constructions in this new morphology–syntax projection architecture, we first have to decide on an appropriate c–structure for diverse types of auxiliaries in French. We will briefly summarize some arguments given by Abeillé and Godard (1996) and follow them in proposing a flat c–structure for temporal auxiliaries and an embedded VP for passive and copular structures. The architecture proposed here is, however, not dependent on the choice of this c–structure.

3.2.1 Temporal auxiliaries

C–structure accounts of the verbal complex in French have proposed nearly all imaginable structures:

(19) a.

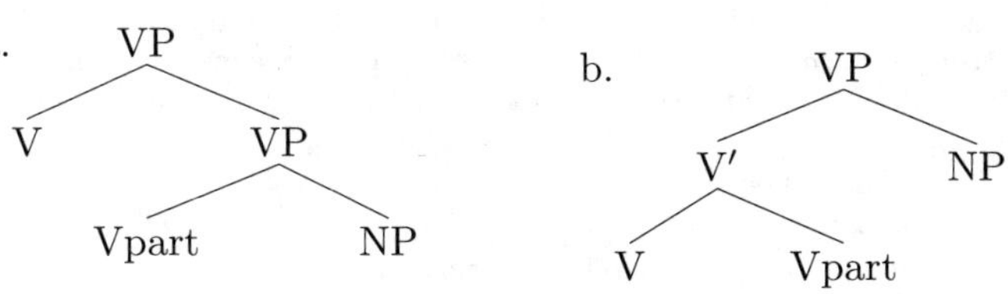

hierarchical VP

verbal complex

c.

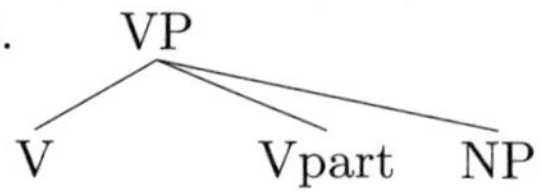

flat VP

The data that are used to motivate these structures depend in part on the theory adopted. Phrase structure does not play the same role in all syntactic theories. In LFG the role of phrase structure is rather limited but it is in general taken to account for local word order generalisations (see Kaplan and Zaenen (1989), King (1995); see in particular Bresnan (2001) and Dalrymple (2001) for more recent discussion of the type of generalisations to be captured by phrase structure rules in LFG). The position of adverbs, occurrence of sub-constituents and coordination are the type of arguments that in an LFG context bear on the c–structure assignment.

Abeillé and Godard (1996) discuss various possible c–structures and observe the following:

1. Whereas structures with control verbs give some evidence for an embedded VP, auxiliary structures do not argue for a right branching hierarchical structure (19a) of the French complex tenses. In French the participle + complements do not occur separate from their auxiliary as illustrated with the following examples. The bad examples in (a) contrast with the grammatical ones in (b).[16]

(20) a. *Allé aux Etats-Unis, je ne (le) suis pas. (A&G)[17]
Gone to the US, I have not (it).

b. Aller aux Etats-Unis, je n'oserai jamais. (A&G)
Go to the US, I would never dare (it).

(21) a. *Ce que Jean a, c'est bu trop de vin. (A&G)
What John has, is drunk too much wine.

b. Ce que Jean voudrait, c'est partir immediatement. (A&G)
What John would like to, is leave immediately.

The only exception to this generalisation is coordination:

[16]In fact, not all infinitival structures give this kind of distributional evidence for a VP structure either. Apart from the notorious *faire* construction, there are verbs like *courir*, *descendre*, etc. that cannot be clefted in the construction illustrated in (i) and (ii):

(i) Il court chercher le journal.
He runs get the newspaper.

(ii) *Ce qu'il court c'est chercher le journal.
What he runs is get the newspaper.

[17]Examples taken from Abeillé and Godard (1996) are marked A&G.

(22) Paul a parlé avec Marie et compris son erreur. (A&G)
Paul talked to Mary and understood his error.

This structure can, however, also be derived via a rule that allows the auxiliary (or the tensed verb) to be gapped (see e.g. Sag et al. (1985) and Brun (1996) on gapping).

2. Adverb placement does not argue for either the VP adjunction or the V adjunction of adverbs in tensed constructions. The principles governing the placement of French adverbs are not completely worked out but a large class of adverbs can occur between auxiliaries and participles: e.g.

(23) Jean a attentivement écouté son professeur. (A&G)
John has listened carefully to his professor.

There is, however, no evidence that this type of adverb is VP initial in all types of VP's. In fact infinitival VP's do not allow this adverb to appear initially:

(24) a. *Il detestait attentivement prendre des notes. (A&G)
He detested carefully taking notes.
b. Il detestait prendre attentivement des notes. (A&G)
He detested taking notes carefully.

The scope of adverbs like *attentivement* also provides some evidence against the VP adjunction (to the left) or the V adjunction (to the right) of these adverbs. In a sentence like (25), *attentivement* takes only scope over the first conjunct:[18]

(25) Jean a (attentivement écouté son professeur) et (pris des notes). (A&G)
John has (carefully listened to his professor) and (taken notes).

An adjunction to VP or to V as shown in (26) correlates in general with scope over both.

(26)
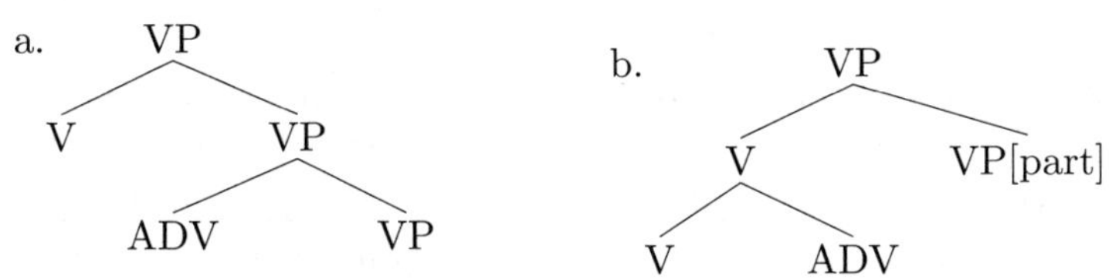

Of course, we can propose another way to map from this representation to scope assignment but this would further undermine the rationale for the hierarchical structure.

[18]Not all speakers agree with these judgements, which Abeillé and Godard restrict to manner adverbials, as opposed to temporal ones.

The facts summarized above can be accounted for if, following Abeillé and Godard (1996) we assume that manner adverbs have two positions in French, one in flat tensed clauses after the tensed element and before the participle, and another in some (but not all) VP's, left or right adjoined to them. In the next section we discuss some cases of embedded VP's, here we give a simplified phrase structure rule for the facts discussed above:

(27) VP $\rightarrow$ V[+tense] (Adv[+manner]) (V[+part]) ....

3. The verbal complex hypothesis (diagrammed in (19b)) does not allow a straightforward treatment of coordination with *ainsi que*: *ainsi que* can be used to coordinate complements and sequences of complements but not sentences or tensed VP's, as shown in (28):

(28) a. Cet été, Jean voudrait écrire une nouvelle ainsi qu'un petit roman. (A&G)
This summer Jean would like to write a short story as well as a small novel.

b. Paul donnera un disque à Marie ainsi qu'un livre à Jacques. (A&G)
Paul will give a record to Mary as well as a book to Jacques.

c. *Cet été, Jean écrira une nouvelle ainsi que Marie peindra des paysages. (A&G)
This summer John will write a short story as well as Mary will paint landscapes.

d. *Cet été Jean écrira une nouvelle ainsi que composera une petite sonate. (A&G)
This summer John will write a short story as well as will compose a small sonata.

The coordination in (29) can be taken to be the result of the auxiliary gapping rule, hypothesized above:

(29) Paul a mangé des fraises ainsi que bu du vin. (A&G)
Paul has eaten strawberries as well as drunk wine.

But this presupposes a flat VP and not one with a verbal complex. In the case of the verbal complex analysis one would have to complicate the conditions further to exclude sentences like (30):

(30) *Paul a mangé des fraises ainsi qu'a bu du vin. (A&G)
Paul has eaten strawberries as well as has drunk wine.

Under the analysis sketched above, coordination facts have then to be handled as nonconstituent coordination in all cases but the data about clefting and topicalization follow if we assume that only constituents can be clefted or topicalized.[19]

We could also take the facts just discussed to show that clefting and topicalization only apply to dependent f–structure constituents, i.e. the preposed XP should be equipped with an equation like $(\uparrow \text{OBJ}) = \downarrow$ or $(\uparrow \text{XCOMP}) =\downarrow$. This is, however, not the case in other languages. E.g. in German or Dutch a sentence like (31) is perfectly ok.

(31) Aangekomen is hij nog niet.
Angekommen ist er noch nicht.
Arrived he isn't yet.

Moreover this view would make the facts discussed in the next section difficult to account for without substantial revisions in the account of passive.

In subsection 3.2.3 we will follow Abeillé and Godard (1996) and assume a flat VP structure.

The assumption of a flat c–structure (19c) for temporal auxiliary constructions does not invalidate the architecture proposed in Butt et al. (1996a). The m–structure equations will have to be slightly rewritten to account for VP rules with more than two V nodes (e.g. for surcom-

[19] Abeillé and Godard (1996) take cross-sentential pronominalization by *le* or by a null anaphor also to be a test for VP-hood. We do not follow them in this regard: it is well-known that *it* in English can refer back to entities that are not surface constituents as in:

(i) The garbage had to be taken out. So Bill did it.

(See e.g. Hankamer and Sag 1976)

The same is true in French for both *le* and null anaphora as the following examples show:

(ii) Cet arbre est facile à abattre mais Jean ne le fera pas.
This tree is easy to fell but John will not do it.

(iii) Les ordures n'ont pas été sorties. Jean a oublié.
The garbage has not been taken out. John has forgotten.

So the antecedent of *le* or the null anaphor does not have to be a VP. Could we claim that the anaphor itself has the category VP or replaces constituents of that type? This would need a detailed argumentation because we would need to investigate which semantic types *le* can have as an antecedent (see Asher (1993) for some discussion of English *it* in that respect) and which verbs subcategorize for *le*. In fact, accepted wisdom has it that *le* only occurs with verbs that allow also nominal complements (see e.g. Huot (1980)).

In any case in other languages, the argument for constituency based on topicalization and clefting does not correlate with the occurrence of *it* or null anaphors. In Dutch and German the preposing of participles with their dependents is grammatical but sentences like the following are as bad as they are in French:

(iv) *Jan heeft een brief geschreven en Piet heeft (het) ook.
John wrote a letter and Pete has (it) too.

posed tenses as in *il a eu travaillé*). The respective V nodes will have to be annotated with equations $\widehat{*}_{\mu} = *_{\mu}$, $(\widehat{*}_{\mu}$ DEP$) = *_{\mu}$, and $(\widehat{*}_{\mu}$ DEP DEP$) = *_{\mu}$, respectively, to build up a hierarchical m–structure from a flat c–structure. In other words, there is no isomorphism between the c–structure and m–structure any more and the potential advantage of being able to encode the hierarchical m–structure without iteration of DEP annotations is no longer available.

3.2.2 Passive and predicational auxiliaries

Abeillé and Godard (1996) follow Couquaux (1979) in distinguishing the structure of passives and copular expressions from that for tense auxiliaries discussed above. With passive *être*, we find a different pattern of acceptability judgements from that found with the tense auxiliaries. This is illustrated by the following examples.

(32) Bien des bâtiments publics ne furent pas épargnés par les bombes, mais, heureusement, la cathédrale le fut. (A&G)
Several official buildings were not spared by the bombings but, luckily the cathedral was.

(33) Qu'est-ce qu'elle a été, la maison de Paul, détruite ou seulement touchée? (A&G)
What has Paul's house been, destroyed or only hit?

(34) Epargnées par les bombes, peu de bâtiments publics le furent, dans cette ville. (A&G)
Spared by the bombs few buildings were, in that town.

(35) C'est délestée de son portefeuille qu'elle a été, la malheureuse. (A&G)
It is robbed of her billfold that she has been, the unlucky woman.

Moreover VP adverbs can occur in the beginning of a passive complement as in (36):

(36) Attentivement écouté par tous les participants, l'orateur reprenait confiance en lui. (A&G)
Carefully listened to by all the participants, the speaker refound his self confidence.

In copular expressions like the following (37) Abeillé and Godard observe the same pattern of pronominalisation of the complement as with passive *étre*:

(37) Paul est trés attaché à son choix. (A&G)
Paul is very attached at his choice.

One can also duplicate the preposing examples:

(38) Tres attaché à son choix, Paul l'est.
Very attached to his choice, Paul is it.

and the clefting ones:

(39) C'est très attaché à son choix qu'est Paul.
It is very attached to his choice that Paul is.

(40) Ce qu'est Paul, c'est très attaché à son choix.
What Paul is is very attached to his choice.

So, it seems reasonable to give the same representation to both these uses of *être*.

The copular and the passive construction seem to exhibit embedded VP structures, just like most infinitival complements. Abeillé and Godard note two kinds of differences between infinitival constructions and the complements of passive or copular *être*:

– With *être* we find partial topicalisation or clefting, as illustrated in (41):

(41) Rassuré il l'est sur mes compétences mais pas sur mon avenir.
Reassured he is about my competence but not about my future.

This contrasts with

(42) *S'adresser, il le veut au directeur et pas à la secrétaire.
Talk he wants it to the director and not to the secretary.

– Although manner adverbs can take scope over all conjuncts of a coordination as in (43)

(43) L'orateur sera attentivement écouté par ses amis et observé par ses adversaires.
The speaker will be carefully listened to by his friends and observed by his enemies.

this scope is not obligatory. (43) is ambiguous between a reading where *attentivement* has scope over both conjuncts and one where it only takes scope over the first conjunct.

Abeillé and Godard take this to be evidence that we need a double structure for passives and copular constructions. In LFG, this double structure is unnecessary. Given the way unification works with f-structure, partial topicalization is automatically allowed, and it occurs in certain languages, e.g. German. In cases where it is not allowed, LFG uses ordering rules insuring the right results (see Zaenen and Kaplan (1995) for discussion). This allows us to propose just one structure for passive and copular *être* as adverb scopes can be taken care of by allowing the manner adverb to occur before the embedded VP.

3.2.3 The LFG account

Problems with the parallel architecture of the morphology–syntax interface led us to a sequenced architecture, where m–structure is projected off the f–structure. In sections 3.1.4 we have shown that both local and long–distance agreement phenomena can be easily stated in this setup. In the previous section we have seen that empirical arguments favor a flat VP structure for tense auxiliaries in French, as opposed to the hierarchical structure proposed in Butt et al. (1996a). We now turn to investigate how to account for complex morphological constraints in the verbal complex within this new architecture.

Sublexical rules in the Xerox Linguistics Environment (XLE)

Before we enter the discussion of how to treat complex tense formation as well as passive and predicative auxiliary structures in the sequenced projection architecture, we want to introduce the *technical* morphology–syntax interface that is provided by the LFG grammar development platform XLE (Xerox Linguistics Environment). This interface will prove useful, later on, to define ordering constraints on the verbal elements in the sequenced architecture.

The XLE system provides so-called *sublexical rules*, which allow us to dispense with fully inflected LFG lexicon entries. These rules are designed to match the structure of the entries in a morphological lexicon, which is encoded as a finite–state transducer. These entries consist of a *lemma* followed by a sequence of word class specific *morphological tags*. E.g., the inflected verb *voit* can be looked up in morphology, and delivers the information: `voir +Pres +Sg +3rd +Verb`.

This structure of the morphological entries (a lemma followed by morphological tags) is recognized by the sublexical rules, which expand to the appropriate sublexical constituents. The resulting sublexical structure is not to be confounded with a genuine word–internal constituent morphological structure. What the sublexical structures represent is the interface to a *formal morphology lexicon structure* assigned to fully inflected forms. This device of XLE proves extremely helpful in designing generalized rules that specify which type of morphological, functional, or even semantic information can be associated with and projected from morphological information encoded in these entries. But it should be kept in mind that nothing hinges on this device. The formalization we propose in subsequent sections can be restated without sublexical rules, by using an LFG lexicon with fully inflected word forms.

The definition of subject verb agreement, dealt with in section 3.1.4, serves as a simple example to illustrate the usage of sublexical rules.

Instead of fully inflected verb forms, the lexicon contains stem entries with category V (see (44a)), which matches the sublexical constituent V_BASE in the sublexical rule (44b). morphological tags like +Pres, +Sg, and +3rd that are provided by the morphological transducer are defined in the sublexical lexicon (44c) to project the appropriate features in terms of functional or morphological annotations. subject verb agreement can thus be defined locally, in a very general way, by annotations of the sublexical constituents VS_NUM and VS_PERS of finite verbs. By trivial functional equations in the sublexical rule (44b) the partial structures defined in (44c) are projected to the mother node of the sublexical rule, which constitutes the lexical V category of ordinary c–structure rules.

(44) a. tourner: V $(\uparrow \text{PRED})=$ 'tourner$\langle(\uparrow \text{SUBJ})(\uparrow \text{OBJ})\rangle$'
$(\uparrow_\mu\ \text{AUX})= -$.

b. V → V_BASE: $\uparrow = \downarrow$;
TNS: $\uparrow = \downarrow$
$(\uparrow_\mu\ \text{FIN})= +$
VS_NUM: $\uparrow = \downarrow$;
VS_PERS: $\uparrow = \downarrow$;
VERB .

c. +Pres TNS: $(\uparrow \text{TENSE})=$ PRESENT.
+Fut TNS: $(\uparrow \text{TENSE})=$ FUTURE.
...
+Sg VS_NUM: $((\uparrow \text{SUBJ})_\mu\ \text{NUM})=$ SG.
+Pl VS_NUM: $((\uparrow \text{SUBJ})_\mu\ \text{NUM})=$ PL.
+3rd VS_PERS: $((\uparrow \text{SUBJ})_\mu\ \text{PERS})=$ 3.

The flat analysis of auxiliary constructions

With the sequenced projection architecture (13) the analysis of auxiliary constructions as defining a monoclausal functional structure must differ substantially from the analysis proposed in Butt et al. (1996a). In the sequenced architecture, the hierarchical m–structure of complex auxiliary constructions cannot be defined in terms of c–structure annotations.

In the parallel architecture ϕ– and μ–projections are independent. It is therefore possible to project a monoclausal f–structure and a hierarchical m–structure from a single c–structure node, as depicted in (45a). This is not possible in the sequenced architecture, where the m–structure is defined off the f–structure. If we were to add the equation $(\uparrow_\mu\ \text{DEP})= \downarrow_\mu$ to the right daughter node in (45b), as stated within brackets, we would obtain an unwarranted, cyclic m–structure.[20]

[20]For ease of exposition, we discuss this point by referring to the hierachical VP

(45) a.

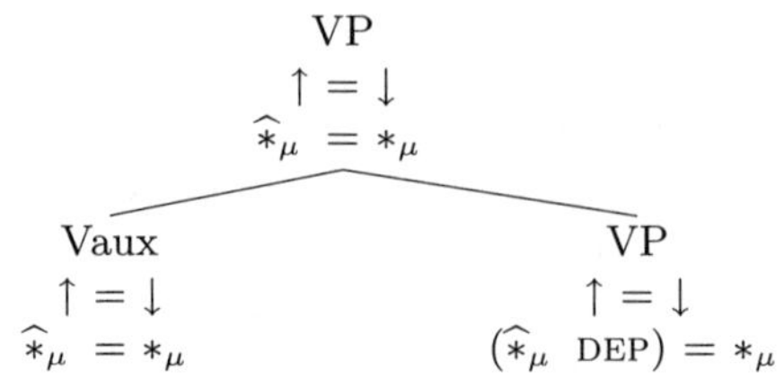

parallel architecture

b.

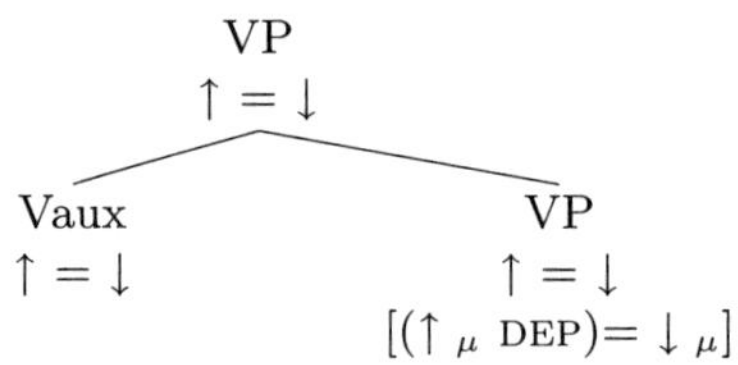

sequenced architecture

In section 3.2.1 we argued that the hierarchical tree structure is not motivated for French tense auxiliaries so that the proposal for a parallel morphology–syntax interface in Butt et al. (1996a) relies in fact on the wrong c–structure assumptions. Instead of (45b), we therefore assume the flat VP structure (46) for tense auxiliaries.

(46)

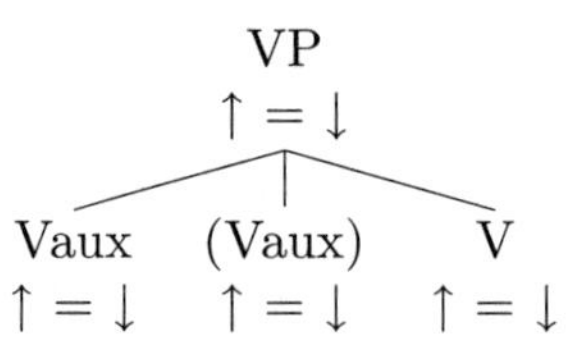

sequenced architecture, flat c–structure

Due to the sequenced architecture, the hierarchical morphological structure of complex auxiliary constructions can only be defined in the lexicon. Below we illustrate how the lexical entries for *est* and *a* spell out in our analysis.[21] The finite auxiliaries define their own morphological features AUX and FIN, and impose constraints upon the morphological features of their DEPendents. Furthermore, the constraints control the regularities of auxiliary selection and tense formation in French.

---

structure proposed by Butt et al. (1996a). But the argument carries over straightforwardly to a flat VP structure, such as the one adopted in (46).

[21] At this stage the lexicon entries for auxiliaries are stated for fully inflected forms. See below for a more general treatment by way of sublexical rules.

(47)

est:	Vaux	$(\uparrow_\mu$ AUX$)= +$	
		$(\uparrow_\mu$ FIN$)= +$	
		$(\uparrow_\mu$ DEP AUX$)= -$	
		$(\uparrow_\mu$ DEP AUX-SEL$)=_c$ ÊTRE	
		{ $(\uparrow_\mu$ DEP VFORM$)=_c$ PERFP	est venu; *a venu
		$(\uparrow$ PASSIVE$)= -$	
		$(\uparrow$ TENSE$)=$ PAST	
		| $(\uparrow_\mu$ DEP VFORM$)=_c$ PASSP	est vu
		$(\uparrow$ PASSIVE$)=_c +$	
		$(\uparrow$ TENSE$)=$ PRESENT }.	
a:	Vaux	$(\uparrow_\mu$ AUX$)= +$	
		$(\uparrow_\mu$ FIN$)= +$	
		$(\uparrow$ PASSIVE$)= -$	
		{ $(\uparrow_\mu$ DEP AUX$)= -$	
		$(\uparrow_\mu$ DEP AUX-SEL$)=_c$ AVOIR	a travaillé; *est travaillé
		$(\uparrow$ TENSE$)=$ PAST	
		| $(\uparrow_\mu$ DEP AUX$)= +$ }	a eu travaillé, a été arrivé
		$(\uparrow_\mu$ DEP VFORM$)=_c$ PERFP.	a été vu

In (47), both *est* and *a* constrain their DEPendent verbs to be main verbs, in which case their properties of auxiliary selection have to be met. In the lexicon, main verbs that select *être* for complex tense formation are marked by the feature $(\uparrow_\mu$ AUX-SEL$)=$ ÊTRE, those that select *avoir* introduce the equation $(\uparrow_\mu$ AUX-SEL$)=$ AVOIR. Thus, the constraining equation in the first disjunct of the entry for *est* captures the past tense formation for unaccusative verbs like *venir* (come). Correspondingly, the entry for *a* captures past tense formation for unergative verbs like *travailler* (work). The constraining equations further distinguish between two values for VFORM, PERFP and PASSP, the latter being restricted to passivized main verbs.[22] As in the original account of Butt et al. (1996a), the values of the functional feature TENSE can be defined in virtue of this type of morphological information: TENSE is set to PAST for tense formation with the perfect participle (*est venu*), and to PRESENT for the passive construction *est vu* (is seen), restricted to participles with VFORM= PASSP. Since *avoir* cannot be used to build passive constructions in the present tense, the entry *a* is missing a corresponding disjunct. By contrast, *avoir* can be used to build so-called "surcomposed" tense forms like *a eu travaillé* (has had worked), or *a été arrivé* (has had arrived). Here the auxiliary selection of the main verb is only observed by the embedded participle auxiliary, whereas both *été (être)* and *eu (avoir)* are embedded under the finite auxiliary

[22]The f–structure feature PASSIVE is set to + in the passive lexical rule. We do not go into any further detail as to the treatment of passive.

avoir in this complex tense formation. It is therefore only the entry for (finite) *avoir* that allows for surcomposed tense formation, i.e., it allows its direct DEPendent to be a past participle auxiliary.

The most important difference with respect to the parallel architecture of Butt et al. (1996a) emerges when we turn to the annotations of participles, both main verb and auxiliary participles, that build such more complex constructions. As noted above, the hierarchical m–structure for verbal dependencies cannot be defined in terms of c–structure annotations. The entries for the auxiliary past participles in (48), since they occur in more deeply embedding constructions, specify the complete paths of DEP features that characterize these various constructions.

(48) été: Vaux ($\uparrow_{\mu}$ DEP AUX)= +
($\uparrow_{\mu}$ DEP DEP AUX-SEL)$=_c$ ÊTRE
{ ($\uparrow_{\mu}$ DEP DEP VFORM)$=_c$ PERFP — a <u>été</u> arrivé
($\uparrow$ PASSIVE)= –
($\uparrow$ TENSE)= PAST-ANTERIOR
| ($\uparrow_{\mu}$ DEP DEP VFORM)$=_c$ PASSP — a <u>été</u> vu
($\uparrow$ PASSIVE)$=_c$ +
($\uparrow$ TENSE)= PAST }.

eu: Vaux ($\uparrow_{\mu}$ DEP AUX)= + — a <u>eu</u> travaillé
($\uparrow_{\mu}$ DEP DEP AUX-SEL)$=_c$ AVOIR
($\uparrow_{\mu}$ DEP DEP VFORM)$=_c$ PERFP
($\uparrow$ PASSIVE)= –
($\uparrow$ TENSE)= PAST-ANTERIOR.

+PaPrt PART { ($\uparrow_{\mu}$ DEP* VFORM)= PERFP
| ($\uparrow_{\mu}$ DEP* VFORM)= PASSP };
AUXPART ($\uparrow_{\mu}$ DEP VFORM)= PERFP.

The auxiliary participle *eu* (of *avoir*) can only participate in the formation of the *passé surcomposé* of verbs selecting *avoir*. The corresponding constraints are now stated relative to the m–structure path DEP DEP, as opposed to the entry for *a* in (47), and we assign the f–structure feature TENSE= PAST-ANTERIOR.[23] The surcomposed form for unaccusative verbs (*a été arrivé*) is defined, in similar ways, in the entry for *été*. Finally, the second disjunct in this entry accounts for the past of the passive *il a été vu*, again restricting the main verb's morphological form to VFORM = PASSP.

Finally, note that the functional annotations for main verb past or

[23] Again, we do not attempt to give any semantic definition of tenses in this paper.

passive participles (characterized by the morphological tag +PaPrt and its sublexical morphological category PART in (48)) contain an uncertainty path over the m–structure attribute DEP. Since the participle can be embedded at various levels of embedding (*a vu*, *a été vu*, etc.), this "uncertainty" of the level of embedding is to be projected from the lexicon entry in terms of the uncertainty path DEP*: the participle must "reckon" with the fact that it can be embedded by an undetermined number of auxiliaries. The resolution of the m–structure path DEP* is however severely restricted by the various constraints on morphological form.

Ordering constraints in the sequenced architecture

The sequenced architecture has important implications for the definition of the linear order of auxiliaries in complex tense formation. Note that the grammar has to rule out ungrammatical sequences like **eu a travaillé* for 'surcomposed' tenses, or **été a vu* for the past of the passive.[24] Since the complex m–structure of auxiliary constructions is a projection of the monoclausal f–structure, we cannot simply constrain the first auxiliary node in (49) to be finite in terms of an annotation ($\downarrow_{\mu}$ FIN)= +: given the equation $\uparrow = \downarrow$ this constraint is satisfied by both the grammatical and the ungrammatical sequences.

(49)

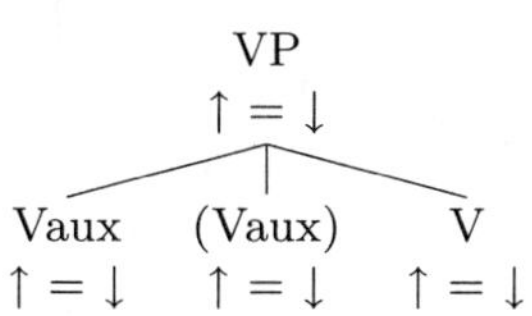

sequenced architecture, flat c–structure

A solution to this problem is to introduce more specific c–structure categories for the respective finite or infinite verbal categories, in order to constrain their correct relative order in the c–structure rules. To capture the ordering constraints of French complex tense formation, we have to define more fine–grained c–structure distinctions between auxiliary and main verbs, as well as between finite, infinite and participle verb forms.[25]

Parameterized rules, a formal construct provided by the XLE grammar development platform, are an elegant device for defining such

[24] The rule fragment for passive and predicational structures will be discussed in more detail below.

[25] In a language like English we would need further categories, in particular for progressive verb forms.

complex categories.[26] Ordinary phrase structure rules – both regular grammar rules, as well as sublexical rules in the syntax-morphology interface – can be formulated as *rule schemata* that take parameters as arguments. With instantiated parameters, these rule schemata are compiled into corresponding ordinary rules.

A simple example is given in (50). (50a) defines a parameterized rule, or rule schema for NPs with a singular or plural head noun. Due to the parameter `_num` with possible instantiations `sg` and `pl`, the parameterized rule represents the family of rules stated explicitly in (50b,c). A grammar rule that calls the complex category `NP[_num]` with the parameter `_num` instantiated to, e.g. `sg` (`NP[sg]`) effectively calls the instantiated rule (50b), with appropriate instantiation of both the embedded complex category `N[sg]` and the m–structure feature NUM= sg.

(50) a. NP[_num] $\rightarrow$ N[_num]: ($\uparrow_{\mu}$ NUM)= _num.
b. NP[sg] $\rightarrow$ N[sg]: ($\uparrow_{\mu}$ NUM)= sg.
c. NP[pl] $\rightarrow$ N[pl]: ($\uparrow_{\mu}$ NUM)= pl.

(52) shows how the crucial distinctions between auxiliary and main verbs, as well as finite, infinite and participle verb forms can be encoded in a system of parameterized (sublexical) rules. The two parameters used are `_type`, with possible values `aux` or `main`, and `_fin`, which allows for the values `fin`, `inf`, or `part` (for participle forms).

The important thing to note here is the effect of parameterization. Without any constraining parameter, any of the three alternative sublexical verb rules could be used to derive a V–category in grammar. With parameterization, however, it is possible to constrain certain positions in a grammar rule to specific complex V–categories. E.g., specifying `V[aux,fin]` in a grammar rule will constrain the V–category to *finite auxiliary* verbs, as defined in the sublexical rule for finite verbs in (52). In this way, reference to complex V–categories will allow us to hard-wire the relative order of main and auxiliary verbs in the flat VP structure, as illustrated in (51).

(51)

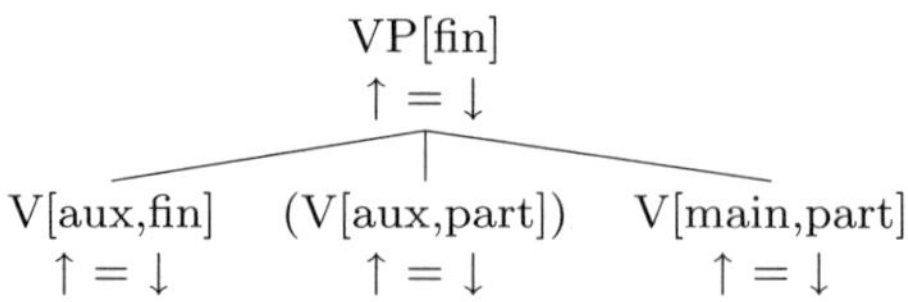

[26]The idea of using parameterized rules to formalize ordering constraints in terms of fine–grained categories was also suggested by John Maxwell. The notion of a *complex category* defined by parameterized rules is due to Ron Kaplan.

By trivial functional equations $\uparrow=\downarrow$ in the sublexical rules (52) the equations that are stated in the morphological lexicon (53) contribute to define partial f– and m–structures for the various complex V–categories.[27] Moreover, the sublexical constituents are annotated with equations that define, or instantiate the respective parameters. Thus, the complex V-type `V[main, fin]`, e.g., is restricted to sublexical structures with sublexical constituent TNS.

In virtue of the distinct morphological features AUX= – and AUX= +, projected from the lexicon, the `type` parameter of auxiliaries is correctly set to `aux` and, correspondingly, the parameter `type` is instantiated to `main` for main verbs. Finally, the distinction between main verb and auxiliary *participles* (cf. (48) above) is now captured in terms of the complex sublexical category `PART[_type]`, which is defined in the morphological lexicon for the respective types `main` and `aux` (see (53)).

[27] We are using the actual XLE syntax, where a trivial equation $\uparrow=\downarrow$ is added by default if no $\downarrow$ arrow appears in the annotation, but often state the trivial equation explicitly, for better readability.

(52) $V[\_type, \_fin] \rightarrow$

{	V_BASE:	{ _type = main $(\uparrow_{\mu}$ AUX$) = -$ | _type = aux $(\uparrow_{\mu}$ AUX$) = +$ };
	TNS:	$\uparrow = \downarrow$ _fin = fin;
	VS_NUM:	$\uparrow = \downarrow$
	VS_PERS:	$\uparrow = \downarrow$
	V_TAG	
|	V_BASE:	{ _type = main $(\uparrow_{\mu}$ AUX$) = -$ | _type = aux $(\uparrow_{\mu}$ AUX$) = +$};
	INF:	$\uparrow = \downarrow$ _fin = inf;
	V_TAG	
|	V_BASE:	{ _type = main $(\uparrow_{\mu}$ DEP* AUX$) = -$ | _type = aux $(\uparrow_{\mu}$ DEP AUX$) = +$};
	PART[_type]:	$\uparrow = \downarrow$ _fin = part;
	VPART_NUM:	$\uparrow = \downarrow$;
	VPART_GEND:	$\uparrow = \downarrow$
	V_TAG	}

Parameterized sublexical rules for complex V–category (preliminary version)

(53)

+Pres	TNS	$(\uparrow$ TENSE$) =$ PRESENT $(\uparrow_{\mu}$ FIN$) = +$.
+PaPrt	PART[main]	{ $(\uparrow_{\mu}$ DEP* VFORM$) =$ PERFP | $(\uparrow_{\mu}$ DEP* VFORM$) =$ PASSP };
	PART[aux]	$(\uparrow_{\mu}$ DEP VFORM$) =$ PERFP.
+Pl	VS_NUM	$((\uparrow$ SUBJ$)_{\mu}$ NUM$) =$ PL.
+3rd	VS_PERS	$((\uparrow$ SUBJ$)_{\mu}$ PERS$) = 3$.
+Pl	VPART_NUM	{ $((\uparrow$ SUBJ$)_{\mu}$ NUM$) =_c$ PL | $((\uparrow$ OBJ$)_{\mu}$ NUM$) =_c$ PL } ...
+Fem	VPART_NUM	{ $((\uparrow$ SUBJ$)_{\mu}$ GEND$) =_c$ FEM | $((\uparrow$ OBJ$)_{\mu}$ GEND$) =_c$ FEM } ...

Morpho–syntactic annotations for sublexical constituents

Based on the parameterized V–category defined in (52) and the (partially stated) functional annotations for the morphological tags in (53) we can impose fine–grained distinctions on the order of verbal elements

in complex verb phrases by explicitly stating the order of the respective instantiated complex verb categories in the c–structure rules.
The following (parameterized) c–structure rule for temporal auxiliary constructions encodes two possible structures for finite (`_fin = fin`) or infinite (`_fin = inf`) phrases.[28] The first disjunct allows for a single main verb of the appropriate finiteness-type. The second disjunct captures a verbal sequence consisting of an (obligatory) auxiliary of the instantiated finiteness type, followed by a participle main verb, and an optional intervening participle auxiliary.

(54) VP[_fin] → { V[main,_fin]
| V[aux,_fin] (V[aux,part]) V[main,part] }
. . . other VP-complements . . .

This rule accounts for the following sentence types. With `_fin` set to `fin`:

(55) a. Il vient.
b. Il est venu.
c. Il a eu travaillé.

with `_fin` set to `inf`: *Il peut ...*

(56) a. ... venir.
b. ... être venu.
c. ... avoir eu travaillé.

Temporal auxiliary vs. passive verbal structures

Abeillé and Godard (1996) argue for the following distinction.

(57) a.

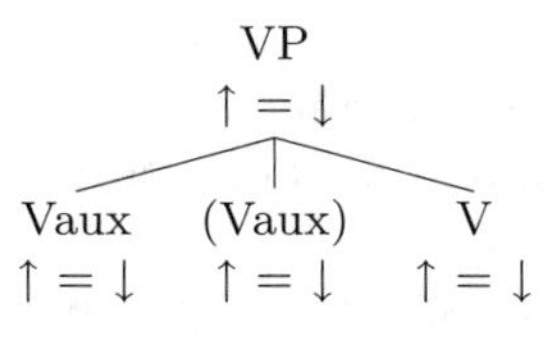

flat c–structure
(temporal auxiliaries)

[28]This rule does not take into account complex predicate formation, as e.g. with causative *faire*.

b.

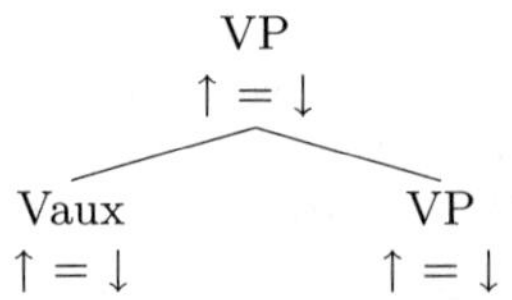

hierarchical c–structure
(passive, predicational constructions)

To account for both the flat VP structure for temporal auxiliaries, as well as the hierarchical VP structure for passive and predicational constructions, the rule system presented above has to be slightly refined because passive constructions are constrained to c–structure configurations with an embedded VP, as opposed to a flat VP structure for non–passive, temporal constructions.[29]

(58) VP[_type,_fin] → { V[main,_fin]
| V[aux,_fin] (V[aux,part]) V[main,part]:
($\uparrow$ PASSIVE)= –
| V[aux,_fin] (V[aux,part]) VP[main,part]:
($\uparrow$ PASSIVE)$=_c$ + }
. . . other complements

The disjuncts in rule (58) are devised for the following construction types, respectively:

(59) a. il vient / de venir / venant / venu
b. il est venu / il a travaillé / il a eu travaillé
c. il est attendu / il a été attendu / d'avoir été attendu

The order of the verbal elements in complex verbal structures is captured in c–structure by reference to complex (parameterized) verbal categories, which we defined in the sublexical rules (52) and (53). With these rules in place, the LFG verb lexicon will consist of entries for verb stems rather than fully inflected forms. The morphological features of inflected verb forms are projected from the annotations of the sublexical rules and sublexical constituents.

For auxiliaries of type aux, however, the lexicon has to encode a distinction between *participle* auxiliaries and other morphological forms. In order to define the correct formation of complex tenses, the participles *été* and *eu* must specify morphological annotations that are *distinct*

[29]In the rule fragment given below, we restrict ourselves to temporal and passive auxiliaries. The predicative auxiliary *être* could either be defined as only contributing morphological and aspectual features, along the lines of the passive auxiliary, or else as a PRED-bearing element which subcategorizes for an XCOMP complement.

from those of their finite (or infinitival) forms (recall this fact by reconsulting (47) vs. (48) above). At the same time, the annotations for these two auxiliary participles *été* and *eu* are also distinct, and must therefore be specified in the corresponding lexical (stem) entries.

In the refined sublexical rule for verbs (61) we therefore define a complex stem category `V_BASE[part]` for (temporal) auxiliary participles.[30] This category shows up as the stem category V[part] in (60), the auxiliary stem lexicon for the *temporal* and *passive* auxiliaries *avoir* and *être*. It distinguishes participle forms `V[part]` from other morphological forms, which are covered by the category `V`. The annotations of the respective disjuncts correspond fully to the ones given for fully inflected forms in (47) and (48).

(60)				
	être:	V	$(\uparrow_{\mu}\ \text{AUX})=+$	
			$(\uparrow_{\mu}\ \text{DEP AUX})=-$	
			$(\uparrow_{\mu}\ \text{DEP AUX-SEL})=_c\ \text{ÊTRE}$	
			$\{\ (\uparrow_{\mu}\ \text{DEP VFORM})=_c\ \text{PERFP}$	est venu
			$(\uparrow\ \text{PASSIVE})=-$	
			$(\uparrow\ \text{TENSE})=\text{PAST}$	
			$\mid\ (\uparrow_{\mu}\ \text{DEP VFORM})=_c\ \text{PASSP}$	est vu
			$(\uparrow\ \text{PASSIVE})=_c\ +$	
			$(\uparrow\ \text{TENSE})=\text{PRESENT}\ \};$	
		V[part]	$(\uparrow_{\mu}\ \text{AUX})=+$	
			$(\uparrow_{\mu}\ \text{DEP AUX})=+$	
			$(\uparrow_{\mu}\ \text{DEP DEP AUX-SEL})=_c\ \text{ÊTRE}$	
			$\{\ (\uparrow_{\mu}\ \text{DEP DEP VFORM})=_c\ \text{PERFP}$	a été arrivé
			$(\uparrow\ \text{PASSIVE})=-$	
			$(\uparrow\ \text{TENSE})=\text{PAST-ANTERIOR}$	
			$\mid\ (\uparrow_{\mu}\ \text{DEP DEP VFORM})=_c\ \text{PASSP}$	a été vu
			$(\uparrow\ \text{PASSIVE})=_c\ +$	
			$(\uparrow\ \text{TENSE})=\text{PAST}\ \}.$	
	avoir:	V	$(\uparrow_{\mu}\ \text{AUX})=+$	
			$(\uparrow\ \text{PASSIVE})=-$	
			$\{\ (\uparrow_{\mu}\ \text{DEP AUX})=-$	a travaillé
			$(\uparrow_{\mu}\ \text{DEP AUX-SEL})=_c\ \text{AVOIR}$	
			$(\uparrow\ \text{TENSE})=\text{PAST}$	
			$\mid\ (\uparrow_{\mu}\ \text{DEP AUX})=+\ \}$	a eu travaillé, a été arrivé
			$(\uparrow_{\mu}\ \text{DEP VFORM})=_c\ \text{PERFP};$	a été vu
		V[part]	$(\uparrow_{\mu}\ \text{AUX})=+$	
			$(\uparrow\ \text{PASSIVE})=-$	
			$(\uparrow_{\mu}\ \text{DEP AUX})=+$	a eu travaillé
			$(\uparrow_{\mu}\ \text{DEP DEP AUX-SEL})=_c\ \text{AVOIR}$	
			$(\uparrow_{\mu}\ \text{DEP DEP VFORM})=_c\ \text{PERFP}$	
			$(\uparrow\ \text{TENSE})=\text{PAST-ANTERIOR}.$	

[30] We assume that `V_BASE` and `V_BASE[part]` are considered as distinct categories.

The sublexical rule for the complex category *verb* now reads as follows. Note that it differs from (52) only with respect to the parameterization of the stem category V_BASE for auxiliary participles.

(61)	V[_type, _fin] $\rightarrow$	{	V_BASE:	{ _type = main
				($\uparrow_\mu$ AUX)= −
				| _type = aux
				($\uparrow_\mu$ AUX)= + };
			TNS:	$\uparrow = \downarrow$
				_fin = fin;
			VS_NUM:	$\uparrow = \downarrow$;
			VS_PERS:	$\uparrow = \downarrow$;
			V_TAG	
		|	V_BASE:	{ _type = main
				($\uparrow_\mu$ AUX)= −
				| _type = aux
				($\uparrow_\mu$ AUX)= + };
			INF:	$\uparrow = \downarrow$
				_fin = inf;
			V_TAG	
		|	{ V_BASE:	_type = main
				($\uparrow_\mu$ DEP* AUX)= −
			| V_BASE[part]	_type = aux
				($\uparrow_\mu$ DEP AUX)= + };
			PART[_type]:	$\uparrow = \downarrow$
				_fin = part;
			VPART_NUM:	$\uparrow = \downarrow$;
			VPART_GEND:	$\uparrow = \downarrow$;
			V_TAG	}

Parameterized sublexical rules for complex V–category (final version)

With the above rules and lexicon entries, we can now illustrate the relevant aspects of the analysis for *Il a été vu*. The finite VP rule instantiates the parameter `_fin` to `fin`. The finite auxiliary *a* can fill the first position in the second disjunct of rule (58). The categorial parameters and functional annotations of both *été* (`V[aux,part]`) and *vu* (`V[main,part]`) are appropriate to expand the structure further as given in (62).

(62)

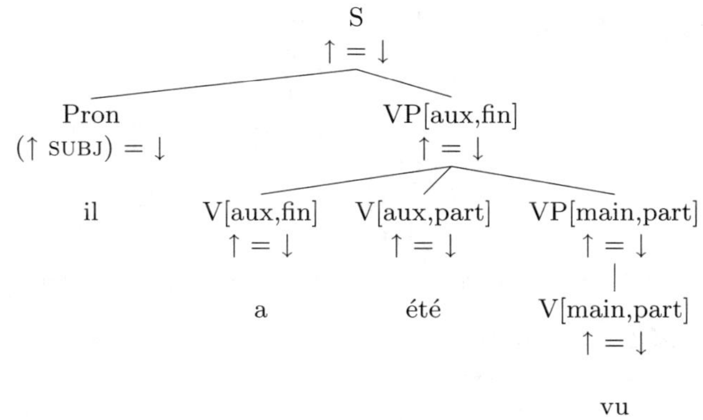

The reader may verify, on this basis, the morphological and functional annotations that are defined by the lexical entries and sublexical rules in (60) and (61), and how they resolve to the wellformed morphological and functional structures (63).

(63)

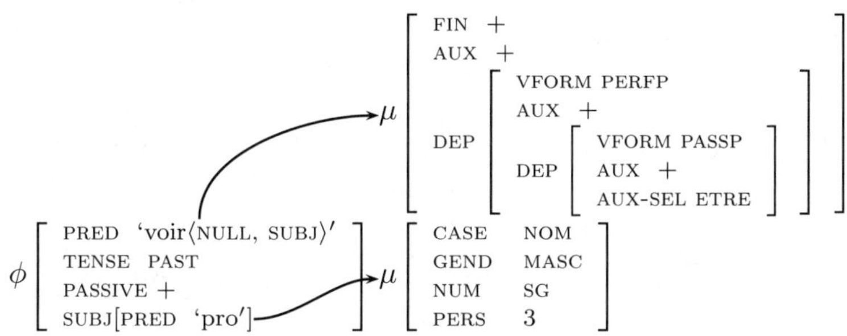

The corresponding German sentence *Er wurde gesehen* will be assigned an equivalent f–structure representation, but a distinct m–structure, which misses one level of embedding. In German the tense information is introduced by a single *past passive* auxiliary *wurde*.

3.2.4 Some consequences and some possible extensions

Where do clitics go?

As the reader might already have observed, the proposed system allows us straightforwardly to do away with most cases of clitic climbing in French. Clitics are local arguments in the f–structure and their functional annotations reflect this. We will assume a phrase structure rule that introduces the clitics as independent words which are attached to the verb. We could also consider them to be part of the verb, in LFG nothing hinges on this.

(64) VP[_type,_fin] → (CL: { (↑ OBJ) = ↓
(↓ $_\mu$ CASE)=$_c$ ACC
| (↑ OBJ2)=↓
(↓ $_\mu$ CASE)=$_c$ DAT}
(CL: (↑ OBJ) = ↓ ...)
(CL: (↑ OBJ2) = ↓ ...))
V[_type,_fin]: ↑ = ↓.

The annotations on the personal clitics will be as illustrated in (65).

(65) la : CL (↑ PRED) = 'pro'
(↑ $_\mu$ NUM)= SG
(↑ $_\mu$ GEND)= FEM
(↑ $_\mu$ CASE)= ACC.

The above clitic rule can be integrated into the complex VP rule established above as in (67). It not only allows for the ordinary cases of "clitic climbing" with auxiliaries like (66a), but in fact prevents illicit clitic positions as in (66b).

(66) a. Il les a vu.
b. *Il a les vu.

(67) VP[_type,_fin] → (CL: { (↑ OBJ) = ↓ ... | (↑ OBJ2)=↓ ...}
(CL: (↑ OBJ) = ↓ ...)
(CL: (↑ OBJ2) = ↓ ...))
{ V[main,_fin]
| V[aux,_fin] (V[aux,part]) V[main,part]:
(↑ PASSIVE)= −
| V[aux,_fin] (V[aux,part]) VP[main,part]:
(↑ PASSIVE)=$_c$ +}
...other complements

The equations of *y* and *en* will have to be more complicated as it is well known that they can represent material that is not a direct argument or even a direct adjunct of the main predicate of the sentence as for example in (68).

(68) J'en ai vu la première partie.
I saw the first part of it.

We do not go into that aspect of French syntax in this paper.

Possible extensions

The copular construction is not limited to *être* but can also occur with verbs like *sembler*, *rester*, etc. For those verbs we could not claim that they have no contribution to make beyond a morphological feature bundle and tense or aspect information. An explicit account of them is beyond the scope of this paper but sentences like the one in (69) indicate that the complex predicate approach proposed for causative constructions will need to be extended to them.

(69) Il lui reste fidèle.
He remains faithful to him/her.

If we do not want to complicate the clitic rules, these verbs will combine with their adjectival complements in the way *faire* combines with its verbal complements. LFG proposals for the treatment of complex predicates have been made, among others, in Alsina (1996), in Butt (1995) and for French in Frank (1996) and Dalrymple and Zaenen (1997). They need to be adapted to the proposal made here. This should not create any problems. The extension to *rester*, etc. should be straigthforward as these cases are simpler than the causative ones given that the subcategorization of the adjective does not change under the various types of embedding.

Possible problems

Problems for an approach that is uniform across languages arise, however, in several other cases. French has not only a synthetic future tense it also has synthetic modal e.g. *je travaillerais*, 'I would work'. Should the English conditional be analysed like the French one? We assume the answer is yes but a further type of problem is raised by the existence of tenses like the immediate future in French as illustrated in (70):

(70) Il va le faire.
He will do it.

The value of *aller* in this context is very similar to that of a verb like *will/shall* in English or a morpheme like *-ai/-as/-a/*etc. in French. Here, however, the clitic placement facts do not plead in favor of a flat f–structure solution, whereas the general consideration about the relation between syntax/morphology and semantics do. It would not be impossible to extend the proposal made above to this case but further investigations will show whether the advantages of bringing the f–structure closer to a semantic structure are compatible with a perspicuous description of the syntax of individual languages.

3.3 Open conceptual issues

Our proposal of a morphology–syntax interface that separates functional-syntactic from morphological information in a sequenced projection architecture raises a number of important conceptual issues.[31]

LFG has been very successful in abstracting away from order constraints and in that way bringing out the similarities between typologically distinct languages. As we stated in the introduction this is important, not only from a theoretical point of view but also from a practical one. The typological distinction between synthetic and analytic languages is also adressed within the theory. LFG accounts in a straightforward way for the fact that the same functional information can be encoded in one word in one language and spread over several words in another without giving up lexical integrity and without loosing the distinction between sentential syntax and word internal morphology (see e.g. Bresnan and Mchombo (1995)). However, as Butt at al. (1996a) observed the level of abstraction is pushed less far here. To push it further we need a careful study of what the informational content of various elements is.

Extending Butt et al. (1996a) we propose here an architecture that would make a distinction between coding projections, such as the c–structure and the m–structure and informational projections, such as the f–structure and the semantic structure. The c–structure manages the order constraints among syntactic elements whereas the m–structure manages the purely morphological dependencies between word forms. Of course the same element will typically play a role in various projections: the c–structure orders e.g. an NP before a VP but this does not prevent this NP from contributing the functional role of a subject, on the contrary, in a language like English it is by virtue of its position that it contributes this information. Similarly, the tense markers which can be independent words or affixes, play a role in the c–structure and/or the m–structure but of course also in the f–structure and the semantics. In this paper we have not discussed these issues but it is obvious that the main raison d'être of auxiliaries is not to take participle complements. What our proposal embodies is the claim that the functional contribution of the various morphological elements is not a one-to-one correspondence with the form of their encoding. As shown e.g. in Bresnan and Mchombo (1987) (on pronoun incorporation in Chicheŵa), the same morphological form can have different functional roles in one and the same language and across languages. Case has distinct functions across and within languages. In the spirit of several authors (e.g. T. Mohanan, A. Wierzbicka) we distinguish between morphological *content* and morphological *forms*. A same morphological form, e.g. a specific case can have a different content in

[31] We are grateful to Joan Bresnan, who raised several of the following issues.

different contexts. Under our proposal morphological form information would go into the m–structure whereas morphological content would contribute to the f–structure. The separation of representation levels lets us encode various kinds of mismatches across levels for features like number, person and gender in a straightforward and explitit way. Such a multilayered representation could also allow us to be more explicit about the presence or absence of morphological marking in a particular language.

It is not possible to give an a-priori answer to what belongs to the various projections without detailed analysis of morpho–syntactic phenomena across a variety of languages. A case in point is a puzzle in asymmetric agreement under coordination in Welsh, studied and discussed in Sadler (1999). One of the alternative approaches Sadler proposes to solve the problem is to postulate agreement features at both f–structure and m–structure, following the projection architecture proposed in the present paper.

A related but more formal issue arises from the proposed sequenced, as opposed to a parallel projection architecture. The sequenced architecture that we proposed implies a functional mapping from f–structure to m–structure. This architecture does not permit a single partial f–structure to map to distinct m–structures. Now, could we be confronted with languages where two expressions that bear distinct morphological markings unify at the level of f–structure? Such a one–to–many relation could not be represented in the sequenced projection architecture. Possible examples could be case attraction phenomena, for example with relative pronouns that appear in the case of the head noun, as opposed to the case of the syntactic argument they represent within the relative clause. Again, it has to be studied whether such cases can be accommodated by distributing inconsistent assignments over distinct levels of representation, or whether alternative approaches, such as the set–based feature theory of Dalrymple and Kaplan (1997,2000) – which is successfully applied to similar agreement problems – can accommodate such facts.

Complex predicate formation is another example where elements with distinct morphological (and functional) features are mapped to a single f–structure unit. This has been discussed in Frank(1996), where a restriction–based approach (including a parallel m–projection) was proposed to account for various problems in the standard LFG treatment of complex predicate formation.

In general, constructions which involve expressions with distinct morphological markings that are unified to the same f–structure unit are difficult to handle in the standard LFG architecture. The sequenced m–structure architecture can only handle such configurations if the mismatching elements are appropriately distributed over the distinct levels of representation, or else by adopting additional formal devices, such as the restriction operator originally introduced by Kaplan and Wedekind (1993), or the set–based approach to feature resolution by Dalrymple and Kaplan (2000).

Finally, and on a more technical note, one might wonder whether the formal device of complex c–structure categories that we used above to capture order constraints in the sequenced architecture could be extended to an approach where all morphological constraints are encoded in terms of complex c–structure categories. A separate level of representation for morphological constraints would then be unneccesary. At first glance it seems, though, that not all morphological distinctions can be naturally encoded in terms of c–structure categories. In the case of the French auxiliary system, for example, one has to express certain restrictions on tense formation which preclude ungrammatical constructions like **est eu travaillé* as opposed to the well-formed *a eu travaillé*, and similarly for **est été arrivé* as opposed to *a été arrivé*. To capture these restrictions, an analysis that relies on purely c–structure categorial distinctions will have to encode the lexical form of the auxiliary, *être* vs. *avoir*, as a c–structure parameter of auxiliary categories. Here we would have to decide whether this kind of lexicalization is still within the range of a natural complex c–structure category.

3.4 Conclusion

In this paper we have proposed a new architecture for the μ–projection in LFG. Our proposal has the advantage that it does not need to reproduce essentially functional information about syntactic arguments in the m–struture. We illustrated our approach with the description of a substantial fragment of the French auxiliary system and in doing so we showed that the problem of stating ordering constraints in the sequenced μ–projection architecture can be solved in a rather elegant way through the use of parameterized rules. The discussion of the French data elaborates further on the advantages of the μ–projection approach advocated by Butt et al. (1996a) but it also points to further phenomena that need to be investigated to get to a crisper view of what the division between language specific and universal aspects of syntax should be. The approach raises numerous interesting and intricate theoretical questions about the partitioning of linguistic features across the various levels of representation.

References

Abeillé, Anna and Daniele Godard. 1996. La complémentation des auxiliaires français. *Langages* 122:32–61.

Alshawi, Hiyan. 1992. *The Core Language Engine*. Cambridge, MA: MIT Press.

Alshawi, Hiyan and Richard Crouch. 1992. Monotonic semantic information. In *Proceedings 30th Annual Meeting of the Association for Computational Linguistics*, pages 32–38.

Alsina, Alex. 1996. *The Role of Argument Structure in Grammar: Evidence from Romance*. Stanford, CA: CSLI publications.

Asher, Nicholas. 1993. *Reference to Abstract Objects in Discourse*. Dordrecht: Kluwer Academic Publishers.

Bresnan, Joan, ed. 1982. *The Mental Representation of the Grammatical Relations*. Cambridge, MA: MIT Press.

Bresnan, Joan. 1995. Lexical-functional syntax. Lecture Notes, ESSLI 7, Barcelona.

Bresnan, Joan. 2001. *Lexical-Functional Syntax*. Oxford: Blackwell.

Bresnan, Joan and Sam A. Mchombo. 1987. Topic, pronoun, and agreement in Chicheŵa. *Language* 63:741–782.

Bresnan, Joan and Sam A. Mchombo. 1995. The lexical integrity principle: Evidence from Bantu. *Natural Language and Linguistic Theory* 13:181–352.

Brun, Caroline. 1996. Using priority union for non-constituent coordination in LFG. In M. Butt and T. H. King, eds., *Proceedings of the First LFG Conference*. Stanford, CA: CSLI Publications.

Butt, Miriam. 1995. *The Structure of Complex Predicates in Urdu*. Stanford, CA: CSLI Publications.

Butt, Miriam, Mary Dalrymple, and Anette Frank. 1997. An architecture for linking theory in LFG. In M. Butt and T. H. King, eds., *Proceedings of the LFG97 Conference*. Stanford, CA: CSLI Publications.

Butt, Miriam, Christian Fortmann, and Christian Roher. 1996a. Syntactic analyses for parallel grammars: Auxiliaries and genitive NPs. In *Proceedings of COLING 1996*, pages 182–187.

Butt, Miriam, Tracy Holloway King, María-Eugenia Niño, and Frédérique Segond. 1999. *A Grammar Writer's Cookbook*. Stanford, CA: CSLI Publications.

Butt, Miriam, María-Eugenia Niño, and Frédérique Segond. 1996b. Multilingual processing of auxiliaries in LFG. In D. Gibbon, ed., *Natural Language Processing and Speech Technology*. Berlin: Mouton de Gruyter. Also reprinted in this volume, pages 23-65.

Couquaux, Daniel. 1979. Sur la syntaxe des phrases prédicatives en français. *Linguisticae Investigationes* III:245–284.

Dalrymple, Mary. 2001. *Lexical Functional Grammar*, vol. 34 of *Syntax and Semantics*. San Diego: Academic Press.

Dalrymple, Mary and Ronald Kaplan. 1997. A set-based approach to feature resolution. In M. Butt and T. H. King, eds., *Proceedings of the LFG97 Conference*. Stanford, CA: CSLI Publications.

Dalrymple, Mary and Ronald Kaplan. 2000. Feature indeterminacy and feature resolution. *Language* 74:759–798.

Dalrymple, Mary and Annie Zaenen. 1997. Les verbes causatifs "polymorphiques": les prédicats complexes en français. *Langages* 122:79–95.

Dorna, Michael, Anette Frank, Josef van Genabith, and Mmele Emele. 1998. Syntactic and semantic transfer with f-structures. In *Proceedings of the ACL/COLING Conference*.

Falk, Yehuda. 1984. The English auxiliary system: A Lexical-Functional Grammar analysis. *Language* 60:483–509.

Frank, Anette. 1996. A note on complex predicate formations: Evidence from auxiliary selection, reflexivization, passivization, and past participle agreement in French and Italian. In *Proceedings of the First LFG Conference*. Stanford, CA: CSLI Publications.

Gosselin, Louis. 1996. *Semantique de la temporalité en Français*. Duculot.

Hankamer, Jorge and Ivan A. Sag. 1976. Deep and surface anaphora. *Linguistic Inquiry* 7:391–426.

Huot, Hélène. 1981. *Les constructions infinitives du Français*. Genéve: Librairie Droz.

Kamp, Hans and Uwe Reyle. 1993. *From Discourse to Logic*. Dordrecht: Kluwer Academic Publishers.

Kamp, Hans and Christian Rohrer. 1983. Tense in texts. In R. Bäuerle, C. Schwarze, and A. von Stechow, eds., *Meaning, Use, and Interpretation of Language*, pages 250–269. Berlin: de Gruyter.

Kamp, Hans and Christian Rohrer. 1988. Temporal reference in French. University of Stuttgart.

Kaplan, Ronald. 1987. Three seductions of computational psycholinguistics. In P. Whitelock, H. Somers, P. Bennet, R. Johnson, and M. M. Wood, eds., *Linguistic Theory and Computer Applications*, pages 149–188. London: Academic Press.

Kaplan, Ronald and J. Wedekind. 1993. Restriction and correspondence-based translation. In *Proceedings of the EACL93*, pages 193–202.

Kaplan, Ronald and Annie Zaenen. 1986. Long-distance dependencies, constituent structure, and functional uncertainty. In M. Baltin and A. Kroch, eds., *Alternative Conceptions of Phrase Structure*, pages 17–42. Chicago: University of Chicago Press. Reprinted in Mary Dalrymple, Ronald M. Kaplan, John T. Maxwell III and Annie Zaenen (eds.) *Formal Issues in Lexical-Functional Grammar*. CSLI Publicahtions. Stanford, CA.

Keenan, Edward. 1976. Towards a universal definition of subject. In C. Li, ed., *Subject and Topic*, pages 303–333. New York: Academic Press.

King, Tracy Holloway. 1993. *Configuring Topic and Focus in Russian*. Ph.D. thesis, Stanford University.

King, Tracy Holloway. 1995. *Configuring Topic and Focus in Russian*. Stanford, CA: CSLI Publications.

Reichenbach, Hans. 1947. *Elements of Symbolic Logic*. London: Collier-MacMillan.

Sadler, Louisa. 1999. Non-distributive features and coordination in Welsh. In M. Butt and T. H. King, eds., *Proceedings of the LFG99 Conference*. Stanford, CA: CSLI Publications.

Sag, Ivan A., Gerald Gazdar, Thomas Wasow, and S. Wisler. 1985. *Coordination and How to Distinguish Categories*. Stanford, CA: CSLI Publications.

Schwarze, Christoph. 1996. The syntax of Romance auxiliaries. In M. Butt and T. H. King, eds., *Proceedings of the First LFG Conference*. Stanford, CA: CSLI Publications.

van Genabith, Josef and Richard Crouch. 1996. Direct and underspecified interpretations of LFG f-structures. In *Proceedings of COLING 1996*, pages 262–267.

Vincent, Nigel and Kersti Börjars. 1996. Suppletion and syntactic theory. In M. Butt and T. H. King, eds., *Proceedings of the First LFG Conference*. Stanford, CA: CSLI Publications.

Zaenen, Annie and Ronald Kaplan. 1995. Formal devices for linguistics generalizations: West Germanic word order in LFG. In M. Dalrymple, R. M. Kaplan, J. Maxwell, and A. Zaenen, eds., *Formal Issues in Lexical-Functional Grammar*, pages 215–239. Stanford, CA: CSLI Publications.

4

Morphology - an overview of central concepts

ANDREW SPENCER

4.1 Two models of morphology

In this chapter I review some of the key issues in recent morphological theory, bringing out those aspects which are most important for the syntax-morphology interface.[1] I will concentrate almost exclusively on inflectional morphology, largely leaving aside derivation, compounding, cliticization as well as the relationship between morphology and phonology, syntax and semantics. My aim is to present a picture of morphology as practicing morphologists see the subject.

I begin with two simple concepts. Consider the set of words {cat, cats}. In one important sense we have two words here. In another sense, however, the set illustrates just one word, that is, a single lexical entry, CAT, whose singular form is /cat/ and whose plural form is /cats/. On the one hand we need to say that CAT is a lexeme, which we can think of as a Saussurean sign, a pairing of meaning and a set of forms (Matthews 1972, 160–1). On the other hand we need to associate the two word forms {cat, cats} with the lexeme CAT, realizing the morphosyntactic description 'singular form of CAT' and 'plural form of CAT'. Our set of forms {cat, cats} is the concrete realization of a paradigm, with two cells which can be labelled with morphosyntactic features: [Number:Sg],

[1] I am grateful to two anonymous reviewers and to one of the editors for useful suggestions on an earlier draft. I am also grateful to the British Academy and Leverhulme Trust for a Senior Research Fellowship which helped support the final preparation of this chapter.

Projecting Morphology.
Louisa Sadler and Andrew Spencer (Eds.).

[Number:Pl].

At the same time, it's apparent that the form *cats* consists of a root *cat-* and a suffix *-s* and that the lexical meaning of CAT is expressed by *cat-* while the functional meaning, or morphosyntactic property 'plural' is expressed by *-s*. In the American Structuralist tradition associated with such authors as Bloomfield, we would say that the forms /cat/ and /s/ are morphemes, the minimal meaningful components of a word. The full semantic characterization of the word results from combining the meaning of the parts (some sort of unification is generally presupposed). This way of thinking is crucial to syntactically-based approaches deriving from the proposals of Pollock (1989), and I have called this set of assumptions Radical Agglutination (Spencer 1992).

The two notions 'lexeme' (or 'lexical entry') and 'morpheme' are both very important in the development of contemporary morphology. It's therefore a little disturbing to think that these concepts are almost completely incompatible with each other. Under the morpheme theory, both /cat/ and /s/ are Saussurean signs and they are both lexical entries in their own right. This means that *cats* is no different structurally from a compound such as *catfood*. To be sure *-s* is a 'bound morph(eme)', but in English compounds, too, can consist of bound forms (see below). It is therefore impossible to reconstruct the notion that cats is a form of a more abstract object, a lexeme CAT which is associated with various (inflected) word forms which serve to realize various morphosyntactic properties in the paradigm associated with the appropriate (class of) lexemes.

In this chapter I shall explore the tension that results from these observations against the background of recent research in morphology and morphosyntax. A sizable number of morphologists reject the classical morpheme concept and Radical Agglutination (though perhaps to varying degrees) especially where inflection is concerned. To begin with I review the key concepts in greater detail.

4.1.1 Morphemes as signs (form-meaning pairs)

In this subsection I review some of the considerations which motivate the view that there is no difference between affixes and words, and that morphotactics should therefore be subsumed under syntax. In classical morpheme theory the concatenation of morphemes ('morphotactics') is only superficially different from compounding and, to be sure, the similarity between compound and affixation is apparent in many cases in which affixes are homophonous with free standing words. In many cases we find homophony with function words such as adpositions or pronominals. Thus, Russian has a series of prefixes which are homophonous with prepositions. From the verb *bežat′* 'to run' we obtain the following:

(1) v 'in'
vbežat′
'to run into'

(2) do 'up to'
dobežat′
'to run up to, as far as'

(3) za 'behind'
zabežat′
'to run behind'

In Chukchee predicatively used nouns and adjectives agree in person/number with the subject (where the 1sg person/number affix is attached by means of a connecting vowel/glide 'i/j' or 'e' depending on vowel harmony):

(4) a. čawuw 'reindeer herder'

b. gəm čawuwaj-gəm
I reindeer herder-1SG
'I am a reindeer herder'

c. muri čawuwa-more
we reindeer herder-1PL
'We are reindeer herders'

(5) a. -erme- 'strong'

b. gəm n-ermej-gəm
I ADJECTIVE-strong-1SG
'I am strong'

c. muri n-erme-muri
we ADJECTIVE-strong-1PL
'We are strong'

In 3rd person forms there is no suffix but in 1st/2nd persons the person/number suffix is homophonous with the Absolutive Case form of the pronoun. We can tell that the pronominal suffix is a suffix because it undergoes vowel harmony (cf. *muri* ~ *more* in the (c) examples), and vowel harmony takes the morphological word as its domain.

In English plural suffixation the suffix is a bound form and it exhibits phonologically-conditioned allomorphy. This means that the phonological shape of the suffix is in part determined by the phonology of the base to which it attaches. Interestingly, neither boundedness nor allomorphy is sufficient to distinguish affixation from compounding in general. In so-called neo-classical compounds such as *cytophage* or *phagocyte* we have two elements, *cyt-* and *phag(e)*, of which *phag(e)* shows non-automatic allomorphy, that is, lexically conditioned changes in phonological shape. (Note also that the components are joined by a meaningless connective or 'intermorph', *-o-*). These words are largely borrowed or specially coined, of course, but we find similar features in native compound structures in other languages. In Lithuanian (Mathiassen 1996, 57) the first component of many compound nouns takes a special form with a stressed connecting vowel:

(6) a. dáiktas 'thing'
 b. var̃das 'name'
 c. daiktãvardis 'noun'

(7) a. sáulė 'sun'
 b. tek- 'rise' (verb)
 c. saulėtekis 'sunrise'

(8) a. avìs 'sheep'
 b. kailis 'skin'
 c. aìkailis 'sheepskin'

(9) a. vidùs 'middle'
 b. vasaris 'summer'
 c. vidùvasaris 'midsummer'

In other cases there is no connecting vowel:

(10) a. laĩk(as) 'time'
 b. rãštas 'writing'
 c. laĩkraštis 'newspaper'

These compounds all belong to the 3rd (i-)Declension, even though their heads (the right hand members) may fall into other declensions (e.g. *var̃das* 'name', 1st Declension). Thus, both elements of compounds in Lithuanian may exhibit non-automatic allomorphy.

However, allomorphy isn't in any case restricted to affixes or elements of compounds. It's not uncommon for function words to exhibit allomorphy, a well-known example being the English indefinite article *a(n)*. Clitics, too, in many languages show unique patterns of allomorphy even if their placement in c-structure is determined by syntactic or prosodic principles. Hayes (1990) provides interesting discussion of a number of cases of allomorphy being triggered by syntactic rather than morphologically defined contexts.

It is sometimes assumed that allomorphy, and particularly the kind of idiosyncratic, lexically governed allomorphy that doesn't result from automatic phonological alternations, is a property, or even a diagnostic of affixhood. However, we have seen that even idiosyncratic allomorphy doesn't identify a formative as an affix or even as a bound element. This means that the principles that govern the distribution of allomorphs of morphemes in classical morpheme theory must go beyond the word domain in the strict sense. This means that the mere fact of allomorphy is insufficient to motivate a principled difference between morphology and syntax. For this reason classical morphotactics treats morphological structure and sentence structure as essentially the same, namely a string of morphemes. This is an architectural assumption which has been inherited in generative grammar.

4.1.2 Lexemes and word forms

We have seen that 'lexeme' refers to a (rather complex) pairing of form and meaning, which abstracts away from inflectional forms. The lexeme can be conveniently thought of as an abstract object defined by (at least) three dimensions, which I shall label MOR, SYN, SEM. The MOR dimension specifies the phonological representation of a basic root form (or perhaps root forms for certain lexemes), the SYN dimension specifies syntactic category and subcategory membership, together with argument structure properties, and the SEM dimension is a specification of the meaning, as shown in (11):

(11)		a.	b.
	MOR	/dog/	/sing/ [Tense:Past] = /sang/ [Form:PastPart] = /sung/
	SYN	N	V(SUBJ, OBJ)
	SEM	$[_{\text{Thing}}$ DOG(x)]	$[_{\text{Event}}$ SING(x, y)]

All theories of morphosyntax postulate sets of features. In fact, it's obvious that in general the grammar of a language has to contain two lists of features, one the list of all the grammatical features that the syntax makes reference to and the other the list of all the features which govern the form of inflected words. These will overlap but won't in general be identical (English has no inflected forms for the feature of DEFINITENESS, for instance). We will see later that there are also morphological features that have no reflex in the syntax, such as 'Conjugation class'.

Once we have a theory of features for morphology we can define a notion of 'morphological paradigm'. Traditionally, the term 'paradigm' is often used to refer to the set of word forms associated with a lexeme. Thus, the 'paradigm' for the verb SING in this sense would be the set {sing, sings, sang, singing, sung}. I do not use the term in that sense in this chapter. Rather, I follow contemporary morphologists in appealing to a more abstract notion of paradigm, one which is at one level of abstraction removed from the list of forms. In this sense, a paradigm is a definition of the set of morphological contrasts that a given class of lexemes can make. Thus, for SING (or any verb in English) a paradigm will be something like the set: {base, 3sg present tense, past tense, present participle, past/passive participle}.

Such a paradigm can be defined, of course, in terms of the set of morphological features, their permissible values, and any cooccurrence restrictions between them. These will jointly define a paradigm space, a set of morphosyntactic properties which find expression in the morphology. A given paradigm will be associated with each lexical (sub)class in the language. For instance, nouns might inflect for number and case, while verbs might inflect for tense, agreement and mood. Inflectional morphology is then the specification of the forms which fill the various cells of the paradigms so defined. Because paradigms are defined entirely in terms of features and their combinatorics, the notion itself is strictly speaking a derived one. It is the algebra of the feature system and the way that system is cashed out in terms of morphological form that is central[2].

The crucial insight behind paradigm-based morphology is that once we have paradigms we don't need (inflectional) morphemes. Inflected word forms are realizations of cells in paradigms, and all we need is a way of accounting for redundancies and regularities in the mapping between form and feature content. This mapping turns out to be rather complex and we frequently find that we can detect regularities in the paradigm structure which go beyond the way that a given feature set is expressed in word forms. For instance, we regularly find syncretisms

[2]Clearly, on this conception of paradigm, any feature system defines a paradigm space.

in paradigms, that is, instances in which the form in one cell is systematically identical to the form in a distinct cell. For instance, in English regular ('weak') verbs, the form of the past/passive participle is always identical to that of the past tense. In languages with more complex paradigms structure we find correspondingly more complex syncretisms. Phenomena such as syncretism are very difficult to capture if the relationship between morphological form and function/meaning is expressed by a form of compounding, as in classical morpheme theory. On the contrary, the compounding assumption, whatever its antecedents in the history of the language, gives rise to more problems than it solves.

This is not to say that compounding (or its close relative, cliticization) can be easily distinguished from true affixation. In fact, it is in the nature of grammaticalization that there is no clear dividing line between the two. But this needn't have any repercussions for the paradigm-based view of morphology. As I have mentioned, any theory which appeals to features ipso facto appeals to paradigms, because paradigms are a logical consequence of a set of feature structures. The crucial question is whether particular subparadigms, and in particular whether individual cells in paradigms, need to be associated with individual formatives (morphemes) in a privileged fashion, or whether we need to work with a more complex mapping which separates form from function and allows us to state generalizations over each independently. This separation of form and function (the 'Separation Hypothesis') is crucial to understanding morphological systems.

4.1.3 morphemes and lexemes

Although the morpheme concept has come in for severe criticism by morphologists, something like a morphemic view is still held by many linguists, including some morphologists. It is essentially the standpoint adopted in Distributed Morphology[3] (Halle and Marantz 1993) and Minimalist Morphology (Wunderlich and Fabri 1995), and a version of it can be found in Lieber (1992). It is also implicit in the work of Carstairs-McCarthy (e.g. 1994), and it is still the dominant mode of thinking for those interested in the morphology-phonology interface. Thus, the theory of Lexical Phonology (Kiparsky 1982) is morpheme-based as is much work in Optimality Theory (McCarthy and Prince

[3]However, the term 'morpheme' itself is used in a rather different sense in Distributed Morphology (something akin to the term 'lemma' in psycholinguistics) and adherents may claim that they do not espouse the classical morpheme concept. In effect, Distributed Morphology operates with a weakened variety of the classical morpheme (the 'Vocabulary Item'). See Stump (1998) for discussion.

1995, 1998). A frequent corollary of this view has been the (sometimes implicit) claim that the notion 'word' is governed by the same principles as sentence structure. This essentially means that word structure is an epiphenomenon (as it was in American Structuralism). Such a view has been argued for by proponents of Word Syntax (Lieber 1983, Selkirk 1982, Toman 1983, 1998, Walińska de Hackbeil 1986) and by a number of others (Baker 1985, Julien 2002). However, increasingly many morphologists have rejected this view and have argued instead that there are linguistically interesting properties of words that can't be derived from other modules such as syntax, semantics or phonology (Anderson 1992, Aronoff 1994, Beard 1995, Booij 2002, Corbett and Fraser 1993, Matthews 1972, Stump 2001, Zwicky 1985). These authors have in common the view that morphology is an autonomous linguistic module, with its own set of organizational principles and a rejection of the classical morpheme concept. I shall briefly expand on the main reasons for the rejection of the morpheme and I shall sketch an alternative based on the related concepts of the lexeme and the paradigm.

4.2 Problems with the morpheme theory of affixation

The conclusions that proponents of American Structuralism drew from examples such as those in Section 4.1.1 are that affixation and compounding are one and the same thing. However, when we look more carefully at such cases we find that there are disturbing deviations from the one-to-one mapping between form and function which is presupposed by the morpheme doctrine. Thus, not all Russian prepositions have a homophonous prefix and there are prefixes which don't correspond to a preposition. In addition, the prefixes generally have meanings which are totally divorced from any of their prepositional meanings (or more accurately, the combination of prefix and verb stem is non-compositional, and thus, strictly speaking, each component is meaningless). For instance, although *za-* is often used with an identifiable inceptive meaning, in other cases it has no meaning of its own at all (e.g. *zapisat′* 'to record, note down' from *pisat′* 'write'). In addition, the consonant-final prefixes exhibit allomorphy of a kind never found with prepositions (except in a handful of idiomatic fixed phrases). Thus, before a lexically defined class of roots, prefixes such as *ot-* 'away from' or *pod-* 'under' assume the form *oto-/podo-*: *ot-beru* 'I take away' from *brat′* 'to take' vs. *otobrat′* 'to take away'. Even straightforward compounding poses problems. Thus, the *black* of *blackbird* can't actually be the adjective BLACK. This is because while 'X is a blackbird' entails

'X is a bird' it doesn't entail 'X is a black bird' (female blackbirds are brown, for instance). Similarly, while *textbook* is headed by the stem *book* of the word BOOK and hence denotes a type of book, the component *text* is meaningless and hence can't be the word TEXT (Spencer 2000).

The problems encountered by the thesis of Radical Agglutination fall into four types. First there are well-known purely formal problems, morphological properties that seem to be signalled by operations over phonological shapes and not by affixation. Second, words (including compounds) often have non-compositional semantics when viewed from the perspective of the morpheme doctrine. Third, a theory of morphology has to make sure that the morphemes are arranged in the right linear order, and there are many examples which pose serious problems for a morphotactics based on the assumptions of Radical Agglutination. Finally, as we have seen there are generalizations over paradigm structure that can only be stated over features, independently of their concrete expression. Not only do these frequently cut across the actual 'morphemes' involved, in some cases the generalizations have to cover synthetic and periphrastic (analytic) constructions. On the other hand, there are few constructions which strongly motivate morphemes.

4.2.1 Morphemes as processes and not things

Hockett (1958) drew a useful distinction between two distinct ways of looking at morphology, which he dubbed 'Item and Arrangement' (IA) versus 'Item and Process' (IP) (see also Spencer 1991, chapter 2). The Item-and-Arrangement theories are those sketched above, based on the classical morpheme-as-sign in which the syntagmatic properties of complex words are effectively reduced to simple compounding, what is often called 'concatenative' morphology. However, it is well-known that morphological properties are often signalled by phonological alternations which are very hard to assimilate to compounding, so-called 'non-concatenative' morphology. Thus, we often find morphological properties being realized by (a) changes in tone, a widespread grammatical device in Bantu languages for instance, (b) stress pattern, as in *cóntrast* - noun vs. *contrást* - verb, (c) vocalism (ablaut or apophony) as in *sing* ~ *sang* ~ *sung* (and *song*?), and (d) consonant mutation, as when we convert the noun *house* /haus/ into a verb by voicing the final consonant *(to) house* /hauz/. In addition, we see replacive morphology, when an affix in a base form seems to have been replaced by another affix to give the derived form (*Marx-ism* ~ *Marx-ist*), and even subtractive morphology, in which a property is signalled by deleting some portion of a word form. For instance, in Russian we can derive personal nouns from latinate names of scientific disciplines by truncating the ending of the word: *biolog-ija* 'biology' *biolog* 'biologist', *fizika* 'physics' *fizik* 'physicist'. One phenomenon which has received considerable attention in recent years is the class of morphological processes known collectively as reduplication.

A summary the various types of morphophonological operation can be found in Spencer (1998) and the references cited there. Reduplication is discussed in detail in McCarthy and Prince (1998). Each of these operations has been recorded as a salient part of the morphology of some language. Item-and-Process approaches stress the existence of non-concatenative phenomena. On such an approach we take a basic form and relate it to a derived form by (a set of) phonological operations, which may include deletion (subtractive morphology) or repetition (reduplication). The morphophonological alternation or relationship is thus the bearer of the semiotic content. On an IP approach classical affixation or concatenative morphology is just a limiting case of non-concatenative morphology. In other words, it is no problem to assimilate the IA approach into the IP approach, since affixation is just one of a number of morphophonological operations employed by morphological systems. However, it requires no little ingenuity (or in some cases artifice) to accommodate non-concatenative morphology to an IA model. Indeed, the problems of such alternations as *sing* ∼ *sang* ∼ *sung* are what prompted Hockett's original discussion.

4.2.2 Deviations from agglutination

Five types of deviation

The next set of problems concern the way that morphemes contribute their content to that of the word as a whole. Under Radical Agglutination morphemes are like words. This means that we might expect them to show synonymy and homophony, as when we have two distinct plural endings in *dog-s* and *ox-en* (synonymy) or as when we have a suffix /z/ which means both 'Plural' and '3sg Present Indicative' (homophony). However, within a word a given morpheme should have exactly one meaning and each identifiable meaning component in the word should be expressed by exactly one morpheme. In other words from the assumption that morphemes are Saussurean signs it follows immediately that we must expect a one:one mapping between form and function, just as we find with compounds. In an expression such as *dog food price war* we don't expect the lexeme FOOD to assume a novel form just because the compound as a whole contains the lexeme WAR, nor do we expect to find that the concept 'price' has to be expressed by two separate words simply because the compound contains the word DOG rather than CAT.

To be sure there are non-compositional compounds (nearly all lexicalized compounds in English show some non-compositionality), and there are abundant non-compositional phrases, namely, idioms. However, even these lexicalized expressions fail to show the full gamut of deviations from agglutination which are routinely seen in morphological systems[4]. Nonetheless, in inflectional morphologies we find all the logically possible deviations from the one:one ideal within single words, even in supposedly 'agglutinating' language types. The four logically possible deviations are listed below:

one meaning	-	zero form	zero morphs
zero meaning	-	one form	meaningless morphs
several meanings	-	one form	cumulation
one meaning	-	several forms	distributed, extended, multiple exponence

I illustrate each in turn and then describe a fifth way in which the form-meaning can be deviant.

Zero morphs

The natural way to interpret the semantics of Radical Agglutination is as unification, as shown in (13):

(12)

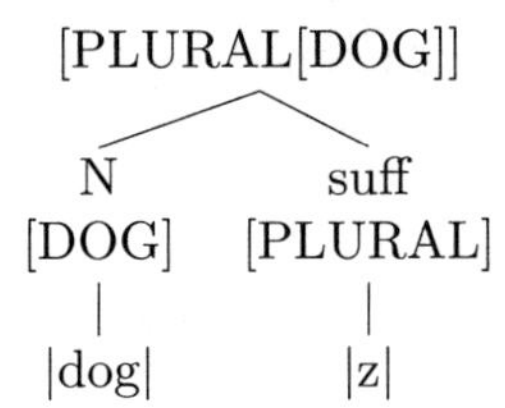

Phon:	/dog/	/z/
Syn:	N	noun suffix
Sem:	DOG	PLURAL

However, as soon as we start looking at slightly more complex cases we find that we need to subvert the principle of Radical Agglutination. In fact, we find this with less complex cases. Consider the singular form

[4]This simple observation is not generally made in the literature, but it points to a very significant difference between the concatenation of genuine lexemes (in semantically compositional compounds or phrases) and the concatenation of grammatical affixes to stems. The point is that real lexemes have a contentful semantics (in LFG terms, they have PRED values) while inflectional formatives realize feature specifications (and hence lack PRED values). I discuss this point in a little more detail in §4.6.

dog. Given that the entry 'dog' isn't inherently either singular or plural, this means that we must assume a zero singular morpheme to ensure that we have a singular marked form:

(13)

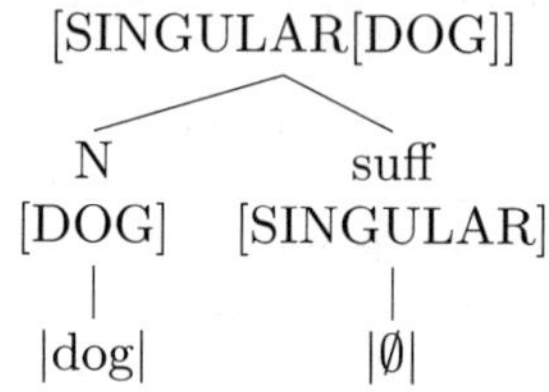

Phon:	/dog/	/∅/
Syn:	N	noun suffix
Sem:	DOG	PLURAL

Here, the zero morpheme is necessary to express the unmarked term of an opposition, and we might call this a 'default zero'. One might wish to say that the bare noun form can be 'pragmatically' interpreted as singular in reference, but that creates a whole host of problems, and in any case is not workable for examples such as Finnish nominative case discussed below.

Clearly, such an approach will require us to posit rather a lot of zero morphemes with different meanings, even in English. Consider a regular verb in the present and past tenses, as in (14):

(14) a. I/we/you walk
he/she/it walk-s
they walk

b. walked

The existence of a contrast between *walks* and *walk* suggests that we must distinguish at the very least 3rd singular from 3rd plural and 3rd person from non-third person. This is a very specific instance of syncretism. The form *walk* is syncretic between (or syncretizes) the feature sets 1st/2nd person and 3rd plural. On the morphemic approach this entails that we need two additional zero morphemes meaning 3rd plural present and 1st/2nd person present (as well as at least two other distinct zero morphemes meaning 'infinitive' and 'imperative')[5]. Other verbs in English provide instances of a different sort of zero. Thus, the past tense of PUT involves no affixation, and the usual *-ed* rule therefore has to be pre-empted. This is not therefore a default zero, but rather an

[5]It is hardly plausible to claim that the non-3rd singular present indicative forms are pragmatically 'unmarked' in some sense compared with 3rd singular forms.

instance of a stipulated zero. On a morpheme theory we would have to say that not only are there zero morphemes meaning 'non-3rd singular present indicative', 'imperative' and so on, but also a zero meaning 'past tense (of PUT, CUT, etc.)'. We'll see presently how a realizational model handles such cases.

Zero morphemes are generally required in languages which permit strings of inflectional affixes. In (15) we see some inflected forms of the Finnish noun TALO 'house':

(15) Finnish noun inflection

talo	'house'	nominative singular
talo-ssa	'in the house'	inessive singular
talo-i-ssa	'in the houses'	inessive plural

Finnish has a rich case system as well as a singular/plural number distinction. As can be seen, the plural suffix is *-i*, which comes between the noun stem and the case suffix. This suggests representations such as (16–18):

(16)

HOUSE	[Num:Pl]	[Case:Iness]
│	│	│
talo	i	ssa

(17)

HOUSE	[Num:Sg]	[Case:Iness]
│	│	│
talo	∅	ssa

(18)

HOUSE	[Num:Sg]	[Case:Nom]
│	│	│
talo	∅	∅

For convenience I've represented the meanings of the affixal morphemes as feature values. Note that we have to assume two distinct zero morphemes here, one for singular number and the other for nominative case.

It's important to realize that the need for zero morphemes such as these is not simply the consequence of a particular model of morphemics. There is a strong sense in which zero morphemes are entailed by any thorough-going theory in which morphemes are treated as Saussurean signs. We might, of course, imagine a host of 'mixed' theories in which the plural morpheme provided the plural number feature to *dogs* but in which the singular meaning of the form *dog* were computed by default feature specification. However, such a theory would encounter interesting technical difficulties. Means would have to be found then to ensure that the component *dog* in the word form *dogs* didn't get incorrectly labelled as 'singular'. This might be done by allowing the plural marking to override the singular reading, or by applying the singular interpretation as a default process in the absence of further marking. In each case we would almost certainly find ourselves appealing to the idea that there is a space of attribute-value pairings such as [Number:{Singular, Plural}], such that each (count) noun must be able to express each of these values. But such a space of feature values is nothing more than a paradigm. Thus, even a slight weakening of the morpheme doctrine leads us directly to some form of paradigmatic morphology. A zero singular morpheme in English can, apparently, only be avoided by conceding that morphology is not based solely on the morpheme-as-sign.

Meaningless morphs

The second deviation occurs whenever it's impossible to assign a meaning to an identifiable recurrent morph. This happens whenever we have a deviation from strict semantic compositionality. This means that any lexicalized compound that has undergone semantic drift without obscuring the identity of its components will be an example, such as BLACKBIRD, TEXTBOOK, PENKNIFE and thousands of other cases. In derivational morphology non-compositionality is the rule rather than the exception. Thus, in a word such as UNDERSTAND we clearly have a prefix *under-* and root *-stand* (because the component *-stand* exhibits exactly the same allomorphy as the verb STAND). However, neither component can be assigned a meaning. Aronoff (1976) discusses this question in detail on the basis of latinate formations such as *refer*, *confer*, *infer*, *defer*, *receive*, *conceive*, *deceive*, *perceive*, etc. These appear to consist of prefix (*re-*, *con-*, *in-*, *de-*, *per-* and so on) and base (*-fer*, - *ceive* and so on). Moreover, the bases show recurrent idiosyncratic allomorphy: *receive* ~ *reception*, *receptive*, *deceive* ~ *deception*, *deceptive*, *defer* ~ *deference*, *deferential*, *infer* ~ *inference*, *inferential*. However, it is quite impossible to assign any kind of constant meaning to either the prefixes or the bases. Thus, although *refer* obviously means something different from *conceive*, neither part of either word has any meaning of its own. Spencer (2000) points out that in inflecting languages such as Russian or German perhaps a majority of the verb lexicon is like this, and since the verbs fall into easily recognizable inflection classes it's even easier to identify morphs despite the non-compositional semantics.

In inflectional morphology it's more difficult to demonstrate meaningless morphs, largely because those who wish to defend a morphemic approach tend to adopt rather loose criteria for what counts as 'meaningful' (thus, for Carstairs-McCarthy (1994), belonging to an arbitrary inflectional class would count as part of the 'meaning'). German compounding provides one example of meaningless inflections. Many German compounds are constructed from a modifying noun in what appears to be an inflected form (Beard 1995, 100). Sometimes this looks like the nominative plural form (*Bücherwurm* 'bookworm' from *Buch* 'book' plural *Bücher*). On other occasions it looks like a genitive singular form: *lebenslustig* 'merry' from *Leben*'life', genitive singular *Lebens*. However, in many instances the linking element can't possibly be an inflection. Thus, in *Universität-s-bibliothek* 'University library' the form **universitäts* is not a legal word form of the word for university. This word is a feminine gender noun and hence doesn't take either a genitive singular or nominative plural ending *-s*. The linking element, or 'intermorph', is therefore meaningless. Similar meaningless linkers are found in the Lithuanian compounds discussed earlier as well as Greek and other languages. In these examples the meaningless morph is part of a compound but at the end of this section we'll see a clear instance of meaningless morphs in inflection.

Cumulation

The third deviation occurs when a more than one meaning is fused or cumulated on a single formative. Indo-European nominal inflection provides innumerable examples of this. In general only one suffix is permitted per noun, but the language group typically distinguishes two morphological categories, number and case. Thus, in Latin, Greek, Russian and so on a word such as *amic-orum*, *fil-on*, *druz'-ej* 'friend, genitive plural' has a single unsegmentable ending which simultaneously conveys the two feature values, a 'portmanteau' affix. However, it isn't just so-called 'inflecting' languages which exhibit this phenomenon. Finnish nouns express number, case and possessor agreement by means of a string of up to three suffixes. Finnish is a classically agglutinating language, so that the three affixes generally realize a single feature value in a transparent manner. In particular, case endings are constant for both singular and plural number. Given this it is mildly ironic that the language illustrates a serious problem with the classical morpheme theory. The problem is posed by the nominative plural form. This has a unique suffix, *-t*:

(19) talo-t 'HOUSE, nominative plural'
*talo-t-ssa ∼talo-i-ssa 'inessive plural'

This plural suffix only occurs in the nominative case; as we have seen the plural marker is *-i-* for other case forms. This means that there are two lexical entries with the meaning 'plural'. How does the grammar know which one to deploy in constructing a word form? The morphotactics of the language (however this is represented in the grammar) first has to select the plural suffix and only then the case suffix. The natural way of representing this is to say that the *-t* suffix is chosen if the case suffix selected on the next round of affixation is going to be nominative, but this requires a kind of prescience on the part of the grammar which is generally not allowed, 'clairvoyant affixation'). The only way to get the right forms is to give the nominative case suffix a special subcategorization frame, selectional restriction or some equivalent feature marking which states that it must appear to the immediate right of the *-t* morpheme. However, that won't quite work, because the same zero suffix realizes nominative case in the singular. Thus, we would need something equivalent to a disjunctive selectional restriction for nominative along the lines of (20):

(20) $\emptyset$: Nom $[\{\emptyset_{Sing}, \text{-t}_{Pl}\}$ _____ $]$

A disjunction of this sort is simply an admission that the analysis is wrong.

It might be thought that we could side-step these problems if we analysed the nominative plural form slightly differently. Suppose we say that the *-t* suffix means not 'plural' but 'nominative'. But in that case it must follow a zero suffix meaning 'plural' and must be marked so as to select a noun with precisely that (zero) suffix. Moreover, all the other case suffixes (of which there are over a dozen) would have to be specially marked to follow the *-i-* plural suffix. Clearly, either approach is equally clumsy and simply fails to capture the obvious generalizations.

Multiple exponence

Matthews (1972, 50) discusses the implications of the 1sg present perfect form of the Latin verb REGO 'rule', *re:xi:* 'I ruled'. The root form of the verb is *reg-*, with a short vowel. In the perfect tenses this vowel is lengthened to give *re:gsi:*. (The *-gs-* cluster is simplified to *-ks-*, orthographically 'x', by regular phonological assimilation.) This present perfect form can be segmented as in (21):

(21)

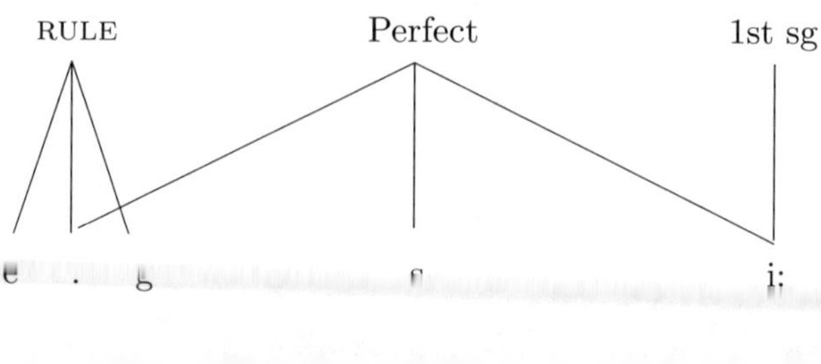

The principal exponent of the property perfect here is the-*s* suffix. However, the allomorph of the 1st singular suffix *-i:* also serves to signal perfect, because in other tenses we find different endings (e.g.*reg-o:*'I rule', present indicative, *reg-am* 'I shall rule', future indicative, and so on). In addition, the basic allomorph of the verb root has a short vowel, but this verb, in common with a number of others of this inflectional class, has a root allomorph with lengthened vowel in perfect tenses. Thus, the vowel length is also a marker of the property perfect. This means that we have instances of cumulation, but in addition a given property can be spread across several formatives (including the lexical root). This is what Matthews (1972, 80) calls 'extended' or 'multiple exponence'.

In his more detailed discussion of these cases, (e.g. Matthews (1972, 93f) he points out that examples like (21) illustrate not only extended exponence but also overlapping exponence, in that the formatives are adjacent. There have also been reported instances of extended exponence in the absence of overlapping exponence. Stump (1991, 1995, 2001) discusses Breton plural diminutives. The word BAG 'boat' has a plural form *bagoù* and a diminutive *bagig*. However, the plural diminutive shows double marking: *bagoùigoù* 'little boats'. This is therefore a simple case of pure extended exponence. It isn't difficult to find examples in other languages in which the extended exponence involves two distinct affixes. A textbook case is the German past participial circumfix in *ge-...-t*, as in *ge-hol-t* 'fetched', from HOLEN (root /hol/). Both parts of the circumfix are required to express the past participle property.

I have now illustrated all four common deviations from agglutination. It is, of course, possible to combine all of these except for the meaningless morphs. Thus, it's possible to have a zero affix which shows cumulation. Likewise, one of the meanings expressed by a cumulative morph may simultaneously be expressed by another morph (cumulation and extended exponence). In principle we can then expect to find cumulative zero morphs which show extended exponence. Actually, matters are worse. We may wish to argue that the standard compounding type in languages such as German, or especially Lithuanian or Greek involves an intermorph. But some compounds lack such an element: *Buchbinder* 'bookbinder'. This makes it look as though there are two very distinct types of compound, one with and the other without an intermorph. However, we can easily solve this problem by assuming that the components of all compounds of the type *Buchbinder* are linked by a zero intermorph. The question is not so much whether such an analysis is desirable, but rather what would stop a morpheme theorist from positing such a zero.

Morphologically complex words as constructions

The discussion has taken as its starting point the assumption that morphemes have meanings but that there are deviations from the normal meaning-form relationship in certain circumstances. However, for many morphologists the real conclusion to draw from these cases is more radical: all affixal morphemes are meaningless. An inflectional morpheme is simply a mark giving us (partial) information about how to construct a full feature specification, while a derivational morpheme is simply a mark telling us that there is some kind of relationship (not necessarily semantic) between two lexical entries. Non-affixal (non-concatenative) 'morphemes' illustrate this point even more forcefully. This means that there is really only one deviation from agglutination, namely, the second in our list.

How, then, do inflected word forms signal their inflectional features? Essentially, we need to think of inflected words as akin to constructional idioms. Even if it may look as though we can identify a meaningful element in an idiom, this is usually an error. The construction metaphor can be illustrated very simply by considering well-known future/conditional forms of Romance verbs. The Spanish conditional provides a particularly complex illustration of deviation from agglutination. This is formed from a stem which for most verbs is identical to the infinitive. The endings of the conditional mood are homophonous with the endings of the 2nd/3rd conjugation imperfect indicative: *beb-ía* 'I was drinking, used to drink'. However, there is no justifiable way of deriving the conditional mood from imperfect tense/aspect in the synchronic grammar. This means that the ending *-ía* cannot be said to convey the property conditional mood on its own, it only serves this function in conjunction with the stem form in *-ar*. This is illustrated in (22) the 1st person singular conditional form, 'I would sing', of the verb CANTAR:

(22)

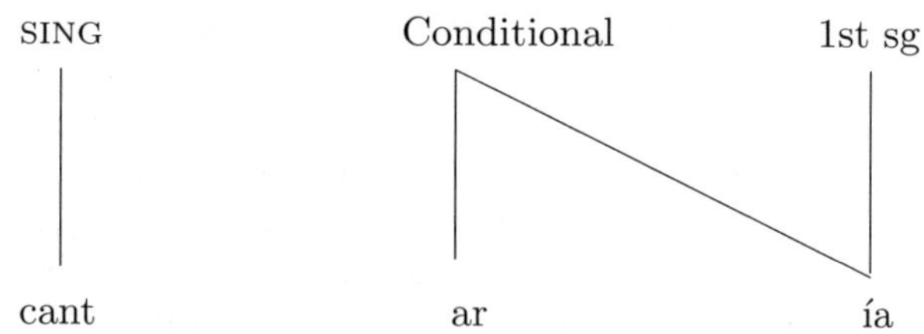

On the other hand, the *-ar* suffix only 'means' conditional when followed by one particular set of endings (namely, those whose primary role is to signal the imperfect indicative!). Furthermore, the form *cantar* looks very much like the infinitive of the verb 'sing', but this, too, must be a mistake. First, the conditional is a finite form and not an infinitive form, so if *cantar* really were an infinitive the features from stem and suffix would fail to unify. Second, if *-ar* is an infinitive ending then it must be a 1st conjugation infinitive. But the *-ía* suffix only combines with 2nd/3rd conjugation verbs. Therefore, we would have to say that the conjugation class membership is changed when the infinitive is formed.

The Romance conditional (and future) can be said to illustrate cumulation and extended exponence (I leave the demonstration as an exercise to the reader), but in a sense this is the wrong way to look at such cases. The problem is not that the meanings are distributed in a non-canonical fashion. The real problem is that the suffixes themselves have no meaning. Indeed, if we were to assume a meaning for these suffixes based on their default usages then we would find that we had to override that meaning in order to compute the meaning of the conditional form. In other words, it is as though the affixes are behaving like parts of a non-compositional idiom such as 'pull someone's leg'. Cases such as this pose particularly serious problems to the classical morpheme concept (see also the discussion in Matthews (1970, 107f), of the Italian verb form *cantarebbero* 's/he would sing'). Aronoff (1994) discusses stems such as the Romance *cantar-* in some detail under the heading of 'Priscianic' word formation, demonstrating conclusively that the stem itself is meaningless, an indexed form (a 'morphome' in his terminology). This theme is developed in some detail in (Stump (2001, chapter 6)) where it is shown that the distribution of the meaningless stems is morphologically defined and can't always be accounted for in terms of morphophonology.

If these five kinds of deviation were rare or contextually restricted we might wish to argue that they were not damaging to the morpheme concept. Unfortunately, it is very easy to find such cases, and many of the most difficult examples come from classically 'agglutinating' languages, or, like, the Romance future/conditional from transparent recently grammaticalized morphosyntax. Morpheme-based approaches therefore find it very difficult to avoid great artificiality when confronted with such examples. However, they also find it very difficult to state obvious generalizations without smuggling in the notion of paradigm in some form.

The conclusion from this survey of form-meaning relationships is that there is no room for the concept of the morpheme as Saussurean sign. This is essentially the Separation Hypothesis according to which any relationships which a linguist can perceive between form and meaning are the result of the operation of grammatical rules, principles or constraints and not form-meaning relationships which are lexically listed. Of course, where the mapping is particularly simple we obtain what appears to be a classical morpheme theory as a special case. But such cases are much rarer than is sometimes appreciated. It's important to understand that under the Separation Hypothesis there is no cumulation, extended exponence or zero exponence as such, because none of the exponents actually has a meaning. Rather the set of features realized by a word form is some complex function of the operations that go to make up that word form. As a consequence all affixes are strictly speaking meaningless.

Discussion so far has been restricted to the form-meaning problem. However, a theory of morphology also has to ensure that roots and affixes are lined up in the right order. This is the problem I next turn to.

4.2.3 Morphotactics

In the Finnish example mentioned above we saw three affixes expressing number, case and possession in that order. How does a morpheme-based theory guarantee this order? In the model proposed by Lieber (1981) morphemes are provided with subcategorization frames stating which other types of morpheme they are allowed to be adjacent to. This encounters serious problems when confronted with cases like the Finnish nominative plural, in which either a zero plural allomorph must 'know' that a special nominative suffix will subsequently be added, or a special 't' plural allomorph must 'know' that a zero nominative suffix will subsequently by added (what I earlier called 'clairvoyant affixation'). Stump (1993b) discusses similar problems in another classically agglutinating language, Swahili, in which even this cumbersome solution is excluded because other affixes may intervene between the two affixes which exhibit the special selection, i.e. the dependency between the two affixes is long-distance. Consider the examples in (23):

(23) a. wa-ta-taka
1PL-FUT-want
'we will want'

b. ha-wa-ta-taka
NEG-1PL-FUT-want
'we will not want'

The verb is inflected by prefixes for polarity (negation), subject agreement and tense.

Now consider (24):

(24) a. wa-li-taka
1PL-PAST-want
'we wanted'

b. ha-wa-ku-taka
NEG-1PL-PAST-want
'we did not want'

The normal past tense prefix is *li*. However, in a negative verb form the past is expressed by a special (cumulative) prefix *ku-*, which occurs nowhere else in the paradigm. Now, the problem for a morpheme-based theory is essentially this. If *ku-* 'means' both [past tense & negation] why isn't (25) grammatical?

(25) *wa-ku-taka

Conversely, if *ku-* is simply a past tense marker that has to cooccur with the ha- prefix, what prevents (26) from being grammatical, given that the unification of past tense and negation will go ahead?

(26) *ha-wa-li-taka

To rule out (26) we must somehow state that there is a dependency between the prefixation ('lexical insertion') of *ku-* and the later prefixation of *ha-*. This is a particularly difficult instance of the 'clairvoyant affixation' seen in Finnish. Stump (1993b) demonstrates in great detail that the subcategorization frame approach can't provide a satisfying analysis of such cases.

A more subtle problem of morphotactics arises with English strong verbs. In §4.2.2 I illustrated the notion of the 'default zero'. Now, not all zeros are default realizations. On occasions any theory will have to stipulate zeros. An example is provided by comparing the irregular past tenses *kept* vs. *sang*. Both involve a vowel change in the root, but *kept* can be said to have a (special) past tense ending *-t*, while *sang* has no such ending. We can say that the-*t* ending of kept is either an irregular suffix which pre-empts the regular *-ed* ending, or, possibly that it is the regular ending. However, what prevents affixation of *-ed* to *sang*? Any grammar has to be able to record the fact that *sang* is not just a past tense root allomorph (like *kep-*) but that it is itself the past tense form. On a paradigmatic theory we capture this by ensuring that the form sang is listed as the form filling the [Tense:Past] cell. There are various technical ways of doing this depending on details of implementation (see §4.3). As Stump (1998, 41) points out a morpheme-based theory requires (yet another!) special zero past tense allomorph here.

4.2.4 Paradigms

There is no obvious place in a morpheme-based approach to morphology for the traditional notion of paradigm. Yet there are many morphological systems in which the paradigm notion seems to be useful, if not indispensible. The commonest situations involve syncretisms. The theoretical interest of this phenomenon is that we frequently encounter situations in which we wish to say that the form which expresses one particular set of feature values is always identical to the form expressing some distinct set of values. That is, we regularly find that we need to identify the contents of cells in different parts of a paradigm. A well-known example of this is provided by Latin declension. Latin nominals distinguish singular/plural number and nominative, accusative, genitive, dative and ablative case. In most nominals (nouns, adjectives, determiners) the dative and ablative singular form is distinct, though in certain classes the forms are identical:

(27) Latin nominals - singular

Class	lexeme	dat sing	abl sing
Nouns			
I	'table' mensa	mensae	mensa:
II	'lord' dominus	domino:	domino:
III	'prince' princeps	principi:	principe
	'head' caput	capiti:	capite
	'rain' imber	imbri:	imbri: (imbre)
	'tower' turris	turri:	turri:
	'cow' bo:s	bovi:	bove
IV	'lake' lacus	lacui: (lacu:)	lacu:
V	'thing' re:s	rei:	re:
Adjectives			
	'good' (fem) bonus	bonae	bona:
	(masc, neut)	bono:	bono:
	'black' (fem) niger	nigrae	nigra:
	(masc, neut)	nigro:	nigro:
	'other' (fem) alter	alteri:	altera:
	(masc, neut)	alteri:	altero:
	'better' melior	melio:ri:	melio:re
Pronouns			
	'this' (fem) haec	huic	ha:c
	(masc, neut) hi:c	huic	ho:c
	1sg ego	mihi	me:
	2sg tu:	tibi	te:

However, in the plural the dative and ablative are invariably the same: *mensi:s, principibus, capitibus, imbribus, turribus, bo:bus* (alternatively *bu:bus*), *lacubus, re:bus, boni:s, nigri:s, alteri:s, melio:ribus, hi:s*. Even the personal pronouns respect this syncretism: 1pl *no:bis*, 2pl *vo:bis*. The syncretism is exceptionless despite the various endings found and the various patterns of stem allomorphy.

Now, as can be seen from the table in (27), some dative and ablative singular forms are also identical (*domino:*, *bono:*, *imbri:* though with alternative ablative singular form). However, the general pattern is clearly for the two cases to be distinct in the singular. Thus, the identity of form in certain singular nouns can't be regarded as a property of the nominal system as a whole, but only of certain declensional classes (the traditional 2nd declension and the i-stems of the 3rd declension). The challenge for linguistic theory is to be able to represent both types of syncretism. It's not obvious how this is to be achieved if each ending is given its own lexical entry. First, the dative singular *-i:* ending only doubles as the ablative singular in words such as *imber* 'rain' or *turris* 'tower', not with *princeps* 'prince' or *caput* 'head'. But perhaps more importantly, in the plural a morpheme based theory would have to assign a dual feature value of [{dative, ablative}, plural] to each of the various dative/ablative plural endings, *-i:s*, (*a:/e:/i/o:/u*)*bus*. But this would make it a complete accident that all dative and ablative plural endings are alike. It is systematic cross-paradigm dependencies of this sort that paradigm-based theories are designed to express. The way it is done is to distinguish in a principled way between the feature content of a cell in the paradigm and the form which occupies that cell.

4.3 Realization- (paradigm-) based approaches

On the classical morpheme-based theory the feature content of the complete word is given by combining the content of the individual morphemes in a manner which in general respects monotonicity. In the taxonomy of Stump (2001) such a bottom-up theory is 'incremental'. In addition, the morphemes themselves are lexical objects listed with their content, so that the theory is 'lexical'. By contrast, in a paradigm-based theory the relationship between form and content is the product of sometimes complex computations, what Stump calls an 'inferential' theory. Since the information flow is top-down, with the complete feature array determining all aspects of exponence, the theory is 'realizational', rather than incremental. Those theories which are generally referred to collectively as word-and-paradigm theories are inferential realizational theories (e.g. Anderson 1992, Aronoff 1994, Corbett and

Fraser 1993, Matthews 1972, Stump 2001, Zwicky 1985).

Aronoff (1976) proposes a different type of theory for derivational morphology. In that theory there are word formation rules (wfr's) which introduce affixes syncategorematically, so that the theory is realizational, not lexical. On the other hand, the affixation process itself contributes the meaning of the affix in a monotonic fashion, so that the theory is incremental, not inferential. Steele (1995) argues for a model of inflection of essentially this type. Finally, the theory of Distributed Morphology (Halle and Marantz 1993) employs default reasoning over feature arrays, making the theory realizational. However, this is done so as to regulate the insertion of lexical listed morphemes ('Vocabulary Items'), so that the theory is lexical, not inferential. It's far from clear how much information should be listed with these Vocabulary Items, and for some morphologists the suspicion is that detailed research will reveal that less and less information can be ascribed to individual morphemes, in which case the theory would become inferential and essentially a notational variant of one of the other word-and-paradigm models that has been proposed.

In this section I shall provide further illustrations of the empirical need for inferential and realizational models. On such top-down models the word form is computed on the basis of prior knowledge of the entire feature array, making it easy to capture complex non-local dependencies. In addition, because the whole feature array is given it's possible to compute the complete abstract paradigm in advance, and this permits reference to the paradigm so as to deploy defaults. In some cases the inferencing is a decidedly non-trivial exercise. Consider, for example, Spanish verbs, which fall into three regular conjugation classes. The endings of the present indicative and present subjunctive 1st conjugation are given in (28) while the present indicative and present subjunctive 2nd conjugation are given in (29):

(28) 1st conjugation

	present indicative	present subjunctive
1sg	o	e
2sg	as	es
3sg	a	e
1pl	amos	emos
2pl	ais	eis
3pl	an	en

(29) 2nd conjugation

	present indicative	present subjunctive
1sg	o	e
2sg	es	as
3sg	e	a
1pl	emos	amos
2pl	eis	ais
3pl	en	an

For non-1st singular forms it is apparent that the endings are identical but switched. Thus, in order to correctly parse a verb form such as *canten* 'they sing (subjunctive)' or *beben* 'they drink (indicative)' it's necessary to know the conjugation class of the lexeme, only then is it possible to determine the grammatical mood feature.

Inflectionally complex languages can provide extremely involved examples. Thus, in (30) we see two verb forms from the Algonquian language, Potawatomi (I have adapted these examples from Stump (2001, 65–66)):

(30) a. k -wapm -a -wa -k
2ND see(TA) DIRECT 2/3PL 3PL
'you (pl) see them'

b. k -wapm -uk -wa -k
2ND see(TA) INVERSE 2/3PL 3PL
'they see you (pl)'

In (30a), knowing all the other paradigmatic contrasts in the language, we can infer the following information:

(31)		
	k-	implies 2nd subject (unless the object is 2nd person, in which case it could also imply that subject is 1st person).
	wapm	transitive verb form with animate arguments
	a	direct marker
	wa	implies 2/3pl object, subject not 1st person and not singular
	-k	implies 3pl object, subject not 1pl

In (30b)we can infer the following information:

(32)		
	k-	implies 2nd object
	wapm	transitive verb form with animate arguments
	uk	inverse marker

wa	implies 2/3pl subject, object not 1st person and not singular
-k	implies 3pl subject, object not 1pl

Potawatomi conjugation illustrates what is known as an 'inverse' system. For certain combinations of person/number features the affixes corresponding to the subject actually refer to the object and vice versa. In Potawatomi, the 'normal' subject-object marking system is indicated by the direct marker *-a*, while the inverse system of marking is indicated by the inverse marker *-uk*. This can be seen from the examples in (30a,b): the word forms *k-wapm-a-wa-k* 'you see them' and *k-wapm-uk-wa-k* 'they see you' are identical except for the presence of the direct/inverse markers, yet they signal opposite subject/object relationships. In other words, (30b) is just like (30a) except that the values for subject/object are switched.

Given the direct form, (30a), how do we determine the person/number features? This is straightforward. First, we know that we have subject and object features to specify because the verb stem belongs to the Transitive Animate class (labelled TA in the glosses). Given the *k*-prefix it seems that the subject bears 2nd person features. However, Potawatomi has an exclusive/inclusive 1pl distinction, and the*k*- prefix is used to indicate 1pl inclusive ('we' = 'you-and-me') as well as pure 2nd person forms, so we can't exclude the interpretation '1pl inclusive'. In addition, the *k*- prefix is also found with a 1st person subject if the object is 2nd person. Now, given the *-wa* suffix we know that the subject must also be 2nd or 3rd plural and that the subject is not 1st person. This tells us that the subject must 2pl. Moreover, the *-k* suffix is incompatible with 1pl (inclusive or exclusive) subjects (though it is found with 1sg subjects). This confirms that the subject is 2pl but not 1pl, and hence not 1pl inclusive. This exhaustively specifies the subject person/number features. The object is uniquely identified as 3pl by the *-k* suffix. However, the final inference is that the definitions of 'subject/object' are as given, because if we were to replace the direct suffix *-a* with the inverse marker-*uk* we would get the opposite specification. Systems of this complexity are not particularly difficult to find in the world's languages.

Any theory that countenances morphosyntactic features and which adopts the Separation Hypothesis is in a position to state regularities over feature sets independently of how those feature sets are realized. This means that it's possible, in principle, to capture syncretisms. It turns out that there are several distinct types of syncretism and these require somewhat different formal devices for their description. A detailed survey is provided in Stump (1993a, 2001) to which I refer the reader. Needless to say, syncretisms pose particularly serious problems for a classical morpheme theory.

4.4 Paradigm Function Morphology

In this section I introduce in simplified form the architecture of the most carefully worked out paradigm-based theory of inflection, that proposed in Stump (2001). I first sketch the theory itself and then turn briefly to the question of allomorphy and why this isn't in practice any greater problem for PFM than for any morpheme-based account.[6]

4.4.1 Paradigm functions and realization rules

A particularly influential type of 'inferential realizational' paradigm-based theory of inflection is Greg Stump's *Paradigm Function Morphology* (PFM). In this model, the cells in the paradigm of a lexeme are defined by a Paradigm Function, which maps the root of the lexeme and the set of features defining the cell onto a word form. I shall illustrate this with a toy example based on the Finnish noun forms given earlier.

Consider the subparadigm in (33):

(33)	a.	talo-ssa	'in the house'	inessive singular
	b.	talo-i-ssa	'in the houses'	inessive plural

The forms in (33a,b) are representative of the dozen or so case forms in the language and so I will first consider just these forms. The Paradigm Function for a Finnish noun has to provide for two suffix slots, one of which contains the Plural suffix *-i*, the other of which contains Case suffixes such as *-ssa*, in that order. First, we need a set of functions which realize the features [Num: Pl] and [Case: Iness], for words of the lexical class 'N' (Noun). This function is labelled 'RR' (for 'realization rule'). In Stump's notation the features to be realized and the lexical class that the function refers to are given as subscripts. The function itself maps a pair consisting of a form (e.g. a stem form for a lexeme) and the complete set of features characterizing the final word form. The output is another form (e.g. a stem+affix) and the same complete feature set . This is shown in (34):

[6] Stump's model represents an amalgam of proposals made by a variety of morphologists over the past three decades. Although the notational devices employed in PFM are unfamiliar to many, they have the advantage of making the theoretical bases much more explicit than in other models of inflection. The PFM model is based entirely on the notion of the function, so that it is eminently open to formalization and comparison with other formalizations.

(34) ia. $RR_{\{Num:Pl\},N}(\langle X, \sigma\rangle) = \langle Xi, \sigma\rangle$
ii. $RR_{\{Case:Iness\},N}(\langle X, \sigma\rangle) = \langle Xssa, \sigma\rangle$

The variable σ stands for the complete feature set of the word being computed (e.g. 'inessive plural'). The rules in (34) state that the plural is formed by adding *-i* to some stem, while the inessive is formed by adding *-ssa* to some stem. These rules will apply whenever the set of features which they realize is to be found as a subset of σ.

When both rules apply we must ensure that (34ii) applies to the output of (34ia). This is achieved by applying the rules in distinct, extrinsically ordered, blocks. The ordering is defined by an index, as in (35):

(35) ia. $RR_{I,\{Num:Pl\},N}(\langle X, \sigma\rangle) = Xi$
ii. $RR_{II,\{Case:Iness\},N}(\langle X, \sigma\rangle) = Xssa$

Since (35ia) is in Block I it applies to a lexically defined stem form (by default the noun's root). Rule (35ii) applies to the output of the Block I rules. Thus, the inessive plural is correctly specified as (33b). For the present we can assume that (35ia) is the only Block I rule in the grammar. This means that the correct form for the inessive singular is automatically generated.

There is no rule in our toy grammar specifying the exponent of [Num: Sg] in any block. If σ contains the specification [Num: Sg], therefore, there will be no rule which realizes any exponent. In Block I this will mean that there is no rule which can apply, which should mean that there is no legal derivation for a singular form. Intuitively, however, we don't need a special rule for the singular form. What we would like to be able to say is that the singular form is expressed by the default form of the lexeme (i.e. the root).

Paradigm Function Morphology assumes a universal principle for such cases, the Identity Function Default. In any Block of rules it is assumed that there is a universal rule triggered by any set of features whatsoever, which delivers the same form as the argument of the function:

(36) Identity Function Default
$RR_{n,\{\},C}(\langle X, \sigma\rangle) = \langle X, \sigma\rangle.$

The Identity Function Default rule is the maximally general rule and left to its own devices it would guarantee that all forms in the paradigm surfaced as the root. However, Paradigm Function Morphology assumes the Elsewhere Principle[7]: whenever two rules are in competition, that

[7] Also known as the 'Elsewhere Condition', 'Maximal Inclusion Principle', 'Maximal Subset Override', 'Paninian Determinism' and various other names.

is, whenever they can apply to one and the same input to give a distinct output, it is the rule with the most specific definition that pre-empts all its competitors. This applies to all rules in a block, with the result that at most one rule per block will be applicable (the 'Narrowest Applicable Rule' or *Nar* in Stump's terminology). Clearly, any rule with any feature characterization at all will be more specific than the Identity Function rule, so that default rule will always be pre-empted provided there is some rule to realize at least one of the feature values associated with the word form[8]. The upshot for our example is that the singular form of TALO is defined as being identical to the current form of the stem, namely, the lexical root *talo*, as required. This root then instantiates the variable 'X' in (35ii) and so the Block II rule will suffix *-ssa* to *talo* to give the form *talossa*.

Finnish grammar also contains no rule in Blocks I, II for realizing the nominative case. Therefore, when $\sigma = \{\text{Num: Sg, Case: Nom}\}$ the Identity Function Default will apply in both Blocks to output the root form *talo*, as required. However, recall that the nominative plural form is exceptional in Finnish. To account for this we add rule (34ib) to Block I:

(34) ib. $\text{RR}_{\text{I},\{\text{Num:Pl,Case:Nom}\},\text{N}}\ (\langle \text{X}, \sigma\rangle) \quad = \quad \langle \text{Xt}, \sigma\rangle$

Notice that (34iib) realizes both number and case features and hence captures the notion of cumulation. If σ contains the feature set [Num: Pl, Case: Nom] then both rules (35ia, ib) are applicable. However, rule (35ib) is more specific than rule (35ia) (in a sense which can easily be made formally precise), and so it constitutes the Narrowest Applicable Rule in the terminology of Stump (2001). It therefore pre-empts (35ia) and gives us the intermediate form *talot*. In Block II there are no rules realizing either [Num: Pl] or [Case: Nom] so the Identity Function Default again applies to output *talot* as the final form, as required.

The Paradigm Function for a class of words can now be defined by reference to the realization rules that go to construct a given word form for a given feature set. If we have a lexeme with root X the Paradigm Function tells us how to construct the word form occupying the cell in the paradigm defined by the feature set σ. For our toy Finnish grammar the Paradigm Function for a noun can be represented informally as in (37):[9]

---

[8]Stump argues that by appropriately defining what is meant by a feature the Elsewhere Principle makes it possible to eradicate all extrinsic ordering of rules within a given block.

[9]A more formal definition is that in (i):

(i) $\text{PF}(\langle \text{X}, \sigma\rangle) =_{def} \text{Nar}_{\text{II},\tau_2,N}\ (\text{Nar}_{\text{I},\tau_1,N}\ (\langle \text{X},\sigma\rangle)$

(37) $\text{PF}(\langle X, \sigma\rangle) =_{def} \text{RR}_{\text{II}}\ (\text{RR}_{\text{I}}\ (\langle X, \sigma\rangle))$

In other words, the Paradigm Function makes explicit the claim that the word form can be generated by successively applying realization rules on a block-by-block basis.

This simple example illustrates the way in which we handle the various deviations from the agglutinative ideal.

Cumulation: When a single affix realizes more than one feature value simultaneously (for instance 'nominative' and 'plural') we have the situation corresponding to cumulation.

'Clairvoyant affixation': Because we can make reference to the complete feature characterization of the word it isn't difficult to make reference to features whose principal exponent is introduced in a later block. In this way we can capture the impression that the selection of an inner affix is dependent on the addition of a later, outer affix. Thus, in the Finnish nominative plural example, because the feature definition for rule (35ib) makes reference both to the Block I number feature and to the (usually Block II) case feature, the nominative plural form doesn't pose any of the problems encountered by classical morpheme theory.

Multiple exponence: The same architectural property also makes multiple exponence easy to handle. Paradigm-based morphology is not 'resource-based': if a given realization rule appeals to some feature specification, this doesn't prevent another rule in a different block from realizing the same feature. Thus, to account for the Swahili negation example, we simply ensure that Block I prefixation includes a cumulative rule realizing both negation and past, as in (38ib), and that Block III prefixation includes a rule realizing just negation, as in (38iii)[10]:

(38)	Block I	ia.	Past, Neg(X)	=	kuX
		ib.	Past(X)	=	liX
	(Block II	subject prefix rules)			
	Block III	iii.	Neg(X)	=	haX

Rule (38ia) will pre-empt rule (38ib) wherever σ contains both [Tense: Past] and [Polarity: Negative], but (38iii) will always apply, even if rule (38ia) has applied. The fact that the feature [Pol: Neg] is mentioned in two rules housed in distinct blocks captures the multiple exponence.

where X is the root of a noun lexeme, 'N' stands for the (morphologically defined) class of nouns, σ is the complete set of features defining the cell in the paradigm, and τ_1, τ_2 are subsets of σ (broadly speaking, the features for number and case respectively), and 'Nar' stands for 'narrowest applicable rule'.

[10]In the interests of readability I simplify the notation here in obvious ways.

Zero realization: It turns out that there are several types of zero realization, with the default zero of singular DOG being just one kind. Where a zero contrasts with a default overt affix we need to stipulate the zero, which can easily be done by means of the identity function restricted to the relevant features:

(39) $\mathrm{RR}_{n,\tau,C}(\langle \mathrm{X}, \sigma\rangle) = \langle \mathrm{X}, \sigma\rangle$.

Rule (39) says that at Block n, for words of class C, the feature set τ is realized by taking the current word form (root, stem, or partly inflected form) and doing nothing to it.

Signhood: Finally, none of the formatives introduced by realization rules is meaningful in the sense of being a Saussurean sign, so that the existence of purely structural intermorphs in compounds or stem forms whose default meaning is completely overridden (such as the Romance infinitive/future/conditional stem) no longer pose problems in principle.

4.4.2 Allomorphy in paradigm-based morphology

One potential defence of the morpheme is to be found in the phenomenon of idiosyncratic allomorphy: if, two affixes realizing different feature sets have the same basic form but undergo different types of allomorphy then this provides prima facie evidence in favour of the existence of some sort of classical morpheme. A (slightly artifical) instance of this can be found in English. There are two derivational prefixes with the basic form *in-*, one of which means 'not', e.g. *inarticulate*, the other of which means 'in', e.g. *inlaid*, *inbred*. The difference in meaning correlates with a difference in morphophonological behaviour: before liquids and bilabials the 'n' of 'negation' *in-* undergoes obligatory assimilation: *illegal* (**inlegal*), *imperfect* (**inperfect*), *immodest* (**inmodest*), but this is not found with the prefix when it means 'in'. This suggests that there are two separate lexical entries, just as would be expected on the morpheme theory. In other languages similar examples can be found in inflection.

In Stump's framework allomorphy is handled by means of morphophonological statements governed by sets of morphological metageneralizations (Stump 2001, 47f). The morphophonological rules are sets of constraints on the operation of realization rules. A simple example of a morphophonological rule from English would be as in (40):

(40) Given $\mathrm{RR}(\langle \mathrm{X}, \sigma\rangle) = \langle \mathrm{Xz}, \sigma\rangle$, then z is realized as follows (stated informally) :

(i) /əz/ if X ends in a sibilant, else

(ii) /s/ if X ends in an unvoiced consonant, else
(iii) /z/

This accounts simultaneously for the allomorphy of the plural, the 3sg and the possessive phrasal affix. In more complex systems certain sorts of allomorphy are associated only with certain realization rules. Stump captures this by means of morphological metageneralizations which stipulate which morphophonological rules apply to which realization rules. For instance, the rule introducing the negative *in-* prefix in *illegal* would be associated with the morphophonological rule which introduces the *in* ~ *il* alternation, while the rule introducing the prepositional *in-* prefix in *inlaid* would not be associated with that rule.

Now Stump's formulations are not couched in any recognized theory of morphology and there are a number of respects in which his proposals are inexplicit. One process that has received considerable attention in the literature on morphophonemics but which isn't discussed by Stump is reduplication. It isn't entirely clear how morphophonological metageneralizations could be deployed to handle all the complexities of that phenomenon (see McCarthy and Prince (1995, 1998), and also Kager (1999), McCarthy (2002) for overview discussion).

One problem is apparent from our simple illustration in (40). It's not obvious how we can identify the 'z' affix phonologically. We could take it to be a fully specified segment /z/ which then gets transformed, as in classical generative phonology, or we could take it to be some kind of underspecified segment. In Stump's architecture the 'z' element is purely phonological. However, there is nothing in principle to prevent us from treating the affixes introduced by realization rules as morphs, that is, as morphological objects with phonological shapes. Essentially this proposal is made (within the framework of HPSG) by Koenig (1999) and Orgun (1996). This would then allow us to deploy much of the machinery of apparently morpheme-based morphophonemics. Although such theories appear to rely on some notion of morpheme, in fact, the notion they actually appeal to is that of 'morph' since the semantics of the morph isn't usually relevant to the morphophonemic behaviour.

I conclude, therefore, that the question of how best to handle allomorphy is as yet somewhat unclear, but it poses no more serious architectural problems to paradigm-based approaches than it does to any other type of approach.

4.5 Justifying the morpheme concept

There is one further potential justification for the concept of morpheme-as-sign which requires discussion. Many formatives are associated with meanings which can be considered to have scopal properties, in a rather broad sense of the term. For example, in many languages verbs can have a causative form and a passive form. In a number of these languages it is possible to combine the two affixes to form the passive of the causative. In a smaller number of languages it is also possible to have the causative of a passive. This is the case in Japanese, for instance. When the causative is 'in the scope' of the passive its affix appears closer to the verb stem than the passive affix, as illustrated in (41), while cases in which the passive is 'in the scope' of the causative show the opposite affix order (42) (Tsujimura 1996, 258f):

(41) a. Taroo-ga Hanako-o waraw-ase-ta.
Taro-NOM Hanako-ACC laugh-CAUS-PAST
'Taro made Hanako laugh.'

b. Hanako-ga Taroo-ni waraw-ase-rare-ta.
Hanako-NOM Taroo-BY laugh-CAUS-PASS-PAST
'Hanako was made to laugh by Taro.'

(42) a. Hanako-ga Taroo-ni sikar-are-ta.
Hanako-NOM Taro-BY scold-PASS-PAST
'Hanako was scolded by Taro.'

b. Ziroo-ga Hanako-o/ni Taroo-ni
Ziro-NOM Hanako-ACC/DAT Taro-BY
sikar-are-sase-ta.
scold-PASS-CAUS-PAST
'Ziro made Hanako be scolded by Taro.'

Syntacticians who wish to derive all word formation from syntactic principles have used facts such as these to motivate a 'Mirror Principle', under which the order of affixation reflects the order of application of syntactic processes (Baker 1985).

Discussing instances of this sort, Stump (1997) argues that it is a straightforward matter in principle to link the affix order with scope properties in the architecture of Paradigm Function Morphology. All that need be done is to ensure that the rule introducing the affix is associated with a rule introducing its semantic effect (construing the term 'semantic' in a broad sense). This is possible because the paradigm function (in the default case) associates the set of indexed rule blocks with a specific linear order of affixation. Thus, affix order and semantic scope will be in tandem (in the default case). While there are innumerable interesting technical questions which arise from this sort of approach it is clear that devices of this sort will have the desired effect without requiring us to resort to an appeal to the classical morpheme[11].

However, it's easy to overestimate the extent to which linear order is correlated with scope, whether in syntax or in morphology. Hyman (2003) provides a salutary illustration of this. He discusses the derivational 'extensions' of Bantu. Typically a Bantu verb stem will admit a string of suffixes realizing argument structure alternations traditionally labelled causative, application, reciprocal and passive (many languages have other suffixes such as a medio-stative, or a reversative). In a number of languages it's possible for one valency alternation to feed another, so that we can have the reciprocal of an applicative (the men worked for each other) or the passive of a causative (as in (41) above). In some cases the order of affixation reflects the order of application but there is a strong tendency for the suffix string to respect a fixed template (the CARP template: Causative-Applicative-Reciprocal-Passive) irrespective of the order of application. This can lead to situations in which the order of application, and hence the meaning, is the opposite of what one would expect from the order of affixation. In fact, matters get even more complex in some languages. In the southern Bantu Nguni group (Zulu, Xhosa and others) there is a restriction that the passive extension must always precede the reciprocal. This violates the pan-Bantu CARP template. As we see from example (43) (Doke 1973, 138) the result may also violate the Mirror Principle:

(43) ku-ya-zond-wa-na lapha.
CLASS:10-ASP-hate-PASS-RECIP here
'There is mutual hatred here.'

This sentence is literally the passive of the reciprocal: *X hate each other* ⇒ *it is hated each other*. It can't be formed by applying the reciprocal to the passive form because reciprocals can't be formed from intransitive predicates.

Claims that morpheme order reflects scope universally should really be taken to reflect tendencies in grammaticalization paths rather than universally valid architectural properties (see Spencer 2003c, 2003b). In particular, attempts to reduce the order of inflectional elements to some sort of principle of semantic scope or syntactic ordering are doomed to failure given the recurrent mismatches in form and function found in

[11] In a wide-ranging and meticulous analysis Rice (2000) proposes that affix order in Athabaskan languages is determined almost exclusively in terms of semantic scope properties. She codes scope in terms of a word syntax model of morphology which thus relies on the classical morpheme concept. However, it would be possible to recast many of her analyses in terms of Stump's suggestion.

inflectional systems. Beard (1995) has argued that the same is true of derivational morphology, though the degree to which uncontroversially derivational morphology deviates from principles of agglutination (that is, compositionality) is generally rather less than that found in inflection.

On the other hand, such mismatches between order and meaning tend to reflect a relatively late stage in grammaticalization. When a semantically compositional construction is at the first stage of grammaticalization we might expect to see a much more direct relationship which conforms much more convincingly to the picture implied by the morpheme doctrine. This is the case with affixes which are in the process of being formed from compounds. For instance, it's very difficult to resist the temptation to treat the formative *-like* in *cat-like* as a morpheme meaning 'similar to (in some respect)' and *cat-like agility/disdain/tail* as essentially no different from *agility/disdain/tail like that of a cat*. (It's also very difficult to know whether to describe *-like* as an affix or a compounded adjective.) Similarly, there are many cases in which a clitic seems to have a fixed meaning or function and shows none of the deviations from strict agglutination common with affixes. Here, too, we are more likely to think in terms of morphemes.

In Spencer (2003a) I discuss these issues in more detail, and I argue that the Paradigm Function architecture allows us to capture the intuition that a formative is associated with a meaning while still being part of a paradigmatic system. All that is needed is to allow certain realization to introduce a semantic predicate rather than simply realizing a feature set. This entails a number of technical changes to the theory, as outlined in Spencer (2003a). One conclusion that can safely be drawn, however, is that typical instances of affixational morphology generally have very different properties from typical instances of compounding in which the elements of the compound are incontrovertibly words in their own right. Since this is not generally made explicit in discussions of the morpheme concept I shall devote the next section to the point.

4.6 How to recognize a morpheme

If we consider purely agglutinating systems then there will be no immediate empirical difference between a realizational theory and a morpheme-based theory. Provided there are no complications with the linear placement of the affix, a rule such as (44) and a lexical entry such as (45) will have identical effects:

(44) $\mathrm{RR}_{\mathrm{I},\{\mathrm{Num:Pl}\},\mathrm{N}}(\langle \mathrm{X}, \sigma\rangle) \quad = \quad \langle \mathrm{X{\scriptstyle Z}}, \sigma\rangle$

(45) MOR z
SYN suffix
SEM [Num: Pl]

Now, given the severe empirical and conceptual difficulties faced by the morpheme concept the onus of proof clearly lies with those who advocate the morpheme. However, there appears to have been no systematic attempt to demonstrate the empirical necessity for classical morphemes.

Such a demonstration would have to take the following form. First, we would need to identify a situation in which a given morph were reliably paired with a given meaning or feature set. For instance, we would need to find word forms such as (46) in some hypothetical language, where [F], [G] are features with values F_1, F_2, ... and G_1, G_2, ... respectively:

(46)

[NOUN]	[F:F_1]	[Num:Pl]	[G:G_1]
|	|	|	|
noun	f	z	g

Suppose now that the plural suffix /z/ induced some idiosyncratic allomorphy on, say, the following suffix morpheme {/g/, [G:G_1]}, so that {/g/, [G:G_1]} assumed the allomorph /g′/. We might then end up with the situation in (47):

(47) a.

[NOUN]	[F:F_1]	[Num:Sg]	[G:G_1]
|	|	|	|
noun	f	s	g

b.

[NOUN]	[F:F_1]	[Num:Pl]	[G:G_1]
|	|	|	|
noun	f	z	g′

In (47b) we see the allomorphic alternation, but in (47a), in which we have the singular suffix, not the plural, we lack the triggering context for that alternation and we obtain the basic or default allomorph realizing [G:G_1], namely, /g/.

This could easily be handled on a morpheme-based account by making the selection of the /g′/ allomorph contingent on the presence of the sign {/z/, [Num:Pl]}. However, provided that there was only one plural affix, this situation could easily be handled on a realization rule approach, too. We would simply make the selection of the /g′/ allomorph contingent on the feature set [Num:Pl], irrespective of its phonological realization. But now suppose that for different classes of nouns or for different choices of [F] there are different [Num:Pl] allomorphs, say, /z, z′/. Suppose further that the g → g′ allomorphy is only triggered by the (basic) /z/ Plural allomorph and not by the ('derived') /z′/ allomorph, and that this fact can't be reduced to any independent phonological or morphophonological generalization. We would then see the situation sketched in (48):

(48) a.

[NOUN]	[F:F_1]	[Num:Sg]	[G:G_1]
|	|	|	|
noun	f	z	g′

b.

[NOUN]	[F:F_2]	[Num:Sg]	[G:G_1]
|	|	|	|
noun	f′	z′	g

In (48b) we see selection of a different morpheme, {/f′/, [F:F_2]} (we might think of F_2 and F_1 as different case forms, for instance). This has triggered selection of the /z′/ allomorph of the Plural. As a consequence we see the 'basic' /g/ allomorph of feature [G].

However, this situation, too, can be handled in principle, at least, in a realization theory. For (48b) we simply make the realization of /g′/ contingent on the conjoint feature set {[F:F_1], [Num:Pl]}:

(49) a. $RR_{\{F:F_1, Num:Pl, G:G_1\}}(\langle X, \sigma \rangle) = \langle Xg', \sigma \rangle$

b. $RR_{\{G:G_1\}}(\langle X, \sigma \rangle) = \langle Xg', \sigma \rangle$

Moreover, rule schema (49) would also work if there were other morphemes with the shape /z/ which could occur before /g/ but which didn't trigger the allomorphy. For instance, suppose that there were a feature specification [F:F_z] with realization /z/, homophonous with the Plural morpheme. Suppose further that the [Num] suffix is realized as a prefix /z/, when [F] is given feature specification [F:F_z]. Finally, suppose that the {/z/, [F:F_z]} suffix fails to trigger the /g′/ allomorphy. Then we would have (50):

(50)

[Num:Pl]	[NOUN]	[F:F_z]	[G:G_1]
|	|	|	|
z	noun	z	g

However, even this would not require us to amend rule (49a), because the crucial triggering feature [F:F$_1$] is not present in (50).

But now suppose that selection of the /z′/ allomorph by [F:F$_2$] is an idiosyncratic property of that feature specification of [F], and that the default realization of [Num:Pl] for all other specifications, [F:F$_n$], is /z/. When [Num:Pl] is realized by the default /z/ affix, it triggers the /g′/ allomorphy, but when plural is realized by /z′/ following the [F:F$_2$] affix, the /z′/ fails to trigger the /g′/ allomorphy. This would give us representations such as (51):

(51)

a.

[Noun]	[F:F$_1$]	[Num:Pl]	[G:G$_1$]
|	|	|	|
noun	f	z	g′

b.

[Noun]	[F:F$_2$]	[Num:Pl]	[G:G$_1$]
|	|	|	|
noun	f′	z′	g

c.

[Noun]	[F:F$_3$]	[Num:Pl]	[G:G$_1$]
|	|	|	|
noun	f″	z	g′

Then we would be missing a generalization with a rule schema such as (49), because we would have to amend it to (52):

(52) a. $\mathrm{RR}_{\{\mathrm{F:F}_n, Num:Pl, G:G_1\}}\ (\langle \mathrm{X}, \sigma\rangle) \quad = \quad \langle \mathrm{Xg}', \sigma\rangle$
where n $\neq$ 2

b. $\mathrm{RR}_{\{\mathrm{G:G1}\}}\ (\langle \mathrm{X}, \sigma\rangle) \quad = \quad \langle \mathrm{Xg}, \sigma\rangle$

But rule (52a) with its codicil is just a cumbersome way of avoiding the obvious generalization. What we would like to be able to say it is the basic allomorph, /z/, of the plural morpheme, {/z/, [Num:Pl]}, which triggers the /g′/ allomorphy of [G:G$_1$], and that derived allomorphs fail to condition that alternation. But realization theories such as Paradigm Function Morphology separate form from function, so that there is no way of referring directly to an object such as 'the morpheme {/z/, [Num:Pl]}' and hence no way of referring directly to the notion 'the allomorph so-and-so of morpheme {/z/, [Num:Pl]}'. In the rule block in which the rules of (52) apply, the 'plural morpheme' has already, so to speak, been amalgamated into the derived stem 'X'[12].

[12]The problem for realizational approaches would be more acute if there were several derived allomorphs which failed to trigger the alternation.

Perhaps not surprisingly it's rather hard to detect cases of this sort in the literature, and I am not aware of any convincing examples. But if the reasoning above is correct it is precisely cases of this sort that morpheme-based theories need to appeal to in order to justify retaining such a troublesome descriptive device[13]. Of course, even if a handful of such examples were to turn up it would still leave us with the puzzling question of why the behaviour of morphemes is so different from that of normal signs.

4.7 Conclusions

In this chapter I have presented what is perhaps the dominant view of inflectional morphology amongst morphologists, namely the realizational-inferential model. The classical conception of the morpheme is that of a Saussurean sign, that is a lexical entry which pairs a form with a function or meaning. Word formation is then simply a matter of linearizing these morphemes appropriately (Radical Agglutination). In the more recent approaches this approach has been abandoned, along with the view of morphotactics that this entails. On the classical view sentence structure and word structure are essentially the same, namely, the concatenation of morphemes. This means that there is no real difference in structure between an inflected word like dogs and a compound like dog food. However, on realizational-inferential ('word-and-paradigm') models inflection is seen as a set of processes applying to some stem form to generate a word form occupying a cell in the word's paradigm. Such models generally deploy the full resources of default reasoning and can thereby capture a whole host of intra-paradigm relationships which are generally lost on morpheme-based theories.

I justified this realizational approach by citing what are now classic arguments in favour of the Separation Hypothesis. Inflectional pieces within a single word form can demonstrate all the possible deviations from the one:one mapping between form and function. However, in

[13]Halle and Marantz (1993, 154f) mount an argument for a weaker conception of 'morpheme' based on their analysis of Potawatomi verb inflection. They claim that the feature bundle [1Pl, subject] triggers certain types of deletion in morphological structure. This is an abstract morpheme in that Halle and Marantz adopt a realizational theory incorporating the Separation Hypothesis. Thus, their abstract morpheme is simply a designated feature bundle which can be realized by more than one type of affix. However, in a somewhat more exhaustive analysis of the facts, Stump (2001, 88f) demonstrates that the relevant outcomes can be achieved more neatly within the architecture of Paradigm Function Morphology. Since Halle and Marantz's discussion offers one of the very few attempts in the recent literature to justify any conception of the morpheme, it's interesting to find that there is as yet no strong evidence even for their very much weakened version of the morpheme doctrine.

genuine compounding we simply don't observe such wild deviations. Compounding is thus a very poor analogy for inflection.

In simple cases the morpheme-based approaches and the realizational approaches give essentially the same results, but with more complex paradigms and word forms we see the full advantages of the realizational approach. There remain two possible justifications for morphemes, however. It is often observed that the semantic scope of an affix is reflected in its proximity to the stem. A scope-defining affix placed to the periphery of a word form will generally take in its scope those affixes which occur nearer the stem. However, there are two problems with this justification. First, in many cases the facts are much more complex than might appear, and there are plenty of cases in which linear order fails to reflect semantic scope or the order of morphosyntactic operations. Second, in most cases there is no real difficulty in assuming that the semantic interpretation principles which are associated with morphological realization rules are keyed into the order of application, so that the scope effects are coded by representational devices which don't entail the classical morpheme concept.

I concluded by suggesting that the strongest evidence against the realizational approach would be to find instances of allomorphy which was crucially triggered by the combination of a particular form (allomorph) and its meaning and which failed to be triggered by the same form when it had a different meaning or the same meaning when it was realized by a different form. Morphologists who still hold to the morpheme concept have not troubled to look for such evidence, no doubt because they fail to realize that the burden of proof lies on those who advocate the American Structuralist conception of morphology. It would certainly enrich our understanding of morphological systems if a systematic search of this kind were to be undertaken.

References

Anderson, Stephen R. 1992. *A-morphous Morphology*. Cambridge: Cambridge University Press.

Aronoff, Mark. 1976. *Word Formation in Generative Grammar*. Cambridge, MA: MIT Press.

Aronoff, Mark. 1994. *Morphology By Itself*. Cambridge, MA: MIT Press.

Baker, Mark C. 1985. The Mirror Principle and morphosyntactic explanation. *Linguistic Inquiry* 16:373–416.

Beard, Robert. 1995. *Lexeme Morpheme Base Morphology*. Stony Brook, NY: SUNY Press.

Booij, Geert. 2002. *The Morphology of Dutch*. Oxford: Oxford University Press.

Carstairs-McCarthy, Andrew. 1994. Inflection classes, gender and the Principle of Contrast. *Language* 70:737–788.

Corbett, Greville G. and Norman Fraser. 1993. Network Morphology. *Journal of Linguistics* 29:113–142.

Doke, Clement M. 1973. *Textbook of Zulu.* Cape Town: Longman Southern Africa (PTY) Limited.

Halle, Morris and Alec Marantz. 1993. Distributed morphology and the pieces of inflection. In K. Hale and S. J. Keyser, eds., *The View from Building 20*, pages 111–176. Cambridge, MA: MIT Press.

Hayes, Bruce. 1990. Precomplied phrasal phonology. In S. Inkelas and D. Zec, eds., *The Phonology-Syntax Connection*, pages 85–108. Chicago: University of Chicago Press.

Hockett, Charles. 1958. Two models of grammatical description. In J. Martin, ed., *Readings in Linguistics*. Chicago: Chicago University Press, 2nd edn.

Hyman, Larry M. 2003. Suffix ordering in Bantu. In G. Booij and J. van Marle, eds., *Yearbook of Morphology 2002*, pages 245–281. Dordrecht: Kluwer Academic Publishers.

Julien, Marit. 2002. *Syntactic Heads and Word Formation*. Oxford University Press: Oxford.

Kager, Réné. 1999. *Optimality Theory*. Cambridge: Cambridge University Press.

Kiparsky, Paul. 1982. From cyclic phonology to lexical phonology. In H. van der Hulst and N. H. S. Smith, eds., *The Structure of Phonological Representations Part 1*, pages 131–175. Dordrecht: Foris.

Koenig, Jean-Pierre. 1999. *Lexical Relations*. Stanford, CA: CSLI Publications.

Lieber, Rochelle. 1981. *On the Organization of the Lexicon*. Ph.D. thesis, Massachusetts Institute of Technology. Distributed by Indiana University Linguistics Club.

Lieber, Rochelle. 1983. Argument linking and compounds in English. *Linguistics Inquiry* 14:251–286.

Lieber, Rochelle. 1992. *Deconstructing Morphology*. Chicago: University of Chicago Press.

Mathiassen, Terje. 1996. *A Short Grammar of Lithuanian*. Columbus, OH: Slavica Publishers, Inc.

Matthews, Peter. 1970. Recent developments in morphology. In J. Lyons, ed., *New Horizons in Linguistics*, pages 96–114. Harmondsworth: Penguin.

Matthews, Peter. 1972. *Inflectional Morphology*. Cambridge: Cambridge University Press.

McCarthy, John. 2002. *A Thematic Guide to Optimality Theory*. Cambridge: Cambridge University Press.

McCarthy, John and Alan Prince. 1995. Prosodic morphology. In J. Goldsmith, ed., *Handbook of Phonology*, pages 318–366. Oxford: Blackwell.

McCarthy, John and Alan Prince. 1998. Prosodic morphology. In A. Spencer and A. Zwicky, eds., *Handbook of Morphology*, pages 283–305. Oxford: Blackwell.

Orgun, Cemil Orhan. 1996. *Sign-Based Morphology and Phonology with special attention to Optimality Theory*. Ph.D. thesis, University of California at Berkeley.

Pollock, Jean-Yves. 1989. Verb movement, Universal Grammar and the structure of IP. *Linguistic Inquiry* 20:365–424.

Rice, Keren D. 2000. *Morpheme Order and Semantic Scope. Word Formation in the Athabaskan Verb*. Cambridge: Cambridge University Press.

Selkirk, Elizabeth O. 1982. *The Syntax of Words*. Cambridge, MA: MIT Press.

Spencer, Andrew. 1991. *Morphological Theory*. Oxford: Blackwell.

Spencer, Andrew. 1992. Nominal inflection and the nature of functional categories. *Journal of Linguistics* 28:313–341.

Spencer, Andrew. 1998. Morphophonological operations. In A. Spencer and A. Zwicky, eds., *Handbook of Morphology*, pages 123–143. Oxford: Blackwell.

Spencer, Andrew. 2000. Morphology. In M. Aronoff and J. Rees-Miller, eds., *Handbook of Linguistics*, pages 213–237. Oxford: Blackwell.

Spencer, Andrew. 2003a. Extended paradigm function morphology. Unpublished ms. University of Essex.

Spencer, Andrew. 2003b. Morphological universals? In R. Mairal and J. Gil, eds., *En torno a los universals lingüísticos (On Linguistic Universals)*, pages 130–170. Cambridge: Cambridge University Press.

Spencer, Andrew. 2003c. Putting some order into morphology. review article on Rice (2000) and Stump (2001). *Journal of Linguistics* 39:621–646.

Steele, Susan. 1995. Toward a theory of morphological information. *Language* 71:260–309.

Stump, Gregory T. 1991. A paradigm-theory of morphosemantic mismatches. *Language* 67:675–725.

Stump, Gregory T. 1993a. On rules of referral. *Language* 69:449–479.

Stump, Gregory T. 1993b. Position classes and morphological theory. In G. Booij and J. van Marle, eds., *Yearbook of Morphology 1992*, pages 129–179. Dordrecht: Kluwer Academic Publishers.

Stump, Gregory T. 1995. The uniformity of head marking. In G. Booij and J. van Marle, eds., *Yearbook of Morphology 1994*, pages 245–296. Dordrecht: Kluwer Academic Publishers.

Stump, Gregory T. 1997. Template morphology and inflectional morphology. In G. Booij and J. van Marle, eds., *Yearbook of Morphology 1996*, pages 217–241. Dordrecht: Kluwer Academic Publishers.

Stump, Gregory T. 1998. Inflection. In A. Spencer and A. Zwicky, eds., *Handbook of Morphology*, pages 13–43. Oxford: Blackwell.

Stump, Gregory T. 2001. *Paradigm Function Morphology. A Theory of Paradigm Structure*. Cambridge: Cambridge University Press.

Toman, Jindřich. 1983. *Wortsyntax: Eine Diskussion ausgewählter Probleme deutscher Wortbildung*. Tübingen: Niemeyer Verlag.

Toman, Jindřich. 1998. Word syntax. In A. Spencer and A. Zwicky, eds., *Handbook of Morphology*, pages 306–321. Oxford: Blackwell.

Tsujimura, Natsuko. 1996. *An Introduction to Japanese Linguistics*. Oxford: Blackwell.

Walińska de Hackbeil, Hana. 1986. *The Roots of Phrase Structure: the Syntactic Base of English Morphology*. Ph.D. thesis, University of Washington.

Wunderlich, Dieter and Ray Fabri. 1995. Minimalist Morphology: An approach to inflection. *Zeitschrift für Sprachwissenschaft* 14:236–294.

Zwicky, Arnold. 1985. How to describe inflection. In M. Niepokuj, M. V. Clay, V. Nikiforidou, and D. Feder, eds., *Proceedings of the Eleventh Annual Meeting of the Berkeley Linguistics Society*, pages 372–386. Berkeley: Berkeley Linguistics Society.

5

Paradigms and Periphrastic Expression: A Study in Realization-based Lexicalism

FARRELL ACKERMAN AND GREGORY STUMP

> "paradigms are primarily and mainly of single words but where short groups of words or phrases (e.g., Latin, and some Greek, perfective passives) are syntactically comparable to single words in the corresponding places of a different paradigm they are obviously to be included in paradigms themselves." – Robins 1959, 124

Our intention in this paper is to develop an explanatory account of the special characteristics of periphrastic expressions by refining the traditional notion of PARADIGM employed within inferential-realizational approaches to morphology (Anderson 1992, Aronoff 1994, Zwicky 1990, Stump 1993, 2001). Our proposal draws on this notion in order to develop a substantive reconceptualization of the form and function of the lexicon in constraint-based theories of syntax. In particular, we argue that the paradigms defined by a language's morphology sometimes include periphrastic combinations (PERIPHRASES). As we show, this conclusion affords a simple resolution of a number of neglected problems which periphrases pose for theories of syntax; it also necessitates a radical rethinking of the relation between the form and content of syntactic structures. The proposals developed here are intended to be relatively neutral with respect to the choice among alternative lexicalist theories of syntax (including Lexical Functional Grammar, Head-driven Phrase Structure Grammar, and Construction Grammar); for concrete-

Projecting Morphology.
Louisa Sadler and Andrew Spencer (Eds.).

ness, however, we articulate the details of our claims in the terminology of LFG.[1]

5.1 A purely syntactic conception of periphrasis

LFG, like other lexicalist and non-lexicalist generativist frameworks, has traditionally subscribed to a morpheme-based conception of morphology.[2] In particular, treatments of various lexical phenomena within this theory have generally assumed what Stump (2001) calls a *lexical-incremental* conception of morphology: such treatments are LEXICAL by virtue of the assumption that affixes, like stems, possess their own separate representations in the lexicon, and they are INCREMENTAL in that the grammatical properties of a fully inflected word are associated with it only as an effect of its acquiring the morphological markers bearing those properties.

In LFG, this approach to morphology was originally employed as a means of defining lexical representations for synthetic word forms functioning as syntactic atoms in c(onstituent)-structure. Thus, a lexically listed verb root such as *tickle* combines with the lexically listed past-tense morpheme *-ed* to yield the inflected word *tickled* which composes or, more technically, unifies the meaning of the root with that of the suffix.

The basic unification apparatus, which served well in handling canonical monotonic relations between words in syntax (e.g. the relation of subject-predicate agreement) as well as in the definition of a synthetic word form's properties, was extended to account for the composition of morphosyntactic property sets expressed by periphrastic combinations of word forms. In proposals such as those of Mohanan (1982) (for Malayalam auxiliaries) and Falk (1984) (for English *do* support), it was hypothesized that morphosyntactic information from a main verb's lexical representation may join with the information

[1] A morphological (and lexical) account of the data examined here represents a refutation of the claim made with respect to Uralic languages in Mitchell (1993, 66) that "... a purely lexical account of inflectional morphology is doomed to failure, even if it is capable of explaining the ordering of morphemes: certain aspects of inflectional morphology can only be explained by means of syntactic processes." The specific syntactic process that Mitchell has in mind is a syntactic blocking mechanism that is hypothesized to account for the distribution of functional information on lexical heads. See Niño (1997) for an LFG treatment of periphrastic negative predicates in Finnish. See also Ackerman and Webelhuth (1998), Blevins (2001), Börjars et al. (1997), Koenig (1999), Orgun (1996), Riehemann (2000), Spencer (2001, 2003b, 2003a), and Sadler and Spencer (2001) for comparable proposals.

[2] See Sells (this volume) for a realization-based interpretation of OT-LFG, as well as Ackerman and Webelhuth (1998) for speculation concerning the compatibility of OT-LFG with the sorts of assumptions argued for in the present article.

from an auxiliary's lexical representation in the projection of a single f(unctional)-structure representation.[3] Mohanan (1982), for example, postulates the c-structure patterns in (1), in which both a predicative element and an auxiliary are annotated with the equations ↑=↓ (which in LFG identifies these elements as heads).

(1) Malayalam clause structure (Mohanan 1982)

$$\begin{array}{llll} \text{S} & \rightarrow & \text{V}' & \\ & & \uparrow=\downarrow & \\ & & & \\ \text{V}' & \rightarrow & \text{X}' & \text{V} \\ & & \uparrow=\downarrow & \uparrow=\downarrow \end{array}$$

The effect of this hypothesis is that the lexical information associated with the individual words occupying terminal nodes in the V′ combines to determine the information associated with the f-structure of the V′, hence that associated with the f-structure of the entire sentence. This purely syntactic approach to periphrasis in effect transports the assumptions of lexical-incremental morphology into the domain of syntax: while the morphosyntactic information contained in a predicate's f-structure representation is, in the case of morphologically synthetic forms, projected from a single word's lexical representation via c-structure, it is, in instances of periphrasis, an amalgam of morphosyntactic information distributed among two or more syntactically atomic co-heads in c-structure.

Consider how this purely syntactic approach to periphrasis might apply in the analysis of inflected predicates in Udmurt. As in other Uralic languages, Udmurt clausal negation is expressed periphrastically by means of a negative verb inflected for subject agreement[4] and a dependent 'main' verb, as in (2). In contrast, the affirmative counterpart of (2) is expressed synthetically, as in (3):

(2) Ton ud miniski
you not.2SG go
'You are not going.' (Kel'makov and Hännikäinen 1999, 28)

(3) Ton miniskod
you go.2SG
'You are going.' (Kel'makov and Hännikäinen 1999, 27)

An f-structure representation of the morphologically synthetic predicate *miniskod* in (3) is projected solely from this word form's lexical rep-

[3]See Butt et al. (1996) for a more recent variant of this hypothesis.

[4]We will see below that there is informative syncretism among negative verb forms.

resentation via its presence in c-structure; by contrast, the f-structure representation of the periphrastic predicate *ud miniski* in (2) is, in the purely syntactic approach to periphrasis, an amalgam of the lexical representations of two distinct syntactic atoms–that of *ud* (4a) and that of *miniski* (4b).[5]

(4) a. Lexical representation of *ud*

ud V
$$\left[\begin{array}{ll} \text{POL} & \text{NEG} \\ \text{TNS} & \text{PRES} \\ \text{SUBJ} & \left[\begin{array}{ll} \text{PRED} & \text{PRO} \\ \text{PER} & 2 \\ \text{NUM} & \text{SG} \end{array}\right] \end{array}\right]$$

b. Lexical representation of *miniski*

miniski V
$$\left[\begin{array}{ll} \text{PRED} & \text{`GO } \langle\text{SUBJ}\rangle\text{'} \end{array}\right]$$

Accordingly, the c-structure representation in (5) yields the unified f-structure representation in (6) for the periphrastic construction in (2):

(5)

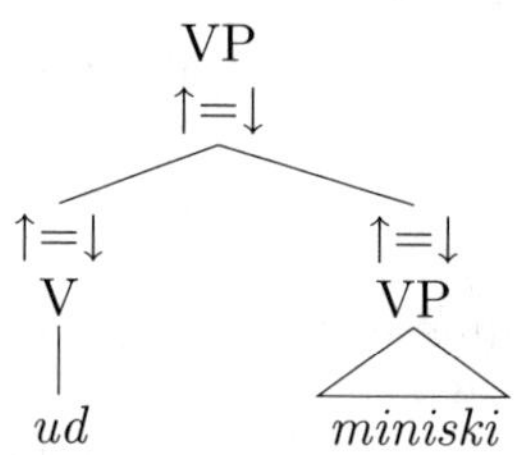

(6)
$$\left[\begin{array}{ll} \text{PRED} & \text{`GO } \langle\text{SUBJ}\rangle\text{'} \\ \text{POL} & \text{NEG} \\ \text{TNS} & \text{PRES} \\ \text{SUBJ} & \left[\begin{array}{ll} \text{PRED} & \text{PRO} \\ \text{PER} & 2 \\ \text{NUM} & \text{SG} \end{array}\right] \end{array}\right]$$

Crucially, in a syntactic treatment of periphrasis such as this there is no single lexical or morphological representation which is associated with the information contained in (6). Instead, an f-structure receives this information as contributions from separate and co-occurring syntactic

[5]We depart from some of the conventions within LFG for depicting lexical representations by using attribute-value matrices; this will help clarify the way in which lexical representations contribute to the definition of f-structures such as (6).

atoms.

5.2 An inferential-realizational conception of periphrasis

The supposition that similar sorts of information are supplied to f-structures by single complex lexical representations, as in (3), or multiple lexical entities co-occurring in c-structure, as in (2), has led to the claim within LFG that "morphology competes with syntax." In this paper we argue that for many instances of periphrasis this slogan is not sufficiently discriminating and should be replaced with the claim that in a language's system of morphological realization, synthesis may compete with periphrasis as a mode of inflectional exponence – in other words, that periphrases are defined realizationally. The essential ingredients of this proposal are the following two claims:

- A lexeme may be realized synthetically (as a single syntactic atom) or periphrastically (by two or more syntactic atoms co-occurring in a c-structure).
- The contentive information associated with a periphrase is not determined by the contentive information associated with its individual, syntactically independent parts through the mediation of unification principles defined on syntactic structures; rather, the contentive information associated with a periphrase is specified morpholexically. That is, syntactic principles of constituency and linearity determine the distribution of a periphrase's individual parts, but not the functional information which that periphrase expresses.

The antecedents of this competing hypothesis can be found in Ackerman (1984, 1987) (where it is employed in the analysis of Hungarian auxiliary constructions) as well as in the descriptive and pedagogical traditions of numerous languages. This proposal shares with those of Mohanan and Falk (and the recent LFG co-head proposals) the claim that periphrases are associated with a single, simple f-structure (rather than with nested f-structures reflecting the hierarchical organization of a periphrase's c-structure); but it differs dramatically in its assumption concerning the source of the information in that f-structure:

> Constructions of these sorts will be referred to as *analytic predicates* . . . they will be interpreted as entities created by morpholexical rules[6] . . . a portion of the analytic predicate, specifically the AUX element, functions as a constituent structure verb, i.e., it is the *categorial* or *structural head* of the lexical composition, while the infinitival

[6] Such rules were hypothesized to be relegated to the lexicon and responsible for word-formation and inflection.

> ... contributes the lexical meaning of the derived grammatical word, i.e., it serves as the *functional head* ... In other words, morpholexical rules produce a grammatical word[7] with discrete structural and functional heads and this analytic composition is associated with a lexical form. (Ackerman 1987, 329)

The assumption, in short, was that the clausal predicate information in f-structures is projected from a single lexical representation which receives either synthetic or periphrastic expression in c-structure.[8]

This approach assumed, but did not develop, a theory of morphology of the type designated as inferential-realizational in Stump's taxonomy. Recently there has been a resurgence of interest in the so-called Word & Paradigm approach to morphology (Robins 1959, Matthews 1972, Zwicky 1985, Anderson 1992, Aronoff 1994, Beard 1995, Stump 2001, etc.); what distinguishes this approach from traditional morpheme-based approaches is its premise that a language's inflectional system is INFERENTIAL rather than lexical (in the sense that it represents inflectional exponents not as lexically listed elements, but as markings licensed by rules by which complex word forms are deduced from simpler roots and stems) and is REALIZATIONAL rather than incremental (in the sense that it treats a word's association with a particular set of morphosyntactic properties as a precondition for – not a consequence of – the application of the rules licensing the inflectional exponents of those properties). Inferential-realizational approaches to morphology are in fact quite consistent with the fundamental assumptions of constraint-based lexicalism, both with respect to general conceptual, design features and in their commitment to comprehensive and rigorous formalization of analyses.

The assumption that a periphrase's f-structure is projected from a single lexical representation is not obviously compatible with usual assumptions in LFG concerning the source of information in f-structures. The standard view is, again, that information associated with lexical representations is projected into c-structure and thence, via correspondence algorithms, to f-structures: the f-structure, thus, represents a

[7]The notion "grammatical word" was intended to reflect Matthews' (1991) hypothesis that wordhood is not a unitary phenomenon and that one dimension of this phenomenon is a contentive one determined by morphosyntactic and lexical-semantic criteria. See Carstairs-McCarthy (2000, 596) for a somewhat different view.

[8]Minimally, within LFG the possibility of multi-word lexical items requires modifying the conventions used for annotating c-structure expressions associated with single-word lexical items so that appropriate lexical information will produce well-formed f-structures. We leave these sorts of implementational issues to another forum in favor of developing general arguments for the morphological status of periphrases.

distillation of syntactically relevant information provided by the lexical elements occupying c-structure terminal nodes. Our claim here, however, is that the syntactic atoms constituting a periphrase may be nothing more than form-theoretic exponents of a unitary content-theoretic element, and that it is this latter element – not its exponents – that determines the periphrase's f-structure. In particular, we claim that rules of morphology define the (potentially periphrastic) realization of a lexeme's pairing with a particular set of morphosyntactic properties, and that the association of such a pairing with an f-structure is insensitive to the manner of its realization.

We develop this inferential-realizational conception of periphrasis in the following sections. In section 5.3, we argue for a theoretical distinction between two types of paradigms and we discuss the relevance of this distinction to an inferential-realizational theory of periphrasis. In section 5.4, we examine a range of empirical evidence favoring the proposed theory over any purely syntactic alternative: focussing primarily on the grammatical characteristics of periphrastically expressed predicates in Udmurt and Mari, we present analyses of these predicates in which the relation between lexical information and its c-structure representation is mediated by realizationally defined paradigms.

5.3 Two types of paradigms and the linkage between them

In distinguishing a lexeme's content-theoretic aspects from its form-theoretic aspects, we will pursue an innovative conception of the lexicon and its relation to c-structure, f-structure, and morphological realization. On this conception, a language's lexicon is bipartite with respect to content and form: one part of its lexicon is its LEXEMICON, whose individual entries are lexemes bearing lexical meanings; the complementary part is its RADICON, whose individual entries are roots, i.e. elements of form. Every member L of a language's lexemicon has an associated CONTENT-PARADIGM C-P(L) such that each cell in C-P(L) consists of the pairing of L with a complete set of morphosyntactic properties;[9] we refer to any such pairing as a CONTENT-CELL. Cru-

[9]The relevant sense of completeness here is that of Stump (2001, 42f): a set σ of morphosyntactic properties for a lexeme of some category is COMPLETE iff σ is well-formed and for any morphosyntactic property set τ such that σ is not an extension of τ, the unification of τ and σ is not well-formed. Thus, although {masc, nom, sg} is a complete property set for Latin nominal lexemes, {masc, sg} is not; and because a property set can be well-formed only if it doesn't have contrasting values for any feature (p.40f), property sets such as {masc, nom, sg, pl} likewise fail to qualify as complete.

cially, content-cells represent ensembles of semantically interpretable information. In contrast, every member r of a language's radicon has an associated FORM-PARADIGM F-P(r) such that each cell in F-P(r) consists of the pairing of r with a set of differentiating morphosyntactic property labels; we refer to any such pairing as a FORM-CELL.[10] A language's paradigms of form-cells house the information necessary to deduce the morphological realization of the cells in that language's content-paradigms.

Consider, for concreteness, the future-tense realizations of the Udmurt verbal lexeme MÏNÏ 'go' in Table 1. In our approach, these forms imply the content-paradigm in (7) and the form-paradigm in (8).

TABLE 1. Future-tense forms of Udmurt MÏNÏ 'go'

		Affirmative	Negative
Singular	1	*mïno*	*ug mïnï*
	2	*mïnod*	*ud mïnï*
	3	*mïnoz*	*uz mïnï*
Plural	1	*mïnom(ï)*	*um mïne(le)*
	2	*mïnodï*	*ud mïne(le)*
	3	*mïnozï*	*uz mïne(le)*

(7) Future-tense content-paradigm of the Udmurt lexeme MÏNÏ 'go'

a. ⟨MÏNÏ, {1st singular future affirmative}⟩
b. ⟨MÏNÏ, {2nd singular future affirmative}⟩
c. ⟨MÏNÏ, {3rd singular future affirmative}⟩
d. ⟨MÏNÏ, {1st plural future affirmative}⟩
e. ⟨MÏNÏ, {2nd plural future affirmative}⟩
f. ⟨MÏNÏ, {3rd plural future affirmative}⟩
g. ⟨MÏNÏ, {1st singular future negative}⟩
h. ⟨MÏNÏ, {2nd singular future negative}⟩
i. ⟨MÏNÏ, {3rd singular future negative}⟩
j. ⟨MÏNÏ, {1st plural future negative}⟩
k. ⟨MÏNÏ, {2nd plural future negative}⟩
l. ⟨MÏNÏ, {3rd plural future negative}⟩

(8) Future-tense form-paradigm of the Udmurt root *mïnï* 'go'

a. ⟨*mïnï*, {1st singular future affirmative}⟩

[10]The concepts developed here are those of Stump (2002), but with different terminology: Stump's 'syntactic paradigms' and 'morphological paradigms' are our 'content-paradigms' and 'form-paradigms'.

b. ⟨*mïnï*, {2nd singular future affirmative}⟩
c. ⟨*mïnï*, {3rd singular future affirmative}⟩
d. ⟨*mïnï*, {1st plural future affirmative}⟩
e. ⟨*mïnï*, {2nd plural future affirmative}⟩
f. ⟨*mïnï*, {3rd plural future affirmative}⟩
g. ⟨*mïnï*, {1st singular future negative}⟩
h. ⟨*mïnï*, {2nd singular future negative}⟩
i. ⟨*mïnï*, {3rd singular future negative}⟩
j. ⟨*mïnï*, {1st plural future negative}⟩
k. ⟨*mïnï*, {2nd plural future negative}⟩
l. ⟨*mïnï*, {3rd plural future negative}⟩

For each cell ⟨L,σ⟩ in the content-paradigm of a lexeme L, there is a corresponding cell in some root's form-paradigm; we refer to this as the FORM-CORRESPONDENT (FC) of ⟨L,σ⟩. Thus, form-cell ⟨*mïnï*, {1st singular future affirmative}⟩ in (8) is the FC of the content-cell ⟨MÏNÏ, {1st singular future affirmative}⟩ in (7).

The REALIZATION of some form-cell ⟨r,σ⟩ is the form defined by the application to r of all relevant morphological rules realizing the property set σ; the realization of some content-cell ⟨L,σ⟩ is the realization of the FC of ⟨L,σ⟩. Thus, the realization of both the form-cell ⟨*mïnï*, {1st singular future affirmative}⟩ in (8) and the content-cell ⟨MÏNÏ, {1st singular future affirmative}⟩ in (7) is the synthetic word form *mïno* (cf. Table 1); similarly, the realization of both the form-cell ⟨*mïnï*, {1st singular future negative}⟩ and the content-cell ⟨MÏNÏ, {1st singular future negative}⟩ is the periphrase *ug mïnï*.[11] We do not assume that the MÏNÏ entry in Udmurt's lexemicon necessarily includes the entire content-paradigm in (7), nor that the *mïnï* entry in Udmurt's radicon necessarily includes the entire form-paradigm in (8); we instead assume that these entries simply contain the information necessary for the projection of these paradigms (and of the realizations of their cells) by well-motivated rules of morphology. Thus, although we shall refer to cells such as ⟨MÏNÏ, {1st singular future affirmative}⟩ and ⟨*mïnï*, {1st singular future affirmative}⟩ as aspects of lexical representation, they might be more accurately characterized as "morpholexical".

The relation between the cells in a root's form-paradigm and the realizations of those cells is mediated by realizational rules of the sort familiar in inferential-realizational ("Word & Paradigm") theories of

[11]Periphrastic negative predicates such as these exemplify the construct "expanded predicate" proposed in Ackerman and Webelhuth (1998); see also Spencer (2003a, 2003b).

morphology. Crucially, however, we also adopt a less usual hypothesis, according to which overt inflectional exponents are not limited to synthetic morphological markings. That is, we adopt the Periphrastic Realization Hypothesis in (9).[12]

(9) The Periphrastic Realization Hypothesis:
Inflectional rules that deduce the realizations of a form-paradigm's cells include rules defining periphrastic combinations as well as rules defining synthetic forms.

While inflectional rules determine the relation between the cells of a root's form-paradigm and their realizations, the relation between the cells in a lexeme's content-paradigm and their form-correspondents is regulated by a different kind of rule: for any content-cell $\langle L,\sigma\rangle$, the FC of $\langle L,\sigma\rangle$ is determined by a RULE OF PARADIGM LINKAGE. In most instances, the operative rule of paradigm linkage is the universal default in (10):

(10) Universal default rule of paradigm linkage:
If root r is stipulated as the primary root of a given lexeme L, then the FC of the content-cell $\langle L,\sigma\rangle$ is the form-cell $\langle r,\sigma\rangle$.[13]

---

[12]See Robins (1959), Matthews (1991), and Haspelmath (2000). See also Börjars et al. (1997), Sadler and Spencer (2001), and Spencer (2001, 2003b) on the periphrasis of the perfect passive in Latin as well as in various Slavic languages; and Stump (2001) on the Sanskrit periphrastic future. Though our discussion here focuses on inflectional instances of periphrasis, it should be noted that periphrastic realization is also "extremely common" (Csúcs, 1998, 295) in the domain of derivation; for instance, Udmurt possesses verbal derivatives consisting of a gerundial form of the main verb and a co-occurring inflected form of a verb encoding properties of tense, aspect, modality, etc. This suggests that synthetic and periphrastic realization obtains for both inflection and derivation and therefore accords with the claims of the Strong Lexicalist Hypothesis; see further Ackerman (to appear).

As it is formulated, the Periphrastic Realization Hypothesis might be taken to portray periphrasis as an intrusion of morphology into the definition of language's syntax; this may not, however, be the most productive interpretation of (9). One might instead assume that a language's realization rules draw upon both morphological and syntactic devices in the expression of its paradigm structure. On such an interpretation a language's "realizational paradigmatics" would span its individual morphological and syntactic components and, consequently, evidence for paradigmatic effects would not necessarily entail morphological status for the entities expressed by realization rules. This is an interpretation whose viability we intend to explore in future work.

[13]Here, we assume that a language's syntactic and form-paradigms involve the same inventory of morphosyntactic properties. Sadler and Spencer (2001), however, argue for a principled distinction between s(yntactic)-features ("functional features which have to be expressed by well-formed phrases and clauses") and m(orphological)-features ("those that regulate the morphophonological structure of words"); in the context of this distinction, one might assume that each form-cell $\langle r,\sigma_m\rangle$ contains a complete set σ_m of m-feature specifications, but that each content-

Thus, if *mïnï* is stipulated as the primary root of the Udmurt lexeme MÏNÏ 'go', then by default, the FC of the content-cell ⟨MÏNÏ, {1st singular future affirmative}⟩ is the form-cell ⟨*mïnï*, {1st singular future affirmative}⟩ (realization: *mïno*), and so on.

The default rule of paradigm linkage in (10) can, however, be overridden. The phenomenon of heteroclisis involves this sort of override Stump (2003). By definition, a heteroclite lexeme is one whose content-paradigm contains two distinct cells $\langle L,\sigma\rangle$, $\langle L,\sigma'\rangle$ such that $\langle L,\sigma\rangle$ has the FC $\langle r,\sigma\rangle$, $\langle L,\sigma'\rangle$ has the FC $\langle r',\sigma'\rangle$, and $r' \neq r$. Thus, Sanskrit has a special rule of paradigm linkage which assigns each direct-case (i.e. nominative, vocative, or accusative) cell in the content-paradigm of the heteroclite noun HṚD 'heart' a FC from the form-paradigm of the root *hṛdaya*, while each oblique-case cell in this content-paradigm is assigned a FC from the form-paradigm of the distinct root *hṛd*; the examples in Table 2 illustrate.

TABLE 2. inflections of the Sanskrit heteroclite noun HṚD 'heart'

Cells in HṚD's content-paradigm	Form-correspondents	Realizations
⟨HṚD, {neut nom sg}⟩	⟨*hṛdaya*, {neut nom sg}⟩	*hṛdaya-m*
⟨HṚD, {neut loc sg}⟩	⟨*hṛd*, {neut loc sg}⟩	*hṛd-i*

Deponence is a phenomenon involving a different sort of override of the default rule of paradigm linkage in (10). A deponent lexeme is, by definition, one whose content-paradigm contains a cell $\langle L,\sigma\rangle$ whose FC is $\langle r,\sigma'\rangle$, where $\sigma \neq \sigma'$. Thus, Latin has a special rule of paradigm linkage which assigns each active cell in the content-paradigm of the deponent verb FATĒRĪ 'confess' a FC from the passive form-paradigm of FATĒRĪ's primary root *fat*; by contrast, the default rule of paradigm linkage associates cells from the passive form-paradigm of the primary root *mon* with passive cells in the content-paradigm of the nondeponent verb MONĒRE 'advise'. The examples in Table 3 illustrate.

cell $\langle L,\sigma_s\rangle$ involves a complete set σ_s of s-feature specifications. On that assumption, the default correspondence between content-paradigms and form-paradigms would have to incorporate the default correspondence of m-feature specifications and s-feature specifications envisioned by Sadler and Spencer (2001, 84). This is a possibility we do not exclude; our present concerns do not necessitate this, however.

TABLE 3. inflections of the Latin verbs FATĒRĪ 'confess' (deponent) and MONĒRE 'advise' (nondeponent)

Cells in content-paradigms	Form-correspondents	Realizations
⟨FATĒRĪ, {1 sg pres act indic}⟩	⟨*fat*, {1 sg pres pass indic}⟩	*fateor*
⟨MONĒRE, {1 sg pres pass indic}⟩	⟨*mon*, {1 sg pres pass indic}⟩	*moneor*

(See Stump (2002) for additional discussion and exemplification of an inferential-realizational approach to heteroclisis and deponence.)

In the grammatical framework advocated here, the interface between content-paradigms and c-structures is regulated by the two principles in (11).

(11) a. Synthetic Realization Principle (= Morphological Expression of Ackerman and Webelhuth (1998)):
Where the realization w of $\langle L,\sigma \rangle$ is a synthetic member of category X, w may be inserted as the head of XP.

b. Periphrastic Realization Principle:
Where the realization of w_1 w_2 of $\langle L,\sigma \rangle$ is periphrastic and w_1 and w_2 belong to the respective categories X and Y, w_1 and w_2 may be inserted as the heads of the respective phrases XP and YP.

As formulated, the Periphrastic Realization Principle makes no claims about the surface constituency relations among the elements of periphrastic constructions; thus, our initial assumption is that the structural relationship between XP and YP in (11b) is determined by RULES OF PERIPHRASTIC SYNTAX at least some of which may be language-specific.

According to (11a), the synthetic form *miniskod* 'go.2SG' in the Udmurt sentence (3) may head a VP which thereby bears the morphosyntactic property set {2nd singular present affirmative}; according to (11b), the parts of the periphrase *ud miniski* 'not.2SG go' in sentence (2) may head separate phrases – presumably the phrases VP_1 and VP_2 in a structure of the form $[_{VP1}$ V VP_2], as in (5). In this way, the individual word forms constituting a realizational periphrase exhibit morphophonological integrity (in accordance with the arguments for Lexical Integrity of Bresnan and Mchombo (1995)), but do not themselves instantiate the Synthetic Realization Principle (11a). Thus the Synthetic Realization Principle does not, on our view, exclude the alternative of analytic realization. By the same token, the lexicality of an entity cannot, on our view, be reliably determined by its surface exponence.

The f-structure corresponding to a c-structure defined by (11a,b) is not projected directly from the forms occupying the individual leaves within this c-structure; rather, its definition depends on accessing the information from the relevant lexeme's content-paradigm – specifically, from the cell $\langle L,\sigma \rangle$ that is realized by the heads in this c-structure. We assume that if $\langle L,\sigma \rangle$ is realized as the periphrase w_1 w_2 in c-structure, then all of the syntactic complement requirements of this periphrase are determined by the lexeme which it realizes (together with the relevant rules of periphrastic syntax). We accordingly conclude that if $\langle L,\sigma \rangle$ has a (synthetic or periphrastic) realization at c-structure and denotes a predicate P, then the subject and complements of $\langle L,\sigma \rangle$'s realization denote P's arguments.

In this framework, the skeletal information associated with a lexeme's f-structural representation is projected strictly from the information in its content-paradigm; on the other hand, the c-structural representation of any cell $\langle L,\sigma \rangle$ in the content-paradigm of a lexeme L is additionally sensitive to this cell's realization. Thus, the realizations associated with a content-paradigm's (content-theoretic) cells do not themselves participate in the determination of f-structure, but are simply the c-structural expressions of information contained in these cells. This permits lexical representations to project their information into clauses, independently of how these lexical representations are formally realized. Thus periphrasis can be construed as a purely formal aspect of lexical representations where the pieces themselves are not annotated with information as they are in co-head analyses within LFG. This system can be viewed as an implementation of Realization-based Lexicalism as discussed in Blevins (2001).[14] The basic organization of lexical representations can be represented as in Table 4.

[14]In some measure, the proposal espoused here represents an elaboration of the intuitions guiding the Sadler and Spencer (2001) treatment of periphrastic constructions in terms of a distinction between s-structures and m-structures: roughly, their s-structure can be construed as the contentive side of the lexical representation embodied by a content-paradigm, while their m-structure is expressed by our notion of form-paradigms (but see footnote 12 above).

Table 4. Lexical representations in the assumed framework

<table>
<tr><th rowspan="2"></th><th colspan="2">Lexical representations:</th><th rowspan="2">Realizations (word forms)</th></tr>
<tr><th>content-cells (⟨L,σ⟩ pairings)</th><th>form-cells (⟨r,σ⟩ pairings)</th></tr>
<tr><td rowspan="2">Associations:</td><td colspan="2">content-cells associated with form-cells by rules of paradigm linkage</td><td></td></tr>
<tr><td></td><td colspan="2">form-cells associated with realizations by realization rules</td></tr>
<tr><td>Information represented:</td><td>Contentive (functional-semantic content, grammatical functions, morphosyntactic properties)</td><td>Formal (morphosyntactic property labels); Diacritic/indexical (inflection class membership, root phonology)</td><td>Purely phonological</td></tr>
</table>

5.4 The lexicality of Mari and Udmurt predicates

In this section we examine instances of periphrasis in two Uralic languages, Mari and Udmurt. We argue that the evidence from these languages strongly favors an inferential-realizational approach to periphrasis – that if principles that are standardly assumed to regulate synthetic exponence in realizational morphological theories are regarded as having periphrastic exponence within their compass as well, then a number of otherwise problematic characteristics of periphrasis turn out to be neither surprising nor unexpected. We develop detailed formal analyses of this data as concrete exemplifications of this approach. Throughout, we explicitly contrast the inferential-realizational approach to periphrasis with the purely syntactic approach, in which morphological synthesis and periphrasis are theoretically segregated (the former being treated as the domain of a language's morphology and the latter as a province of its syntax).

A priori, the development of a morphological theory of periphrasis confronts a number of important issues. Foremost among these is the issue of criteria: how does one decide whether a given multi-word expression is the realization of some cell in a paradigm? That is, how is a periphrase distinguished from a group of words in a relation of syntactic complementation? Though this issue is virtually ignored in modern linguistic theory, it was central to much speculation on the nature of wordhood in the Soviet linguistic tradition. The following remarks from Gukhman (1963, 199) provide a cogent statement of the basic task:[15]

> The need to establish criteria for the differentiation of analytic verbal constructions from other types of word combinations, such as the combination of two or several full words or the combination of an aux-

[15]See also Zhirmunskij (1963, 24).

iliary with a full word, is connected with the question of whether these constructions are considered members of a paradigmatic series, that is, whether they are units of the morphological level.

This is a particularly crucial issue, since constraint-based lexicalist frameworks such as LFG and HPSG conventionally assume that periphrasis should not be treated in the lexical/morphological component of grammar, given that it involves syntactically independent elements. As a consequence these frameworks have developed analyses of such phenomena which employ various modifications of the syntactic apparatus used to address other syntactic phenomena. In effect, the default assumption has been that periphrasis falls within the purview of syntactic frameworks since they possess tools that can be modified to treat them. It hardly needs to be said that this argument from parsimony, shared by Chomskyan syntactocentric approaches, represents an analytic convenience rather than an independently motivated, empirically supported, and well-reasoned theoretical proposal. The irony of this position for lexicalist approaches is that, given their adoption of representational modularity, they are not committed architecturally and conceptually to a syntactic analysis of periphrasis in the same way that Chomskyan approaches are.

In the following discussion, we argue that there are at least three sufficient criteria for the identification of periphrases: the criterion of featurally intersective distribution, that of noncompositionality, and that of distributed exponence.[16] Our discussion will therefore focus on analytic combinations which satisfy one or more of these criteria, and our objective, again, is to demonstrate that combinations which satisfy any of these criteria are most plausibly treated as expressions of a language's morphology. Because the languages Mari and Udmurt possess rich inventories of predicates which receive synthetic and periphrastic expression, they are instructive sources of data for the development of this discussion.

Our discussion proceeds as follows. First, we introduce the criterion of featurally intersective distribution and focus attention on a class of analytic combinations from Western Mari which satisfy this criterion

[16]See Spencer (2001, 2003b) for the postulation of additional criteria which are useful for distinguishing between morphological versus syntactic objects. Ackerman and Webelhuth (1998), additionally, suggested a general criterion derived from the Strong Lexicalist Hypothesis, namely, that all evidence of the derivational modification of information stands as a sufficient condition of lexicality. This was referred to as The Principle of Lexical Adicity. This principle is consistent with the new, and we believe, more compelling criteria presently being adduced from morphology proper.

(section 5.4.1); we argue that the purely syntactic approach to periphrasis does not afford an adequate account of the manner in which periphrasis and synthesis are paradigmatically opposed in the Western Mari data; the inferential-realizational approach, by contrast, does. We present a detailed formal analysis of a fragment of Western Mari verb morphology to give concrete substance to this claim (section 5.4.2). In section 5.4.3, we introduce the criterion of noncompositionality and adduce examples of analytic constructions from Mari and Udmurt which satisfy this criterion; we demonstrate that periphrases of this sort constitute an especially forceful type of evidence against the purely syntactic approach to periphrasis and in favor of the inferential-realizational approach. In section 5.4.4, we discuss the criterion of distributed exponence, which we exemplify with additional evidence from Udmurt; as we show, the inferential-realizational approach to periphrasis affords a superior account of this evidence as well. We conclude (section 5.4.5) with a brief discussion of two kinds of evidence which support the inferential-realizational approach to periphrasis: the close relation between synthesis and periphrasis in language change and the status of periphrasis in a theory of morphological markedness.

5.4.1 The paradigmatic opposition of periphrasis to synthesis

Periphrases commonly stand in paradigmatic opposition to synthetic realizations; that is, they realize contrasting values for the same morphosyntactic features but are otherwise identical in their lexicosemantic content. Mari (known also as Cheremis) exhibits numerous instances of this characteristic of periphrasis, some of which we examine here.

Consider, for example, the present desiderative, first-past, and second-past[17] realizations of the verb KOL 'die' in Western Mari; these are given in Tables 5-7.[18] The second-past realizations in Table 7 are uniformly synthetic, for both the affirmative-polarity and the negative-polarity portions of the paradigm. The desiderative and first-past realizations in Tables 5 and 6, by contrast, are synthetic in the affirmative but periphrastic in the negative; in particular, each of the negative realizations in Tables 5 and 6 involves a finite form of the negative verb AK (the relevant forms of which are isolated in Table 8) and an

[17]According to Kangasmaa-Minn (1998, 229), "[t]he first past refers especially to states and events which the speaker has personally witnessed, while the second past is more or less a record of what has been or happened without any emphasis on the speaker's attitude towards the truth value of the utterance".

[18]The segmentation of Mari formatives assumed here and throughout follows the analysis of Eastern Mari verbs proposed by Sebeok and Ingemann (1961).

essentially invariant form of KOL itself.

TABLE 5. Present desiderative realizations of the Mari *em*-conjugation verb KOL 'die' (Western dialect) [Alhoniemi 1985, 125, 127]

		Affirmative	Negative
SG.	1	*kolə̂-ne-m* 'I want to die.'	*ə-ne-m kolə̂* 'I don't want to die.'
	2	*kolə̂-ne-t*	*ə-ne-t kolə̂*
	3	*kolə̂-ne-žə*	*ə-ne-žə kolə̂*
PL.	1	*kolə̂-ne-nä*	*ə-ne-nä kolə̂*
	2	*kolə̂-ne-ðä*	*ə-ne-ðä kolə̂*
	3	*kolə̂-ne-štə*	*ə-ne-štə kolep*

TABLE 6. First-past realizations of the Mari *em*-conjugation verb KOL 'die' (Western dialect) [Alhoniemi 1985, 113f, 118]

		Affirmative	Negative
SG.	1	*kolə̂-š-ə̂m* 'I died.'	*š-əm kolə̂* 'I didn't die.'
	2	*kolə̂-š-ə̂c*	*š-əc kolə̂*
	3	*kolə̂-š*	*əš kolə̂*
PL.	1	*kolə̂-š-na*	*šə-nä kolə̂*
	2	*kolə̂-š-ta*	*šə-ðä kolə̂*
	3	*kol-eβ-ə*	*əš kolep*

TABLE 7. Second-past realizations of the Mari *em*-conjugation verb KOL 'die' (Western dialect) [Alhoniemi 1985, 114, 118]

		Affirmative	Negative
SG.	1	*kol-en-äm* 'I died.'	*kolə̂-ð e-l-am* 'I didn't die.'
	2	*kol-en-ät*	*kolə̂-ð e-l-at*
	3	*kol-en*	*kolə̂-ð e*
PL.	1	*kol-en-nä*	*kolə̂-ð e-l-na*
	2	*kol-en-dä*	*kolə̂-ð e-l-ð a*
	3	*kol-en-ət*	*kolə-ð e-l-ə̂t*

TABLE 8. Present desiderative and first-past realizations of the Mari negative auxiliary AK (Western dialect) [Alhoniemi 1985, 118]

		Present desiderative	First past
SG.	1	*ə-ne-m*	*š-əm*
	2	*ə-ne-t*	*š-əc*
	3	*ə-ne-žə*	*əš*
PL.	1	*ə-ne-nä*	*šə-nä*
	2	*ə-ne-ðä*	*šə-ðä*
	3	*ə-ne-štə*	*əš*

The distribution of periphrasis in Tables 5-7 can be construed as FEATURALLY INTERSECTIVE, in the sense that there is no one morphosyntactic property among those expressed by the realizations in Tables 5-7 that is always expressed periphrastically rather than synthetically: not all negative realizations are periphrastic, nor are all desiderative or first-past realizations synthetic; instead, it is the intersection of negative polarity with the desiderative mood or with the first-past tense which is expressed periphrastically in Western Mari. Since each of the features expressed in Tables 5-7 has a specification whose exponence is synthetic, these features are clearly available to a system of realization rules; the fact that certain combinations of specifications of these same features are expressed periphrastically suggests that such expression is an effect of this same system of realization rules. featurally intersective distribution is the basis for our first criterion for distinguishing morphologically defined periphrases from other analytic combinations; this criterion is stated in (12). (Note that (12) is merely a sufficient criterion; it does not require that every periphrase have a featurally intersective distribution.)

(12) Criterion I: If an analytic combination C has a featurally intersective distribution, then C is a periphrase.

By this criterion, all of the analytic combinations in Tables 5 and 6 are periphrases.

The paradigmatic opposition of synthesis and periphrasis exemplified in Tables 5-7 raises two crucial questions for a theory of periphrasis. First, why do some morphosyntactic property sets lack single-word realizations? And second, why do single-word realizations exclude the use of synonymous periphrases? The purely syntactic approach to periphrasis implies one set of answers to these questions; the inferential-realizational approach to periphrasis affords a very different set of answers. We now show that of the two approaches, the latter provides a superior account of paradigmatic oppositions of synthesis and periphrasis.

Accounting for paradigmatic oppositions in a purely syntactic approach to periphrasis

Consider first the question of why certain morphosyntactic property sets lack single-word realizations. In inferential-realizational approaches to morphology, it is assumed that a language's morphology provides expression for every association of a lexeme's root with a set of morphosyntactic properties available to that lexeme. The expression of such an association may involve overt morphology, as in the realization *walk-ed* expressing the association of the verbal lexeme WALK with the property set {TNS:past, MOOD:indic, AGR:{PER:1, NUM:pl}}. But overt morphology needn't be involved. For instance, the association of WALK with the property set {TNS:pres, MOOD:indic, AGR:{PER:1, NUM:pl}} is simply expressed by the uninflected root realization *walk*, because English morphology lacks any rule realizing this property set; instances of this sort can therefore be said to exhibit POVERTY OF EXPONENCE.

The affirmative forms in Tables 5-7 and the negative forms in Table 7 show that properties of polarity, mood, and tense are available to verbal lexemes in Western Mari; thus, in the absence of any contrary stipulation, property sets combining negative polarity with desiderative mood or first-past tense should be available to verbal lexemes in Western Mari. Yet, as we have seen, there is no overt synthetic expression of the association of a verb root with a property set specified for negative polarity and either desiderative mood or first-past tense, nor are such associations simply expressed (through poverty of exponence) as uninflected root forms. Why is this?

In a purely syntactic approach to periphrasis in which all synthetic realizations are defined by morphological realization rules and all analytic combinations are defined by ordinary principles of syntax, the absence of one-word realizations in the negative desiderative or negative first past (whether these be synthetically inflected realizations or, through poverty of exponence, simple uninflected forms) would have to be attributed to the following ad hoc stipulation:

(13) Contrary to expectation, property sets specified for negative polarity and either desiderative mood or first-past tense are not available to Mari verbal lexemes.

On this view, a lexeme's form-paradigm would only contain cells for those property sets that are realized synthetically. At the same time, a purely syntactic approach would have to ensure that the syntax of Western Mari defined negative desiderative and negative first-past periphrases; as a consequence, the fact that the negative desiderative and negative first past are realized periphrastically and not synthetically would be improbably portrayed as a coincidental effect of morphological restrictiveness and syntactic permissiveness.

The second critical question raised by the paradigmatic opposition between periphrasis and synthesis concerns the fact that a synthetic realization overrides the use of a synonymous periphrase: why, for example, does each instance of synthesis in Tables 5-7 exclude the use of a periphrastic alternative? A priori, there is nothing about the syntactic approach to periphrasis that entails that property sets expressed by periphrastic means should strictly complement those property sets that are realized synthetically. Proponents of this approach must therefore stipulate this complementarity by appealing to an ad hoc principle of "morphological blocking" (Andrews 1990, Blevins 2000). According to such a principle, the existence of a synthetic expression for a specified morphosyntactic property set excludes the use of a synonymous periphrase. This principle reifies the basic bifurcation of synthetic and analytic marking underlying the purely syntactic approach to periphrasis, stipulating an otherwise unanticipated domain of competition between morphology and syntax; the need to appeal to such a principle is thus an artifact of the purely syntactic approach to periphrasis. On the face of it, the introduction of such a principle acknowledges that the availability of certain syntactic expressions is determined by morphology, but indirectly (rather than directly, as in the account we propose): part of a language's syntax must be treated as effectively the complement of morphology that does not receive synthetic exponence.

Accounting for paradigmatic oppositions in an inferential-realizational approach to periphrasis

An inferential-realizational approach to periphrasis provides a much less stipulative account of the paradigmatic opposition of synthesis and periphrasis. In this approach, morphological rules of synthesis and periphrasis participate competitively – as alternatives – in the realizational definition of a lexeme's forms. The competition, however, is not between morphology and syntax, as in morphological blocking proposals, but between the varieties of exponence employed in realizing the cells in a lexeme's content-paradigm. The fact that some morphosyntactic property sets lack single-word realizations is therefore attributed to (a) the lack of any rules of synthetic exponence realizing those property sets and (b) the existence of a general default rule of periphrastic exponence realizing those sets. No ad hoc stipulation comparable to (13) is needed in this approach: property sets specified for negative polarity and either desiderative mood or first past tense are, as expected, available for realization in the inflection of Western Mari verbal lexemes, but happen to be realized by a default rule of periphrasis.[19] Thus, the inferential-realizational approach is – unlike the purely syntactic approach – fully compatible with the restrictive hypothesis that any property set that is legal in c-structure can also legally drive morphological realization. The fact that synthesis excludes periphrasis in the negative second past follows from the assumption that the default rule of periphrasis defining negative realizations is (in accordance with Pāṇini's principle) overridden by a narrower rule of synthesis defining negative second-past realizations; thus, the inferential-realizational approach also avoids appealing to an ad hoc principle of morphological blocking to account for the exclusion of periphrasis in such instances. In other words, there is no need to posit a special blocking principle to regulate the relation between morphology and syntax: as a general, independently motivated constraint within morphology, Pāṇini's principle suffices to account for the relevant data if periphrasis is defined realizationally (Stump (to appear)).

5.4.2 Formal analysis of a fragment of Western Mari verb morphology

We now develop a formal analysis of the Mari realizations in Tables 5-7 which embodies these advantages of the inferential-realizational approach to periphrasis and which will provide a concrete basis for further discussion. At the core of this analysis is our assumption (noted above, cf. Table 4) that the cells in a lexeme's form-paradigm are associated with their realizations by a system of realization rules.

Basic assumptions

The analysis that we shall propose for the Mari verb forms in Tables 5-7 rests on a number of pretheoretic assumptions, which we now elucidate. Morphologically, the desiderative and first-past realizations in Tables 5 and 6 are built upon KOL's SCHWA STEM, i.e. the result of suffixing schwa to KOL's root *kol*;[20] exceptionally, however, the third-person plural form of the first past (and, in the negative polarity, that of the desiderative) are built on a special stem in *-ep* (prevocalic alternant: *-eβ*). The schwa stem *kolə̂* and the special stem *kolep* will be referred to as KOL'S PRIMARY STEMS. In the affirmative of the present

[19] The default appeal to periphrastic realization parallels the status of periphrastic negative expressions as the unmarked encoding within Uralic.

[20] Because other forms of KOL are also built on this stem and because the full set of forms that are built on it are not unified by any common morphosyntactic property, 'schwa-stem' is a morphomic category (Aronoff 1994).

desiderative and of the first past, the primary stem is augmented by the modal suffix *-ne* and the temporal suffix *-š* (respectively); the *-š* suffix is, however, grammatically restricted to *em*-conjugation verbs and phonologically restricted to postvocalic positions (and is, for this latter reason, absent from the third-person plural affirmative first-past form *kol-eβ-ə*, whose primary stem ends in a consonant). Augmenting a primary stem in these ways produces a SECONDARY STEM. A verb form's subject-agreement terminations are affixed to its secondary stem; in the first past, however, the third person singular is a default realization lacking any overt personal termination. In the periphrastic negative realizations of the present desiderative and first past, the inflections for mood and subject agreement appear not on the stem of KOL itself, but on a primary stem of the negative auxiliary AK (which, though negative in meaning, exhibits the same markers as used in affirmative morphology). The primary stems of AK are irregular: its primary desiderative stem is *ə*; its primary first-past stem is *əš* in third-person realizations, otherwise *šə*.[21]

The affirmative second-past realizations in Table 7 are built on a primary stem identical to KOL's affirmative gerundial stem (which consists of its root plus the *em*-conjugation gerundial suffix *-en*). This primary stem is inflected with person/number markers expressing subject agreement; here also, the third-person singular realization carries no overt agreement marking.[22] The negative second-past realizations are built on a primary stem having two distinct forms – an absolute form identical to its negative gerundial stem (its root plus the negative marker *-ð e*) and a conjunct form arising from the absolute form through the suffixation of *-l*. The conjunct stem is used in the presence of inflectional suffixes, and the absolute form, in their absence; thus, the latter form is restricted to the third-person singular, since it alone is not overtly marked for subject agreement.

Notwithstanding the different degrees of morphological synthesis exhibited by the present desiderative, first-past, and second-past realizations, our assumption is that their content-paradigms are parallel; the relevant differences between these tenses are differences in the modes of exponence exploited in the realization of the content-paradigm's cells

[21]There is clearly a historical connection between the sibilant appearing in the first-past stem of AK and the first-past suffix *š*; but in view of the idiosyncratic variation in the shape of the former, it is not clear that these should be synchronically identified.

[22]Bereczki (1990, 55) reports that in some eastern dialects, the first- and second-person plural affirmative second-past forms are instead periphrastic, consisting of an uninflected gerund and a copula inflected both for present tense and for subject agreement, e.g. *tolân ulâna* 'we came', *tolân ulâð a* 'you came'.

(through the realization of these cells' FCs in the corresponding form-paradigm).

We assume that the relation between a cell in a form-paradigm and the realization of that cell is mediated by realization rules; following Stump (2001, 44), we assume the following format for realization rules.[23]

(14) $\mathrm{X_C}, \sigma : \tau \rightarrow \mathrm{Y}$

A rule stated in this format is to be interpreted as follows: Given a pairing $\langle \mathrm{X},\sigma \rangle$ consisting of a root or stem X belonging to class C and a property set σ that is an extension of τ, the result of applying the rule to $\langle \mathrm{X},\sigma \rangle$ is, by definition, the pairing $\langle \mathrm{Y},\sigma \rangle$. For example, the rule for the realization of an *em*-conjugation verb's affirmative gerund is formulated in (15).

(15) $\mathrm{X_{V[\textsc{conjugation}:em]}}, \sigma$:{VFORM:gerund; POL:aff} → X*en*

This rule applies to the cell ⟨*kol*,{VFORM:gerund, POL:aff}⟩ in the form-paradigm of the *em*-conjugation verb root *kol* 'die' to yield the pairing ⟨*kolen*,{VFORM:gerund, POL:aff}⟩. In formulating rules in which the value of Y doesn't vary according to the value of σ, we henceforth abbreviate the format in (14) as in (16).

(16) $\mathrm{X_C}, \tau \rightarrow \mathrm{Y}$

Every realization rule is a member of some rule block. In general, a realization rule belonging to a particular rule block competes with other members of the same block in the definition of a cell's realization. Rule competition of this sort is resolved by Pāṇini's principle: when two realization rules compete in the definition of a cell's realization, the narrower rule prevails.[24] In such instances, the prevailing rule can be referred to by means of what we call NAR ("narrowest applicable rule") notation (cf. Stump 2001, 52): where

---

[23]The format in (14) is only a superficial departure from the (equivalent) format employed by Stump (2001, 44), in which the realization rule represented in (14) would, as a member of rule block *n*, be expressed as (i).

(i) $\mathrm{RR}_{n,\tau,\mathrm{C}}(\langle \mathrm{X},\sigma \rangle) =_{def} \langle \mathrm{Y},\sigma \rangle$

[24]The relevant notion of narrowness is that of Stump (2001, 52): where (i)-(iii) belong to the same rule block, (i) is NARROWER than (ii) iff ρ is an extension of τ and $\rho \neq \tau$; where $\mathrm{C} \neq \mathrm{C}'$, (i) is NARROWER than (iii) iff $\mathrm{C} \subseteq \mathrm{C}'$.

(i) $\mathrm{X_C}, \sigma : \rho \rightarrow \mathrm{Y}$

(ii) $\mathrm{X_C}, \sigma : \tau \rightarrow \mathrm{Z}$

(iii) $\mathrm{X_{C'}}, \sigma : \upsilon \rightarrow \mathrm{W}$

$X_C, \sigma : \tau \to Y$

is the narrowest rule in block n which is applicable to $\langle X,\sigma \rangle$,

$\langle X,\sigma \rangle : n$

represents the result of applying that rule to $\langle X,\sigma \rangle$ (i.e. the result $\langle Y,\sigma \rangle$). This notation will be useful for defining the systematic resolution of competition among rules of synthetic and periphrastic exponence.

Our assumption is that three rule blocks are necessary for the definition of the Mari realizations in Tables 5-7. The first block (here labelled 'Block I') houses rules which deduce a verb's primary stem forms from its root; the second (labelled 'Block II') houses rules which allow a verb's secondary stem to be deduced from its primary stem; the third ('Block III') houses the various rules specifying the exponents (if any) of subject agreement. On this assumption, we can say that for any cell $\langle r,\sigma \rangle$ in a Mari form-paradigm, w is the realization of $\langle r,\sigma \rangle$ if and only if $((\langle r,\sigma \rangle : I) : II) : III = \langle w,\sigma \rangle$.[25]

Mari realization rules

In this framework, we propose the following formulations for the three blocks of realization rules necessary for the definition of a verb's present desiderative, first-past, and second-past realizations in Western Mari. The rules in Block I (rules **W-Ia** through **W-Ij**) define the primary stems of the realizations in Tables 5-7; the Block II rules **W-IIa** and **W-IIb** determine the secondary stems used in these realizations; and the outer layer of inflectional morphology exhibited by these realizations is regulated by the agreement-marking rules in Block III. We discuss each of these three rule blocks in turn.

Block I: *Rules deducing primary stems from roots (rules* **W-Ia** *through* **W-Ij***)*

By rule **W-Ia**, a verb's schwa stem is its default primary stem; here and in the rules which follow, the variable X ranges over stems but not periphrases.

W-Ia. $X_V, \{\} \to Y$, where Y is X's schwa stem.

[25]This generalization constitutes one clause in the definition of Western Mari's paradigm function; cf. Stump (2001, 50ff).

Example: From the affirmative first-person singular present desiderative cell (17a) in the form-paradigm of *kol* 'die', rule **W-Ia** licenses the pairing (17b), where *kolə̂* is the primary stem of (17a)'s realization *kolə̂-ne-m* 'I want to die'.

(17) a. ⟨*kol*, {POL: aff, MOOD: desid, TNS: present, AGR:{PER: 1, NUM: sg}}⟩
 b. ⟨*kolə̂*, {POL: aff, MOOD: desid, TNS: present, AGR:{PER: 1, NUM: sg}}⟩

As it is formulated, **W-Ia** is the most general possible rule for the definition of a verb's primary stem; as such, it is overridden by the other, narrower members of Block I, in accordance with Pāṇini's principle.

W-Ib. X_V, {POL: aff, TNS: 1st past, AGR: {PER: 3, NUM: pl}}
→ X*ep*

Example: From the affirmative third-person plural first-past cell (18a) in the form-paradigm of *kol* 'die', rule **W-Ib** licenses the pairing (18b), where *kolep* is the primary stem of (18a)'s realization *kol-eβ-ə* 'they died'. Note that in accordance with Pāṇini's principle, the narrower rule **W-Ib** overrides the more general rule **W-Ia** in the definition of *koleβə*'s primary stem.

(18) a. ⟨*kol*, {POL: aff, MOOD: indic, TNS: 1st past, AGR:{PER: 3, NUM: pl}}⟩
 b. ⟨*kolep*, {POL: aff, MOOD: indic, TNS: 1st past, AGR:{PER: 3, NUM: pl}}⟩

W-Ic. X_V,{TNS: 2nd past} → Y,
where Y is identical to the realization of the form-cell
⟨X, {VFORM: gerund, POL: aff}⟩

Example: From the affirmative first-person singular second-past cell (19a) in the form-paradigm of *kol* 'die', rule **W-Ic** (a rule of referral[26]) licenses the pairing (19b), where *kolen* (*kol*'s affirmative gerund; cf. **W-If**) is the primary stem of (19a)'s realization *kol-en-äm* 'I died'. As the narrower rule, **W-Ic** overrides the default rule **W-Ia** in the definition of *kolenäm*'s primary stem.

(19) a. ⟨*kol*, {POL: aff, MOOD: indic, TNS: 2nd past, AGR:{PER: 1, NUM: sg}}⟩
 b. ⟨*kolen*, {POL: aff, MOOD: indic, TNS: 2nd past, AGR:{PER: 1, NUM: sg}}⟩

[26] See Zwicky (1985) and Stump (1993, 2001) for discussion of the special properties of rules of referral.

W-Id. X_V, σ:{POL: neg} → [<u>Y</u> Z], where Y is the realization of ⟨AK,σ⟩, ⟨X,σ'⟩ : I=⟨Z,σ'⟩, and $\sigma' = \sigma/${POL:aff, TNS:1st past}

Rule **W-Id** is central to our analysis of the periphrasis in Tables 5 and 6. By this rule, the default realization of any negative cell ⟨X,σ⟩ in a verb's form-paradigm is a periphrase. Here and throughout, we represent periphrases in brackets: [Y Z]. We further assume that in general, periphrases are headed, and we identify the head of a periphrase by underlining: [<u>Y</u> Z]. The periphrases defined by rule **W-Id** are subject to rule (20) at the morphology-syntax interface; we assume for present purposes that this rule of periphrastic syntax is language-specific.

(20) Rule of periphrastic syntax:
Where [<u>Y</u> Z] (or [Z <u>Y</u>]) is the realization of a cell ⟨r,σ⟩ in a form-paradigm such that r belongs to category X, then in c-structure, Y heads XP[σ] and Z heads an XP complement of Y.

The slash notation $\sigma/\{\text{F}_1{:}\rho_1, \ldots, f_n{:}\rho_n\}$ in **W-Id** refers to that morphosyntactic property set that is like σ except that its value for the feature F_i is ρ_i ($1 \leq i \leq n$). (See Stump (2001, 56) for a more precise definition.) Thus, the rule of referral **W-Id** causes a negative form to be realized – by default – as the periphrastic combination of a finite form of the negative verb AK with the primary stem of the corresponding affirmative first-past realization; note that this rule applies whether the primary stem of the corresponding affirmative first-past realization is a schwa stem (defined by rule W-Ia) or a stem in *-ep* (defined by rule **W-Ib**). In this way, rule **W-Id** applies to pairings such as (21a) and (21b) in the form-paradigm of *kol* 'die' to license the respective pairings (22a) and (22b); by (20), the realizations in these latter pairings have the c-structure representations in (23a) and (23b).

(21) a. ⟨*kol*, {POL: neg, MOOD: indic, TNS: 1st past, AGR:{PER: 1, NUM: pl}}⟩
b. ⟨*kol*, {POL: neg, MOOD: desid, TNS: present, AGR{PER: 3, NUM: pl}}⟩

(22) a. ⟨[<u>*šənä*</u> *kolə̂*], {POL:neg, MOOD:indic, TNS:1st past, AGR:{PERS:1, NUM:pl}} ⟩
b. ⟨[<u>*əneštə*</u> *kolep*], {POL:neg, MOOD:desid, TNS:present, AGR:{PERS:3, NUM:pl}} ⟩

(23) a. [$_{\text{VP}}$[$_{\text{V}}$ *šənä*][$_{\text{VP}}$ [$_{\text{V}}$ *kolə̂*]]]
b. [$_{\text{VP}}$[$_{\text{V}}$ *əneštə*][$_{\text{VP}}$ [$_{\text{V}}$ *kolep*]]]

Because the variable X employed in the language-specific realization rules defined here ranges over stems (including roots) but never over periphrases, none of these rules applies to pairings of the sort defined by **W-Id**; instead, such pairings are subject only to the Identity Function Default (24), a universal realization rule acting as the ultimate default in every rule block of every language (Stump 2001, 53).

(24) Identity Function Default: Where Y ranges over stems *and* periphrases,
Y_{any}, {} → Y

In the inflection of negative second-past forms, rules **W-Ia**, **W-Ic**, and **W-Id** are all overridden by the rule of referral **W-Ie**, according to which the primary stem of a negative second-past verb form has an absolute form Y identical to the verb's negative gerund and a conjunct form resulting from the suffixation of *l* to Y.

W-Ie. X_V, {POL: neg, TNS: 2nd past} → Y,
where Y is an absolute stem form which
(a) is identical in form to the realization of the form-cell ⟨X, {VFORM: gerund, POL: neg}⟩ and
(b) has Y*l* as its conjunct stem form.

Example: From the negative first-person singular second-past cell (25a) in the form-paradigm of *kol* 'die', **W-Ie** licenses the pairing (25b), where *kolə̂ð e* (*kol*'s negative gerund; cf. **W-Ig**) is the primary stem of (25a)'s realization *kolə̂ð elam* 'I didn't die'. As the narrowest applicable rule, **W-Ie** overrides rules **W-Ia**, **W-Ic**, and **W-Id** in the definition of *kolə̂ð elam*'s primary stem.

(25) a. ⟨*kol*, {POL: neg, MOOD: indic, TNS: 2nd past, AGR:{PER: 1, NUM: sg}}⟩

b. ⟨*kolə̂ð e*, {POL: neg, MOOD: indic, TNS: 2nd past, AGR:{PER: 1, NUM: sg}}⟩

The affirmative and negative gerund forms called by the rules of referral **W-Ic** and **W-Ie** are defined by the rules of exponence **W-If** and **W-Ig**. By **W-If**, an *em*-conjugation verb's affirmative gerund arises from its root through the suffixation of *-en*; by **W-Ig**, its negative gerund arises through the suffixation of *-ð e* to its schwa stem.

W-If. $X_{V[\text{CONJUGATION:em}]}$, {VFORM: gerund; POL: aff} → X*en*
W-Ig. $X_{V[\text{CONJUGATION:em}]}$, {VFORM: gerund; POL: neg} → Y*ð e*,
where Y is X's schwa stem.

Rules **W-Ih** through **W-Ij** account for the morphological irregularity of the negative verb AK: **W-Ih** identifies *ə* as AK's primary desiderative stem; **W-Ii** identifies *šə* as the default form of AK's primary first-past stem; and **W-Ij** identifies *əš* as the primary stem for third-person first-past forms of AK. Under the assumed conception of rule narrowness (Stump 2001, 52), these rules are narrower than (and therefore override) any and all competitors among the foregoing rules **W-Ia** through **W-Ig**; in addition, **W-Ij** overrides **W-Ii**.)

W-Ih. $X_{\{\text{AK}\}}$, {MOOD: desid} → *ə*
W-Ii. $X_{\{\text{AK}\}}$, {TNS: 1st past} → *šə*
W-Ij. $X_{\{\text{AK}\}}$, {TNS: 1st past, AGR: {PER: 3}} → *əš*

A careful examination of the realizations in Tables 5, 6, and 8 reveals that the sequence of suffixes used to realize tense, mood, and agreement in each affirmative realization is virtually identical to the auxiliary form introducing the corresponding negative realization.[27] Because the forms of the negative auxiliary are morphologically affirmative, it must be seen as a "deponent" verb (cf. the discussion surrounding the Latin forms in Table 3 in section 5.3): each cell in its content-paradigm contains the property POL: neg, while the corresponding cell in its form-paradigm instead contains the property POL: aff, as in the examples in Table 9.

TABLE 9. Examples of the inflection of the Western Mari negative auxiliary AK (deponent)

Cells in content-paradigm	Form-correspondents	Realizations
⟨AK, {POL: neg, TNS: pres, AGR: {PER: 1, NUM: sg}}⟩	⟨*ak*, {POL: aff, TNS: pres, AGR: {PER: 1, NUM: sg}}⟩	*am*
⟨AK, {POL: neg, TNS: 1st past, AGR: {PER: 2, NUM: pl}}⟩	⟨*ak*, {POL: aff, TNS: 1st past, AGR: {PER: 2, NUM: pl}}⟩	*šəðä* (cf. Table 8)

Thus, we assume that the relation between AK's content- and form-paradigms is regulated by the rule of paradigm linkage in (26).

(26) Rule of paradigm linkage for AK:
Where σ is an extension of {POL: neg}, the FC of the content-cell ⟨AK,σ⟩ is the form-cell ⟨*ak*,σ/{POL: aff}⟩.

[27] This state of affairs is described in the pedagogical grammar of Mari by Z. G. Zorina et al. (1990, 114) in the following way:

> "The negative form of the 1st past tense is formed with the help of negative words, which are represented by the suffixal part of the 1st past tense of 2nd declension verbs and the stem of the imperative."

It should also be noted that this strategy for negative formation is applicable to 1st declension verbs as well, despite the fact that the suffixes in the affirmative 1st past for this class differ from those of 2nd class.

Block II: *Rules deducing secondary stems from primary stems (rules* **W-IIa** *and* **W-IIb***)*

The primary stems defined by Block I may give rise to secondary stems through the application of the rules in Block II. By **W-IIa**, a secondary stem in *-š* is used in defining the affirmative first-past realizations of a verb belonging to the *em*-conjugation.

W-IIa. $X_{V[\text{CONJUGATION:em}]}$, {POL: aff, TNS: 1st past} → X*š*, where X is vowel-final.

Example: In the realization of the affirmative first-person singular first-past cell in the form-paradigm of *kol* 'die', Block I licenses the association of the primary stem *kolə̂* with the property set in (27a); rule **W-IIa** therefore licenses the pairing of the secondary stem *kolə̂š* with this same property set, as in (27b).

(27) a. ⟨*kolə̂*, {POL: aff, MOOD: indic, TNS: 1st past, AGR:{PER: 1, NUM: sg}}⟩
b. ⟨*kolə̂š*, {POL: aff, MOOD: indic, TNS: 1st past, AGR:{PER: 1, NUM: sg}}⟩

By **W-IIb**, a secondary stem in *-ne* is used in defining a verb's affirmative present desiderative realizations.

W-IIb. X_V, {POL: aff, MOOD: desid, TNS: pres} → X*ne*

Example: In the realization of the affirmative first-person singular present desiderative cell in the form-paradigm of *kol* 'die', Block I licenses the association of the primary stem *kolə̂* with the property set in (28a); rule **W-IIb** therefore licenses the pairing of the secondary stem *kolə̂ne* with this same property set, as in (28b).

(28) a. ⟨*kolə̂*, {POL: aff, MOOD: desid, TNS: pres, AGR:{PER: 1, NUM: sg}}⟩
b. ⟨*kolə̂ne*, {POL: aff, MOOD: desid, TNS: pres, AGR:{PER: 1, NUM: sg}}⟩

The Identity Function Default guarantees that for any realization whose secondary stem is not determined by **W-IIa** or **W-IIb**, the relevant secondary stem is simply identical to the primary stem defined by Block I.

Block III: *Rules expressing subject agreement (rules* **W-IIIa** *through* **W-IIIm***)*

The outer layer of a verb's inflectional morphology is regulated by the rules of exponence in Block III. By rule **W-IIIa**, a first-person singular affirmative first-past realization involves the suffixation of *-əm* to the secondary stem defined by Block II:

W-IIIa. X_V, {POL: aff, TNS: 1st past, AGR: {PER: 1, NUM: sg}}
→ X*əm*

Example: In the realization of the affirmative first-person singular first-past cell in the form-paradigm of *kol* 'die', Block II licenses the association of the secondary stem *kolə̂š* with the property set in (29a); rule **W-IIIa** therefore licenses the pairing of the word *kolə̂šə̂m* with this same property set, as in (29b).

(29) a. ⟨*kolə̂š*, {POL: aff, MOOD: indic, TNS: 1st past, AGR:{PER: 1, NUM: sg}}⟩

b. ⟨*kolə̂šə̂m*, {POL: aff, MOOD: indic, TNS: 1st past, AGR:{PER: 1, NUM: sg}}⟩

By rule **W-IIIb**, a second-person singular affirmative first-past realization involves the suffixation of *-at*; and so on. Note that rules **W-IIIf** through **W-IIIj** introduce default expressions of agreement; others are additionally restricted according to both polarity and tense (**W-IIIa**, **W-IIIb**), to both polarity and mood (**W-IIIk**, **W-IIIl**), or to tense alone (**W-IIIc**, **W-IIId**, **W-IIIe**, **W-IIIm**). Because of the Identity Function Default, the absence of any Block III rule realizing third-person singular subject agreement outside of the desiderative entails that a verb's third-person singular first- and second-past realizations will simply lack overt agreement morphology.[28]

[28] A sketch concerning some of the morphophonological properties associated with the realization rules for Mari is provided in the Appendix.

W-IIIb. X_V,{POL:aff,TNS:1st past,AGR:{PER:2,NUM:sg}} → X*əc*

W-IIIc. X_V,{TNS:2nd past, AGR:{PER:1, NUM:sg}} → X*am*

W-IIId. X_V,{TNS:2nd past, AGR:{PER:2, NUM:sg}} → X*at*

W-IIIe. X_V,{TNS:2nd past, AGR:{PER:3, NUM:pl}} → X*ə̂t*

W-IIIf. X_V,{AGR:{PER:1, NUM:sg}} → X*m*

W-IIIg. X_V,{AGR:{PER:2, NUM:sg}} → X*t*

W-IIIh. X_V,{AGR:{PER:1, NUM:pl}} → X*na*

W-IIIi. X_V,{AGR:{PER:2, NUM:pl}} → X*da*

W-IIIj. X_V,{AGR:{PER:3, NUM:pl}} → X*ə*

W-IIIk. X_V,{POL:aff,MOOD:desid,AGR:{PER:3,NUM:sg}} → X*žə*

W-IIIl. X_V,{POL:aff,MOOD:desid,AGR:{PER:3,NUM:pl}} → X*štə*

W-IIIm. X_{DAKV},{TNS:1st past, AGR:{PER:3, NUM:pl}} → X

Analysis summary

In this analysis of Mari verb morphology, periphrasis (as introduced by rule **W-Id**) is treated as a kind of inflectional exponence. Within the morphology itself, periphrasis is theoretically unremarkable, serving alongside various synthetic devices as just another kind of exponence available to inflectional systems. The distinctive character of periphrasis emerges only at the morphology/syntax interface, where the c-structure representation of a periphrase is regulated by the special rule in (20). The paradigmatic opposition of synthesis and periphrasis follows as a necessary consequence of this analysis. The fact that some morphosyntactic property sets lack single-word realizations is not attributed to an ad hoc gap (comparable to (13)) in the inflection of Mari verbs, but is attributed to (a) the lack of any rules of synthetic exponence realizing those property sets and (b) the existence of a default rule of periphrastic exponence realizing those sets. The fact that single-word realizations exclude the use of synonymous periphrases is not attributed to an ad hoc principle of morphological blocking, but follows, more generally, as a direct consequence of the way in which Pāṇini's principle regulates realizational morphology.

5.4.3 Noncompositional periphrases

In Soviet linguistics there is a tradition of distinguishing between an analytic word combination belonging to a lexeme's paradigm and a word combination whose parts stand in a purely syntactic relationship; one of the most reliable and compelling diagnostic criteria for distinguishing combinations of the former type is the noncompositionality of the meanings associated with the individual words of which they are constituted.[29] Thus, Gukhman (1955, 343) concludes with respect to German periphrastic verbal constructions:

> "the grammatical meaning of analytic constructions in German is never equal to the sum of the grammatical meanings of its component parts, but appears as the meaning of a nondecomposable whole."

We regard this noncompositionality as a second sufficient criterion for the identification of periphrases:

(30) Criterion II: If the morphosyntactic property set associated with an analytic combination C is not the composition of the property sets associated with its parts, then C is a periphrase.

The usual view of such composition is that the content of a complex expression follows from the content of its immediate constituents by a principle of property unification; this is consistent with the purely syntactic approach to periphrasis adopted in lexicalist frameworks and elsewhere. In contrast, the Periphrastic Realization Hypothesis implies that a periphrase's membership in a paradigm may have independent consequences for this computation. And indeed, close inspection of periphrastic constructions in Uralic reveals that while some such constructions can be claimed to be compositional in their content, not all can.

As an instance of apparent compositionality, consider again the negative first-past forms of Western Mari *kol* 'die' in Table 6; each of these is construable as an analytic combination of a stem of KOL with a first-past form of the negative auxiliary AK. Ordinary principles of property unification appear to guarantee that in c-structure, a negative first-past verb phrase such as [$_{\text{VP}}$ *šəðä kolə̂*] 'you didn't die' will be associated with the desired morphosyntactic property set (namely {POL: neg, TNS: 1st past, AGR:{PER: 2, NUM: pl}}), since this is the very property set associated with the verb phrase's head (the negative auxiliary) in its content-paradigm.

In many other instances, however, ordinary assumptions about property unification do not suffice to determine the content of a periphrase from the content of its parts. Given this, the challenge for theory construction, of course, is to identify the most principled way of accounting for both apparently compositional and non-compositional phenomena.

---

[29]It is important to convey that by appealing to this criterion we are not repudiating the notion of semantic compositionality: the hypothesis that words are provided with fully specified feature sets defining their grammatical meanings independent of their realization simply means in general that such meanings are not determined by forms. As mentioned below, it is an important task to develop a semantics of grammatical meaning which does not depend upon morpheme-based assumptions.

Consider, for instance, the negative second-past forms of KOL 'die' in the Eastern dialects of Mari in Table 10: each of these is an analytic combination of KOL's affirmative gerundial stem *kolen* with a negative present-tense form of the copula UL (cf. Table 11); this latter form is itself a compound of a present-tense form of the negative auxiliary OK (cf. Table 12) with the stem *ə̂l* of the copula UL.

TABLE 10. Second-past realizations of the Mari *em*-conjugation verb KOL 'die' (Eastern dialects) [Alhoniemi 1985, 110, 116]

		Affirmative	Negative
SG.	1	*kol-en-am* 'I died'	*kolen omə̂l* 'I didn't die'
	2	*kol-en-at*	*kolen otə̂l*
	3	*kol-en*	*kolen oɣə̂l*
PL.	1	*kol-en-na*	*kolen onal*
	2	*kol-en-da*	*kolen oð al*
	3	*kol-en-ə̂t*	*kolen oɣə̂tə̂l*

TABLE 11. Present-tense realizations of the Mari *am*-conjugation copula UL[30] (Eastern dialects) [Alhoniemi 1985, 111, 116]

		Affirmative	Negative
SG.	1	*ul-a-m* 'I am'	*om-ə̂l* 'I am not'
	2	*ul-a-t*	*ot-ə̂l*
	3	*ul-eš*	*oɣ-ə̂l*
PL.	1	*ul-ə̂-na*	*ona-l*
	2	*ul-ə̂-ð a*	*oð a-l*
	3	*ul-ə̂-t*	*oɣə̂t-ə̂l*

TABLE 12. Present-tense realizations of the Mari negative auxiliary OK[31] (Eastern dialects) [Alhoniemi 1985, 115f]

SG.	1	*o-m*
	2	*o-t*
	3	*ok*
PL.	1	*o-na*
	2	*o-ð a*
	3	*oɣ-ə̂-t*

Thus, none of the parts of a negative second-past verbal periphrase expresses the second-past tense; indeed, the exponents of tense carried by the finite head of such a periphrase are expressions of the present

[30]The plural negative realizations in Table 11 exhibit some variation in shape; see section 5.4.5 below.

[31]The present-tense forms of OK sometimes follow the *am*-conjugation, as in the third-person singular realization *oɣ-eš* and the first- and second-person plural realizations as *oɣ-ə̂-na* and *oɣ-ə̂-ð a* (Alhoniemi 1985, 115f).

tense. Consequently, though the verb phrase $[_{\text{VP}}$ *kolen omə̂l* $]$ 'I didn't die' is associated with the property set {POL: neg, TNS: 2nd past, AGR: {PER: 1, NUM: sg}}, this association cannot be seen as an effect of ordinary property unification. The analytic combinations in Table 10 are therefore periphrases by criterion (30).

In an inferential-realizational approach to periphrasis, the association of the periphrase *kolen omə̂l* 'I didn't die' with the property set {POL: neg, TNS: 2nd past, AGR: {PER: 1, NUM: sg}} is effected morphologically. In particular, we propose that the morphology of Eastern Mari defines the second-past realizations of KOL by means of the realization rules in (31). As in our earlier discussion of Western Mari, we assume that for any cell $\langle r,\sigma\rangle$ in a Mari form-paradigm, w is the realization of $\langle r,\sigma\rangle$ if and only if $((\langle r,\sigma\rangle : \text{I}) : \text{II}) : \text{III} = \langle w,\sigma\rangle$; we further assume that the Eastern Mari negative auxiliary OK is subject to a rule of paradigm linkage analogous to (26), and that OK's default root form *ok* has *o* as its regular preconsonantal alternant.[32]

(31) Some realization rules for second-past verb forms in Mari (Eastern dialects)

Block I

E-Ia. X_V, {TNS: 2nd past} → Y,
where Y is the realization of the form-cell
⟨X, {VFORM: gerund, POL: aff}⟩. (= **W-Ic**)

E-Ib. $X_{V[\text{CONJUGATION:em}]}$, {VFORM: gerund, POL: aff} → X*en* (= **W-If**)

E-Ic.[33] X_V, {POL: aff, TNS: present, AGR: {PER: 3, NUM: pl}} → Xə̂

E-Id. $X_{\{\text{UL}\}}$, σ: {POL: negative; TNS: present} → Yə̂*l*,
where Y is the realization of the content-cell ⟨OK,σ⟩.

E-Ie. X_V, σ: {POL: negative, TNS: 2nd past} → [Z $\underline{\text{Y}}$],
where Y is the realization of the content-cell
⟨UL,σ/{TNS: present}⟩, $\langle X,\sigma'\rangle : \text{I} = \langle Z,\sigma'\rangle$,
and $\sigma' = \sigma/$ {POL: aff}. (instead of **W-Ie**)

[32]We also assume that vowel hiatus is avoided by the elision of the second of two adjacent vowels (as in *ona-l* 'we are not', i.e. *o-na-ə̂l*), and that intervocalic obstruents are subject to lenition (as in *oð a* and *oɣə̂t* the second- and third-person plural present-tense realizations of the negative auxiliary OK).

[33]Rule **E-Ic** optionally applies more generally, in all plural affirmative present forms.

Block III

E-IIIa. X_V, {TNS: 2nd past, AGR: {PER: 1, NUM: sg}} → X*am* (= **W-IIIc**)

E-IIIb. X_V, {TNS: 2nd past, AGR: {PER: 2, NUM: sg}} → X*at* (= **W-IIId**)

E-IIIc. X_V, {TNS: 2nd past, AGR: {PER: 3, NUM: pl}} → X*ə̂t* (= **W-IIIe**)

E-IIId. X_V, {AGR: {PER: 1, NUM: sg}} → X*m* (= **W-IIIf**)

E-IIIe. X_V, {AGR: {PER: 2, NUM: sg}} → X*t* (= **W-IIIg**)

E-IIIf. X_V, {AGR: {PER: 1, NUM: pl}} → X*na* (= **W-IIIh**)

E-IIIg. X_V, {AGR: {PER: 2, NUM: pl}} → X*da* (= **W-IIIi**)

E-IIIh. X_V, {AGR: {PER: 3, NUM: pl}} → X*t*

Many of these rules have identical counterparts in Western Mari; note, for example, that rules **E-IIIa** through **E-IIIg** match rules **W-IIIc** through **W-IIIi**. There are, however, two main points of contrast: first, by rules **E-Ie** and **E-Ia**, a verb's negative second-past realizations are built upon its affirmative gerundial stem rather than on its negative gerundial stem (contrast rule **W-Ie**); and second, a verb's negative second-past realizations are, according to rule **E-Ie**, periphrases consisting of a primary second-past stem and a present-tense realization of the copula UL. Each negative present-tense realization of UL is, by **E-Id**, the result of compounding the corresponding realization of the negative auxiliary OK with UL's stem *ə̂l*; cf. Tables 11 and 12. The realization rules relevant for the present-tense inflection of the negative auxiliary OK in (31) are **E-Ic**, and **E-IIId** through **E-IIIh**.

By the rules in (31), the periphrase [*kolen omə̂l*] 'I didn't die' is the realization of the cell ⟨KOL, {POL: neg, TNS: 2nd past, AGR: {PER: 1, NUM: sg}} in KOL's content-paradigm. This association with the property set {POL: neg, TNS: 2nd past, AGR: {PER: 1, NUM: sg}} is transmitted from the periphrase [*kolen omə̂l*] to the verb phrase [$_{VP}$ *kolen omə̂l*] by the rule (20) at the morphology-syntax interface. It is this rule, in concert with the realizational morphology of Eastern Mari, that determines the content of this verb phrase; the usual principles of property unification to which c-structures are ordinarily subject are here overridden.

Comparable phenomena are widely observable. Consider a second example. In Udmurt, the imperfective past tense is a compound tense used to describe "a protracted or repeated activity occurring in the ... distant past" (Csúcs, 1987, 51). This tense is realized by the periphrastic combination of a future-tense form (inflected for subject agreement) with the invariant past form *val* of the copula, as in Table 13; compare the future-tense forms in Table 14.

Table 13. Affirmative imperfective past-tense realizations of Udmurt MÏNÏ 'go' [Suihkonen 1995, 302][34]

SG.	1	*mïno val* 'I used to go (long ago)'
	2	*mïnod val*
	3	*mïnoz val*
PL.	1	*mïnom(ï) val*
	2	*mïnodï val*
	3	*mïnozï val*

Table 14. Affirmative future-tense realizations of Udmurt MÏNÏ 'go' [Csúcs 1988, 142]

SG.	1	*mïno* 'I will go'
	2	*mïnod*
	3	*mïnoz*
PL.	1	*mïnom(ï)*
	2	*mïnodï*
	3	*mïnozï*

Neither part of an imperfective past-tense periphrase such as [*mïno* *val*] carries any exponent of an aspectual property such as durativity or habituality; yet, such a property is associated with the verb phrase [$_{\text{VP}}$ *mïno val*] as a whole. Moreover, while the finite head of [*mïno* *val*] is marked for future tense, the periphrase as a whole expresses the distant past tense. This departure from pure compositionality is, we claim, determined by the morphology of Udmurt: the temporal and aspectual properties of the verb phrase [$_{\text{VP}}$ *mïno val*] aren't deducible from the properties of its individual syntactic atoms by means of ordinary unification, but are instead the effect of a morphological rule of periphrasis realizing certain cells in the content-paradigm of MÏNÏ 'go'. (This rule is formulated as **U-Ia** in (33) below.)

5.4.4 Distributed exponence in periphrases

Though instances of extended exponence are far from rare, there is a tendency for each of the morphosyntactic properties realized by an inflected word form to have no more than a single exponent in that form's morphology. This tendency toward DISTRIBUTED EXPONENCE receives its fullest expression in heavily agglutinating languages. For instance, the Swahili verb form *ha-tu-ta-taka* 'we will not want' has

[34]Though the source for paradigm is Suihkonen (1995), for consistency we utilize the orthography used by Csúcs (1987, 1988, 1998).

exactly one affixal exponent for each of the morphosyntactic properties it expresses: *ha-* expresses the property POL: neg; *tu-*, the property AGR: {PER: 1, NUM: pl}; and *ta-*, the property TNS: future.

Periphrases likewise often exhibit distributed exponence. In Udmurt, for instance, the negative future-tense realizations of MÏNÏ 'go' are periphrastic combinations of a realization of the negative verb U with a "connegative" form of MÏNÏ, as in Table 15; the connegative form realizes number but not person, while the negative verb form realizes person but not number (except in the first person, where the negative verb forms *ug* and *um* apparently express both person and number). Because a verb's imperfective past-tense realizations are built upon its future-tense realizations (cf. again Tables 13 and 14), the negative imperfective past-tense realizations of MÏNÏ 'go' in Table 16 embody this same distribution of exponence.

TABLE 15. Negative future-tense forms of Udmurt MÏNÏ 'go' [Csúcs 1988, 143]

SG.	1	*ug mïnï*
	2	*ud mïnï*
	3	*uz mïnï*
PL.	1	*um mïne(le)*
	2	*ud mïne(le)*
	3	*uz mïne(le)*

TABLE 16. Negative imperfective past-tense realizations of Udmurt MÏNÏ 'go' [Suihkonen 1995, 302]

SG.	1	*ug mïnï val*
	2	*ud mïnï val*
	3	*uz mïnï val* 's/he didn't use to go (long time ago)'
PL.	1	*um mïne(le) val*
	2	*ud mïne(le) val*
	3	*uz mïne(le) val*

We therefore propose distributed exponence as a third sufficient criterion for the identification of periphrases:

(32) Criterion III: If the morphosyntactic property set associated with an analytic combination C has its exponents distributed among C's parts, then C is a periphrase.

In a purely syntactic approach to periphrasis, there is no particular reason to expect that periphrases should exhibit a comparable tendency toward distributed exponence; word combinations in syntax are, after all, sometimes highly redundant in their expression of shared morphosyntactic properties (as in the Swahili sentence *ki-kapu ki-kubwa ki-moja ki-lianguka* 'one large basket fell', every one of whose words carries an exponent of the subject's gender and number). But if the economy of inflectional exponence exhibited by heavily agglutinating languages is seen as a property of rules which realize form-paradigms, then the assumption that periphrases are morphological in their definition entails that periphrases should be no less likely to exhibit this same economy.

The analysis of Urdmurt verb morphology in (33) accounts both for the noncompositionality exemplified in Table 13 and for the distribution of exponence exemplified in Tables 15 and 16.

(33) Some realization rules for future-tense and imperfective past-tense realizations in Udmurt

Block I

U-Ia. $X_{V[\text{NONAUXILIARY}]}$, σ: {TNS:distant past, ASP:durative} → [<u>Y</u> *val*], where Y is the realization of the form-cell ⟨X,σ/{TNS: future, ASP: simple}⟩.

U-Ib. $X_{V[\text{NONAUXILIARY}]}$, {POL: aff, TNS: fut} → X*o*

U-Ic. $X_{V[\text{NONAUXILIARY}]}$, {POL: neg, AGR: {NUM: sg}} → X*ï*

U-Id. $X_{V[\text{NONAUXILIARY}]}$, {POL: neg, AGR: {NUM: pl}} → X*e(le)*

Block II

U-IIa.[35] $X_{V[\text{NONAUXILIARY}]}$, σ: {POL: neg} → [<u>Y</u> X], where Y is the realization of the content-cell ⟨U,σ⟩.

Block III

U-IIIa. $X_{\{U\}}$, {POL:aff, AGR:{PER:1, NUM:sg}} → X*g*

U-IIIb. X_V, {POL: aff, AGR: {PER: 1, NUM: pl}} → X*m*

U-IIIc. X_V, {POL: aff, AGR: {PER: 2}} → X*d*

U-IIId. X_V, {POL: aff, AGR: {PER: 3}} → X*z*

Block IV

U-IVa. $X_{V[\text{NONAUXILIARY}]}$, {POL: aff, AGR: {NUM: pl}} → X*ï*

Rule **U-Ia** causes the cell ⟨MÏNÏ, {POL: aff, TNS: distant past, ASP: durative, AGR: {PER: 2, NUM: pl}}⟩ in the content-paradigm of MÏNÏ 'go' to be realized as the periphrase [<u>*mïnodï*</u> *val*], neither of whose parts is itself an expression of durative aspect and whose head is, on its own, an expression of the future tense; at the morphology/syntax interface, principle (20) associates this periphrase with a c-structure in which the usual, compositional pattern of property unification is suspended.

[35] We assume here that the Udmurt negative verb U is subject to a rule of paradigm linkage analogous to the rule for Western Mari AK in (26).

Moreover, rule **U-IIa** causes ⟨MÏNÏ, {POL: neg, TNS: distant past, ASP: durative, AGR: {PER: 2, NUM: pl}}⟩ to be realized as the periphrase [[<u>*ud*</u> *mïne(le)*] *val*], whose exponence is distributed: the head <u>*ud*</u> is (by **U-IIIc**) an exponent of person but not number, while its nonhead element *mïne(le)* is an exponent of number but not person.

5.4.5 Some confirming evidence

Here we examine two types of evidence confirming the need for an inferential-realizational approach to periphrasis: the close connection between periphrastic realizations and synthetic realizations in language change, and the participation of periphrasis in generalizations about morphological markedness.

Periphrasis and language change

A widely observed phenomenon in historical linguistics is the diachronic development of periphrasis into synthetic morphology. This phenomenon follows very naturally from the conception of periphrasis advocated here. Periphrasis is, in this approach, just one more type of morphological exponence. The development of synthetic morphology from periphrasis is therefore not different, in principle, from the development of fusional morphology from agglutination: both sorts of developments involve an increasing degree of fusion in the inflectional realization of a paradigm's cells. Our approach predicts that just as one can observe different degrees of progress in the development from agglutination to fusionality, one should likewise find different degrees of progress in the development of synthesis from periphrasis; Mari itself provides compelling evidence of this sort of gradation.

Consider again the synthetic negative second-past realizations in Western Mari (given above in Table 7). It is clear that these descend historically from periphrases – in particular, from periphrastic combinations of the negative gerund with affirmative present-tense forms of the copula UL; compare the free forms of this copula in Table 17.

TABLE 17. Affirmative present-tense realizations of the Mari *am*-conjugation copula UL (Western dialects) [Alhoniemi 1985, 114]

SG.	1	*ə̂l-a-m*
	2	*ə̂l-a-t*
	3	*ə̂l-eš*
PL.	1	*ə̂l-ə̂-na*
	2	*ə̂l-ə̂-da*
	3	*ə̂l-ə̂-t*

This development from periphrasis to synthesis in the second past is even more extensively observable in Northwest Mari. Consider the affirmative second-past realizations of *tol* 'go' in Table 18.

TABLE 18. Affirmative second-past realizations of the Mari *am*-conjugation verb TOL 'go' (Northwest dialect) [Bereczki 1990, 55]

SG.	1	*tol-ə̂n-l-am* 'I went'
	2	*tol-ə̂n-l-at*
	3	*tol-ə̂n*
PL.	1	*tol-ə̂n ulna*
	2	*tol-ə̂n ulda*
	3	*tol-ə̂n ult*

Here, the plural realizations consist of an uninflected affirmative gerund with an independent copula inflected for present tense and subject agreement. By contrast, this copular construction has become synthetic in the first- and second-person singular realizations in Table 18; like the negative second-past realizations in Western Mari, the singular affirmative realizations in Table 18 now involve a gerundial stem whose absolute form appears in the third-person singular and whose conjunct form (suffixed with *l*) otherwise appears with the appropriate person/number marker. The development from periphrasis to synthesis has progressed partway across the affirmative second-past paradigm.

In an inferential-realizational approach to periphrasis, the affirmative second-past realizations of Northwest Mari in Table 18 and their Western Mari counterparts in Table 7 express the same content-paradigm; that is, the relevant difference between these dialects is a difference not in the inventory of cells available for realization but in the morphological rules by which these cells are realized. In particular, the Northwest dialect's system of realization rules differs from the system in section 5.4.2 in two relevant ways. First, it has an additional rule of periphrasis whose effect is to license periphrases in plural realizations of the affirmative second past; second, it employs a single rule to define the default primary stem of the second past. These rules are formulated in (34):

(34) Realization rules for second-past verb realizations (Northwest dialect)

Block I (as in section 5.4.2 except that **NW-Ia** takes the place of **W-Ic** and **W-Ie**)

NW-Ia X_V, {POL: α, TNS: 2nd past} → Y,
where Y is an absolute stem form which
(a) is identical to the realization of the form-cell
⟨X, {VFORM: gerund, POL: α}⟩ and
(b) has Y*l* as its conjunct stem form.

Block II (as in section 5.4.2 except for the additional rule **NW-IIa**)

NW-IIa X_V, σ: {POL: aff, TNS: 2nd past, AGR: {NUM: pl}}
→ [X Y], where Y is the realization of the content-cell
⟨UL,σ/{TNS: pres}⟩.

Block III (as in section 5.4.2)

It is a virtue of the inferential-realizational approach to periphrasis that it allows the Western/Northwest contrast in the affirmative second past to be so simply localized in the morphology.

The Northwest forms in Table 18 suggest a change in progress: gradually, the copulative verb used in the periphrastic expression of the affirmative second past has become enclitic, then reanalyzed as synthetic morphology. A similar change in progress is actually documented in Eastern Mari, where the plural realizations of the copula *ul* in the negative present tense appear sometimes as single-word forms (as in Table 11), but sometimes as periphrases (as in Table 19); presumably the periphrastic realizations are losing ground among innovative speakers.

TABLE 19. Variation in negative present-tense realizations of the Mari *am*-conjugation copula UL (Eastern dialects) [Alhoniemi 1985, 111, 116]

SG.	1	*om-əl* 'I am not'
	2	*ot-əl*
	3	*oɣ-əl*
PL.	1	*ona-l* ~ *oɣə̂na-l* ~ *oɣə̂na ul*
	2	*oð a-l* ~ *oɣə̂ð a-l* ~ *oɣə̂ð a ul*
	3	*oɣə̂t-əl* ~ *oɣə̂t ul*

Periphrasis and morphological markedness

Very often, the types of exponence observable among the realizations of a lexeme's paradigm correlate with the degree of markedness of the morphosyntactic property sets which those forms realize. For instance, exponents of more highly marked morphosyntactic properties tend to be less fusional (cf. Greenberg 1966, Mayerthaler 1988): in Sanskrit, for instance, the nominative singular is often expressed purely by stem gradation (e.g. PITAR 'father', nom. sg. *pitā*, RĀJAN 'king', nom. sg. *rājā*), while the dative singular is always expressed suffixally (*pitr-e* 'to the father', *rājñ-e* 'among the kings'); in Swahili, negation and first-person singular subject agreement are expressed by a portmanteau prefix *si-* (e.g. *si-ta-taka* 'I will not want') while negation and first-person plural subject agreement are expressed separately by the respective prefixes *ha-* and *tu-* (*ha-tu-ta-taka* 'we will not want'); and so on.

In a theory in which periphrasis is regarded as a kind of morphological exponence, periphrastic exponence would be expected to participate in this same correlation. In particular, since periphrasis is by definition nonfusional, one would expect that in paradigms in which synthesis and periphrasis exist side by side, the incidence of periphrasis will be associated with more highly marked morphosyntactic properties. And such is indeed overwhelmingly the case. For instance, among the Northwest dialect realizations in Table 18, it is those whose property sets include the marked number specification 'plural' which preserve periphrasis; similarly, periphrasis is the default expression of the marked polarity specification 'negative' in Western Mari. This phenomenon is dramatically evident in the Samoyedic language Tundra Nenets as illustrated in Table 20.

TABLE 20. Declension of *ti* 'reindeer' in Tundra Nenets [Salminen 1997]

		Singular	Dual	Plural
Grammatical cases	Nominative	*ti*	*tex*^{o}*h*	*tiq*
	Accusative	*tim*	*tex*^{o}*h*	*tí*
	Genitive	*tih*	*tex*^{o}*h*	*tíq*
Local cases	Dative	*ten*^{o}*h*	*tex*^{o}*h nyah*	*tex*^{o}*q*
	Locative	*tex*^{o}*na*	*tex*^{o}*h nyana*	*tex*^{o}*qna*
	Ablative	*texød*^{o}	*tex*^{o}*h nyad*^{o}	*texøt*^{o}
	Prosecutive	*tew*^{o}*na*	*tex*^{o}*h nyamna*	*teqm*^{o}*na*

Periphrastic expression in Nenets nominals, consisting of the dual stem plus an appropriately case-inflected form of the postposition NYA, occurs solely for those cells which contain the most marked value for case (namely the local cases) as well as the most marked value for number (namely dual); all other morphosyntactic property sets receive synthetic expression.

A theory whose notion of exponence encompasses synthetic but not periphrastic markings affords no coherent articulation of the overarching generalization which such cases embody; in the grammatical ontology of such a theory, the phenomena which ought to be subsumed under this generalization – phenomena such as fusion, agglutination, periphrasis – fail to constitute any kind of natural class.

5.5 Conclusions

Drawing on the assumptions of inferential-realizational morphology, we have argued that certain periphrastic expressions are directly projected from form-paradigms by realization rules. We have adduced criteria for distinguishing morphologically defined periphrases from ordinary syntactic complementation in Uralic. These criteria motivate the adoption of the Periphrastic Realization Hypothesis (given above in (9)). They also require a modification of the basic principle regulating the relation between morphology and syntax, permitting the exponence of lexical representations to be realized as independent and possibly discontinuous elements in c-structure. Finally, this type of analysis is facilitated by appealing to standard inferential-realizational assumptions concerning the strict separation of content from form and, in effect, represents a trivial extension of these assumptions so that they apply to periphrastic expressions. This is implemented here by interpreting lexical representations in terms of cells in content- and form-paradigms which are put in correspondence by rules of paradigm linkage and by providing realization rules which account for the surface syntactic exponence of roots and stems in form-paradigms.

Appendix: Remarks on the morphophonology of Mari

The morphophonology of Mari is quite complex; here we merely describe those rules relevant to the definition of the forms in Tables 5-8. Among the vowels introduced by the realization rules in section 5.4.2, some are subject to vowel harmony (those in **W-IIIa** through **W-IIIe**, **W-IIIh**, and **W-IIIi**) and some are not (those in **W-Ib**, **W-If**, **W-Ig**, **W-IIb**, **W-IIIl**, and **W-IIIm**). Moreover, a suffixal vowel which is subject to vowel harmony only harmonizes when the suffix joins with a stem whose last vowel is a trigger; vowels are triggers by default, but the vowel introduced by rule **W-Ig** is not a trigger (so that even though *kolenäm* 'I went' exhibits vowel harmony, *kolə̂ð elam* 'I didn't go' does not).

The stops introduced by rules **W-Ib** and **W-IIIi** are subject to intervocalic lenition (as in *kolə̂neðä* 'you (pl.) want to die' and *koleβə* 'they died') and to obstruent voicing assimilation (as in *kolə̂šta* 'you (pl.) died').

All of the rules in Block III which apply in the definition of negative second-past realizations select the conjunct primary stem (e.g. *kolâð el-*) over its absolute counterpart (*kolâð e-*).

In the definition of the negative verb AK's affirmative first-past realizations, the ə-ə hiatus occasioned by the application of rules **W-IIIa** and **W-IIIb** is eliminated by vowel coalescence.

We assume that all of the morphophonological rules described here have the status of morphological metageneralizations; see Stump (2001, 47ff) for discussion.

References

Ackerman, Farrell. 1984. Verbal modifiers as argument taking predicates: Complex verbs as predicate complexes in Hungarian. In *Gröningen Working Papers in Linguistics*, pages 23–71. Gröningen: University of Gröningen.

Ackerman, Farrell. 1987. *Miscreant Morphemes: Phrasal Predicates in Ugric.* Ph.D. thesis, University of California, Berkeley.

Ackerman, Farrell. to appear. Grammatical wordhood and degrees of morphological fusion. In F. Ackerman, J. Blevins, and G. Stump, eds., *Periphrasis and Paradigms*. Stanford, CA: CSLI Publishcations.

Ackerman, Farrell and Gert Webelhuth. 1998. *A Theory of Predicates*. Stanford, CA: CSLI Publications.

Alhoniemi, Alho. 1985. *Marin Kielioppi.* Helsinki: Suomalais-Ugrilainen Seura.

Anderson, Stephen R. 1992. *A-Morphous Morphology*. Cambridge: Cambridge University Press.

Andrews, Avery D. 1990. Unification and morphological blocking. *Natural Language and Linguistic Theory* 8:507–557.

Aronoff, Mark. 1994. *Morphology by Itself*. Cambridge, MA: MIT Press.

Beard, Robert. 1995. *Lexeme-Morpheme Base Morphology*. Albany, NY: SUNY Press.

Bereczki, Gábor. 1990. *Chrestomathia Ceremissica*. Budapest: Tankönyvkiadó.

Blevins, James. 2000. Markedness and blocking in German declensional paradigms. In B. Stiebels and D. Wunderlich, eds., *Lexicon in Focus*, vol. 45 of *Studia Grammatica*, pages 83–103. Berlin: Akademie-Verlag.

Blevins, James. 2001. Lexemic stems in Western Germanic. Unpublished ms. University of Cambridge.

Börjars, Kersti, Nigel Vincent, and Carol Chapman. 1997. Paradigms, periphrases and pronominal inflection: A feature-based account. In G. Booij and J. van Marle, eds., *Yearbook of Morphology 1996*, pages 155–179. Dordrecht: Kluwer Academic Publishers.

Bresnan, Joan and Sam A. Mchombo. 1995. The lexical integrity principle: evidence from Bantu. *Natural Language and Linguistic Theory* 13:181–254.

Butt, Miriam, María-Eugenia Niño, and Frédérique Segond. 1996. Multilingual processing of auxiliaries in LFG. In D. Gibbon, ed., *Natural Language Processing and Speech Technology: Results of the 3rd KONVENS Conference*, pages 111–122. Berlin: Mouton de Gruyter. Also reprinted in this volume.

Carstairs-McCarthy, Andrew. 2000. Lexeme, word-form, paradigm. In Geert Booij, Christian Lehmann, and Joachim Mugdan (in collaboration with Wolfgang Kesselheim and Stavros Skopeteas), eds., *Morphologie: Ein Internationales Handbuch zur Flexion und Wortbildung/Morphology: An International Handbook on Inflection and Word-formation*, pages 595–607. Berlin & New York: Walter de Gruyter.

Csúcs, Sándor. 1987. *Chrestomathia Vottaca*. Budapest: Tankönyvkiadó.

Csúcs, Sándor. 1988. Die wotjakische Sprache. In D. Sinor, ed., *The Uralic Languages: Description, History and Foreign Influences*, pages 131–146. Leiden: E. J. Brill.

Csúcs, Sándra. 1998. Udmurt. In D. Abondolo, ed., *The Uralic Languages*, pages 276–304. London & New York: Routledge.

Falk, Yehuda. 1984. The English auxiliary system: A Lexical-Functional analysis. *Language* 60:483–509.

Greenberg, Joseph H. 1966. *Language Universals, with Special References to Feature Hierarchies*. The Hague: Mouton.

Gukhman, M. M. 1955. Glagol'nye analiticheskie konstruktsii kak osobye sochetaniia chastichnogo i polnogo slova (na materiale istorii nemetskogo iazyka). In V. V. Vinogradov, ed., *Voprosy grammaticheskogo Stroia*. Moscow: Academic Sciences.

Gukhman, M. M. 1963. Kriterii vydelenia glagol'nikh analiticheskikh struktsij iz drugikh tipov slovosochetanij. In V. M. Zhirmunskij and O. P. Sunik, eds., *Morfologicheskaia struktura Slova v Iazykakh Razlichnykh Tipov*, pages 199–202. Moscow: Nauka.

Haspelmath, Martin. 2000. Periphrasis. In Geert Booij, Christian Lehmann, and Joachim Mugdan (in collaboration with Wolfgang Kesselheim and Stavros Skopeteas), eds., *Morphologie: Ein Internationales Handbuch zur Flexion und Wortbildung/Morphology: An International Handbook on Inflection and Word-formation*, pages 654–664. Berlin & New York: Walter de Gruyter.

Kangasmaa-Minn, Eeva. 1998. Mari. In D. Abondolo, ed., *The Uralic Languages*, pages 219–248. London & New York: Routledge.

Kel'makov, Valentin and Sara Hännikäinen. 1999. *Udmurtin Kielioppia ja Harjoituksia*. Helsinki: Suomalais-Ugrilainen Seura.

Koenig, Jean-Pierre. 1999. *Lexical Relations*. Stanford, CA: CSLI Publications.

Matthews, Peter H. 1972. *Inflectional Morphology: A Theoretical Study Based on Aspects of Latin Verb Conjugation.* Cambridge: Cambridge University Press.

Matthews, P. H. 1991. *Morphology*. Cambridge: Cambridge University Press. Second edition.

Mayerthaler, Willi. 1988. *Morphological Naturalness*. Ann Arbor: Karoma.

Mitchell, E. 1993. *Morphological Evidence For Syntactic Structure: the Finno-Ugric Languages and English.* Ph.D. thesis, Cornell University.

Mohanan, K. P. 1982. Grammatical relations and clause structure in Malayalam. In J. Bresnan, ed., *The Mental Representation of Grammatical Relations*, pages 504–589. Cambridge, MA: MIT Press.

Niño, Maria-Eugenia. 1997. The multiple expression of inflectional information and grammatical architecture. In F. Corbin, D. Godard, and J.-M. Marandin, eds., *Empirical Issues in Formal Syntax and Semantics*, pages 127–147. Berne: Peter Lang.

Orgun, Orhan. 1996. *Sign-based Morphology and Phonology with special Attention to Optimality Theory*. Ph.D. thesis, University of California, Berkeley.

Riehemann, Susannah. 2000. Type-based derivational morphology. *Journal of Comparative Germanic Linguistics* 2:49–77.

Robins, Robert H. 1959. In defence of WP. *Philological Society of London* pages 116–144.

Sadler, Louisa and Andrew Spencer. 2001. Syntax as an exponent of morphological features. In G. Booij and J. van Marle, eds., *Yearbook of Morphology 2000*, pages 71–96. Dordrecht: Kluwer Academic Publishers.

Salminen, Tapani. 1997. *Tundra Nenets Inflection.* Helsinki: Suomalias-Ugrilainen Seura.

Sebeok, Thomas and Frances J. Ingemann. 1961. *An Eastern Cheremis Manual: Phonology, Grammar, Texts and Glossary*, vol. 5 of *Uralic and Altaic series*. Bloomington: Indiana University publications.

Sells, Peter. this volume. Syntactic information and its morphological expression.

Spencer, Andrew. 2001. The Word-and-Paradigm approach to morphosyntax. *Transactions of the Philological Society* 99:279–313.

Spencer, Andrew. 2003a. Paradigm-based lexicalism: Negation in Japanese. Unpublished ms. University of Essex.

Spencer, Andrew. 2003b. Periphrastic paradigms in Bulgarian. In U. Junghanns and L. Szucsich, eds., *Syntactic Structures and Morphological Information*, pages 249–282. Amsterdam: John Benjamins.

Stump, Gregory T. 1993. On rules of referral. *Language* 69:449–479.

Stump, Gregory T. 2001. *Inflectional Morphology: A Theory of Paradigm Structure*. Cambridge: Cambridge University Press.

Stump, Gregory T. 2002. Morphological and syntactic paradigms: arguments for a theory of paradigm linkage. In G. Booij and J. van Marle, eds., *Yearbook of Morphology 2001*, pages 147–180. Dordrecht: Kluwer Academic Publishers.

Stump, Gregory T. 2003. A theory of heteroclite inflectional paradigms. Unpublished ms. University of Kentucky.

Stump, Gregory T. to appear. Morphological blocking and Pāṇini's principle. In F. Ackerman, J. Blevins, and G. Stump, eds., *Periphrasis and Paradigms*. CSLI Publications.

Suihkonen, Pirkko et al. 1995. *Udmurt-English-Finnish Dictionary with a Basic Grammar of Udmurt*. Helsinki: Suomalais-Ugrilainen Seura.

Zhirmunskij, V. M. 1963. O granitsakh slova. In V. M. Zhirmunskij and O. P. Sunik, eds., *Morfologicheskaia struktura Slova v Iazykakh Razlichnykh Tipov*, pages 3–33. Moscow: Nauka.

Zorina, Z. F. et al. 1990. *Mariiskii iazyk Dl'a Vsekh*. Ioshkar-Ola: Mariiskoe Knizhnoe Izdatelstvo.

Zwicky, Arnold M. 1985. How to describe inflection. In M. Niepokuj, M. Van Clay, V. Nikiforidou, and D. Feder, eds., *Proceedings of the Eleventh Annual Meeting of the Berkeley Linguistic Society*, pages 372–386.

Zwicky, Arnold M. 1990. Inflectional morphology as a (sub)component of grammar. In W. U. Dressler, H. C. Luschützky, O. E. Pfeiffer, and J. R. Rennison, eds., *Contemporary Morphology*, pages 217–236. Berlin: Walter de Gruyter.

6

Relating Morphology to Syntax

LOUISA SADLER AND RACHEL NORDLINGER

6.1 Introduction

Relatively little attention in theoretical work in LFG has focussed on the nature of the interface between morphology and syntax, or indeed on the role of morphology proper.[1,2] While the contribution of morphology to the definition of f-structures is firmly established, and the separation of external structures by the principle of lexical integrity is the backbone of LFG's lexicalist outlook, the internal operation of the morphological component and how words come to contribute the relevant f-descriptions have not generally been at the forefront of theoretical work.

From a syntactic point of view this is unsurprising, for in the general case nothing much hangs on precisely how matters internal to inflectional morphology are dealt with. In the typical case "pieces" of inflectional morphology contribute information to the f-structure of the word itself (e.g. $(\uparrow \text{TNS}) = \text{PAST}$) or to the f-structure of a dependent of

[1]Thanks for discussion of relevant material to Mary Dalrymple and Andrew Spencer. We are also grateful to Ryo Otoguro and two anonymous reviewers for comments on this paper. Remaining errors are of course solely our own responsibility. Sadler is grateful to the University of Essex for a period of sabbatical leave during which this work was completed, and Nordlinger for the support of the Australian Research Council, grant F9930026, held at the University of Melbourne.

[2]Existing work touching on, or having consequences for, these issues includes Ackerman 1990, Sadler 1997, Sells 2000 and this volume, and Kaplan and Butt 2002, amongst others, and in particular the work on verbal periphrasis including Butt et al 1996, Börjars et al 1997, Sadler and Spencer 2001 and Frank and Zaenen 2002.

Projecting Morphology.
Louisa Sadler and Andrew Spencer (Eds.).

the word (e.g. (↑ SUBJ PRED) = 'PRO'), and thus the syntactic contributions of discrete "pieces" of inflectional morphology do not interact in any complicated way. This means that a simple, word-syntactic, incremental view may be taken of the syntactic contribution of inflectional morphological processes such as affixation, in which f-descriptions are associated directly with morphological forms or features.

However, more complex data makes it evident that the simple incremental view can be problematic. Difficulties may arise in several domains. For example, there is a considerable body of morphological data which suggests that an incremental approach is insufficient or inappropriate on purely morphology-internal grounds of the adequacy of morphological description, although we will not be concerned with such evidence in this paper (see Stump 2001 and Spencer this volume for more discussion). Additionally, there is a further type of complex data where the complexity relates to the interaction between the syntax and the morphology, more particularly, the interaction between the pieces of syntactic information which are encoded morphologically. Such data pose fundamental issues for the mapping between syntax and morphology, showing that the simple view, under which all that is required is to (incrementally) associate syntactic information with morphological features (or forms), is incorrect. This paper is concerned with data of this sort, and in particular with the phenomenon of case stacking, which shows in a clear fashion both that morphological structure *does* matter, and that there are interesting issues to be addressed in the morphology-syntax interface itself.

The phenomenon of case stacking, dramatically illustrated in (1) from the Australian language Martuthunira, demonstrates in an extreme form the role that morphology can have in building and constraining syntactic structures.

(1) Ngayu nhawu-lha ngurnu tharnta-a mirtily-marta-a
I saw-PST that(ACC) euro-ACC joey-PROP-ACC
thara-ngka-marta-a.
pouch-LOC-PROP-ACC
'I saw the euro with a joey in (its) pouch.' (Martuthunira, Dench 1995a:60, (3.15))

In this example the most deeply embedded nominal 'pouch' carries three case markers, each one relating to a successively higher syntactic relationship. First 'pouch' is inflected with the locative case marking the f-structure function of 'pouch', then with the proprietive case indicating that the locative nominal is embedded within the proprietive NP 'joey in (its) pouch', and finally with the accusative case, marking the whole proprietive NP as being contained within the object NP. Case stacking data such as that in (1) pose some interesting challenges for morphological description because it demonstrates that morphosyntactic features may be iterated. More importantly, it casts light on the nature of the interface between syntax (f-structure) and morphology because capturing these data necessitates a complex mapping between morphological sequencing and syntactic structure.

In earlier work, Nordlinger (1998) provides an incremental, morpheme-based account of these data in LFG. The morphology (or lexical component) constructs fully inflected wordforms with multiple case markers — for this Nordlinger adopts an essentially word-syntactic approach to inflectional morphology. Functional (f-structure) information is associated directly with morphemes (which are conventionally thought of as listed as (sub-)lexical entries). The role of morphology in defining or constraining the larger syntactic environment within which the word appears is straightforwardly captured by the use of so-called *inside-out* statements. For example, on a morphemic approach the Martuthunira accusative case marker *-yu* can itself be associated with a functional description which states that it specifies or defines an OBJ function. This model of constructive morphology has been widely adopted in recent morphosyntactic research in LFG (Nordlinger 1998, Barron 1998, Sadler 1998, Sells 2000, Lee 1999, Sharma 1999, Nordlinger 2000, Nordlinger and Sadler 2000, O'Connor 2002, Ørsnes 2002). To accommodate case stacking, Nordlinger formulates a combinatorial principle (the Principle of Morphological Composition (PMC)) which correctly constrains the interaction of f-structure information associated with different morphemes in the inflected word. However, an important issue which arises in this connection is that the PMC is not formalized within the LFG description language in that work.[3] As should become clear as we proceed, one reason why the mapping between morphemes (or morphological features) and syntactic functions is problematic to formalize on a word syntactic view is precisely because the incremental morphemic view under which affixes are added hierarchically by means of a binary X → X Aff rule provides an inappropriate structure for the felicitious combination of f-descriptions.

The purpose of this paper is to explore more fully the mapping between morphological and syntactic descriptions, with primary reference to the case stacking data. In particular we aim to show how the insights of Nordlinger's (1998) Principle of Morphological Composition can be

[3]Note however that the appendix to Nordlinger (1998) suggests an approach to restating the PMC with standard LFG tools which prefigures in some respects the approach to formalization which we adopt here.

incorporated into a model of the morphology/syntax interface which is fully compatible with the description language of LFG, but on the basis of different assumptions about the nature of the morphological representation itself. We will not be concerned here with actual morphological forms, nor with the theory of inflectional morphology which generates the inflected word forms. In specifying the mapping between morphology and syntax in this paper our starting point will be the sorts of structured representations delivered by the inferential-realizational account of the morphology of case-stacking proposed in Sadler and Nordlinger (to appear).[4]

The rest of this paper is structured as follows. Section 6.2 provides the background necessary to understand the problem we focus upon. It begins with a brief review of the relevant case stacking data and then illustrates the constructive morphology approach to these data which our analysis builds on. The section concludes with an evaluation of the Principle of Morphological Composition. With this background in place, section 6.3 outlines our proposal for the interface between morphological structures and f-descriptions and section 6.4 concludes.

6.2 Composition and F-Descriptions

6.2.1 Case stacking

The following is a straightforward example of adnominal multiple case in the Australian language Thalanyji. Here the possessor is coded by the dative case marker *-ku* DAT, and also takes the case of the head that it modifies (ACC).

(2) kupuju-lu kaparla-nha yanga-lkin wartirra-ku-nha
child-ERG dog-ACC chase-PRES woman-DAT-ACC
'The child chases the woman's dog.' (Thalanyji, Austin 1995:372, (22))

The fully inflected word *wartirra-ku-nha* 'woman-DAT-ACC' projects the functional information shown in (3), in which f_1 is the f-structure

[4]Sadler and Nordlinger (to appear) propose a morphological analysis in the framework of Paradigm Function Morphology (PFM), which has several advantages over the morpheme-based account of Nordlinger (1998). In particular, it is quite straightforward in PFM to set up the morphology to appropriately constrain the interaction of different case functions (e.g. the relational, modal, associating and complementizing case functions of Kayardild (Evans 1995a)), whereas in the original work by Nordlinger, the morphology overgenerates on this front, with the syntax effectively playing a filtering role. Additionally, the separation of function from exponence in a realizational framework permits various exceptional forms, such as portmanteau affixes and case substitutions, to be correctly treated. See Sadler and Nordlinger (to appear) for further discussion.

of the nominal itself, and contains the dative case feature, while the accusative case feature belongs in a higher f-structure (namely, that of the head noun 'dog').

(3) $$\left[\begin{array}{ll}\text{CASE} & \text{ACC}\\ \text{POSS} & f_1\left[\begin{array}{ll}\text{PRED} & \text{`WOMAN'}\\ \text{CASE} & \text{DAT}\end{array}\right]\end{array}\right]$$

A more complex case stacking example is the following from Martuthunira, repeated from (1) above.

(4) Ngayu nhawu-lha ngurnu tharnta-a mirtily-marta-a
I saw-PST that(ACC) euro-ACC joey-PROP-ACC
thara-ngka-marta-a.
pouch-LOC-PROP-ACC
'I saw the euro with a joey in (its) pouch.'

The information projected from the single inflected nominal *thara-ngka-marta-a* 'pouch-LOC-PROP-ACC' is shown diagrammatically in (5) — once again, the f-structure of the nominal itself is f_1. In this example, the innermost (locative) case marks the locative adjunct 'pouch'. The proprietive case signals the proprietive adjunct relation between 'joey' and 'euro', and the outermost (accusative) case signals the relation between 'euro' and the verb (the object relation).

(5) $$\left[\begin{array}{ll}\text{OBJ} & \left[\begin{array}{ll}\text{CASE} & \text{ACC}\\ \text{ADJ}_{prop} & \left[\begin{array}{ll}\text{CASE} & \text{PROP}\\ \text{ADJ}_{loc} & f_1\left[\begin{array}{ll}\text{PRED} & \text{`POUCH'}\\ \text{CASE} & \text{LOC}\end{array}\right]\end{array}\right]\end{array}\right]\end{array}\right]$$

The case system of the Tangkic language Kayardild (see Evans 1995a) is still more complex, additionally permitting the use of case markers in modal function (where case morphology partially specifies temporal and modal information at the level of the clause) and case markers in complementizing function, where case markers are used to mark interclausal relations on complementized clauses (Dench and Evans 1988, Evans 1995a). The word *thabuju-karra-nguni-na* in (6) illustrates the combination of two case markers in core function with a case marker in modal function. The modal ablative case (M.ABL) marks the clause as having past tense. The instrumental case marks 'brother' as belonging to an instrumental argument of the verb and the genitive case marks ‘brother’ as the (adnominal) possessor argument within the instrumental NP. The information projected from the nominal *thabuju-karra-nguni-na* is shown in (7)— again, the f-structure of the nominal itself is f_1.

(6) Ngada yalawu-jarra yakuri-na thabuju-karra-nguni-na
I catch-PST fish-M.ABL brother-GEN-INST-M.ABL
mijil-nguni-na.
net-INST-M.ABL
‘I caught the fish with brother’s net.’ (Kayardild, Evans 1995b: 400, (10))

(7)
$$\begin{bmatrix} \text{TNS} & \text{PAST} \\ \text{ADJ}_{instr} & \begin{bmatrix} \text{CASE} & \text{INSTR} \\ \text{POSS} & f_1\begin{bmatrix} \text{PRED} & \text{‘BROTHER’} \\ \text{CASE} & \text{GEN} \end{bmatrix} \end{bmatrix} \end{bmatrix}$$

As a further complication to the data, note that number marking may be interleaved with case marking in these languages, with each instance of number marking modifying a different referent according to its position in the morphological structure, as shown in the Kayardild example (8), in which the ablative case marks the possessor function.

(8) maku-yarr-nurru-naba-walad
woman-DU-ASSOC-ABL-MANY(NOM)
‘the many belonging to (those) having two wives’ (Kayardild, Evans 1995a:123)

Similarly, in the following Martuthunira noun phrase, the pronominal stem is SG, the genitive case marks the possessor function and the subsequent dual number marking is interpreted with respect to the possessed noun *pawulu-* ‘child’.

(9) nganaju-wu-tharra-a pawulu-tharra-a
1SG.OBL-GEN-DU-ACC child-DU-ACC
‘my two children’ (Dench 1995a:95, (4.154))

(10)
$$\begin{bmatrix} \text{NUM} & \text{DU} \\ \text{CASE} & \text{ACC} \\ \text{POSS} & f_1\begin{bmatrix} \text{CASE} & \text{GEN} \\ \text{PRED} & \text{‘PRO’} \\ \text{NUM} & \text{SG} \\ \text{PERS} & 1 \end{bmatrix} \end{bmatrix}$$

The fact that number marking interacts with the stacking of case markers in this manner is significant because it demonstrates that more is at issue here than a simple "quirk" of the case systems of these languages. Rather it is evident that the morphological structure itself is complex and that the successive levels of case marking define syntactic structures which are referenced by other f-structure descriptions expressed word-internally, thereby providing additional support for the constructive view itself.

6.2.2 Constructive Morphology: Inside-Out Constraints

Such case stacking clearly demonstrates the fundamental role that morphology can play in encoding complex syntactic relations. In order to account for such data Nordlinger (1998) develops the model of constructive case within LFG whereby morphological constituents/processes may actively define properties of their clausal environment independently of syntax (see also Simpson 1983, 1991 and Andrews 1996). The model of constructive case consists essentially of two distinct ideas.

The first of these is the use of inside-out constraints (e.g. Halvorsen and Kaplan 1988, Dalrymple 1993, see also Andrews 1996:41-43) associated with the lexical elements, morphological features or processes to enable nominal constituents to define the larger syntactic (f-structure) context in which they are embedded.[5] In this way, case-marked nominals can specify the grammatical function of the higher clause of which their f-structure is the value. Thus the f-structure information associated with accusative case in an example such as the Martuthunira (4) is as in (11), and the accusative-case nominal (e.g. 'euro-ACC') projects the f-structure in (12).

(11) ACC: $(\uparrow \text{CASE}) = \text{ACC}$
$(\text{OBJ} \uparrow)$

(12)
$$f_2\begin{bmatrix} \text{OBJ} & f_1\begin{bmatrix} \text{PRED} & \text{`EURO'} \\ \text{CASE} & \text{ACC} \end{bmatrix} \end{bmatrix}$$

By virtue of the inside-out designator (OBJ ↑), the information associated with the accusative case constructs a higher f-structure (f_2) which contains an OBJ to which the f-structure associated with the case-inflected nominal itself (f_1) belongs. Thus, on this analysis, a nominal

[5]Inside-out function application is well-established in LFG through work in such areas as quantifier scope (Halvorsen and Kaplan 1988), anaphoric binding (Dalrymple 1993), internally-headed relative clauses (Culy 1990), Russian genitive of negation (King 1995), Urdu case (Butt 1995), and topicalization (Bresnan 2001).

inserted into the syntax already defines its grammatical function by virtue of the case marker attached to it.

While the use of the inside-out constraints enables nominals to construct information about the higher f-structure in which they are embedded (e.g. by specifying a grammatical function for it), this alone does not provide an analysis of the case stacking data presented above. The constructive case model also contains a second component to compose the information contributed by multiple morphological elements, for each case marker contributes information about a successively higher f-structure. This is the Principle of Morphological Composition, which we discuss in the following subsection.

6.2.3 Interfacing Stacking Morphology with Syntax

On a standard LFG view of how the f-description associated with an inflectionally complex word comes about, the syntactic information associated with each morphological element is simply conjoined. For a word with multiple case markers, such as *thara-ngka-marta-a* 'pouch-LOC-PROP-ACC' in (4), this essentially corresponds to positing the following sub-lexical annotated tree, in which each case marker introduces a CASE value and makes reference to a (different) grammatical function:

(13)

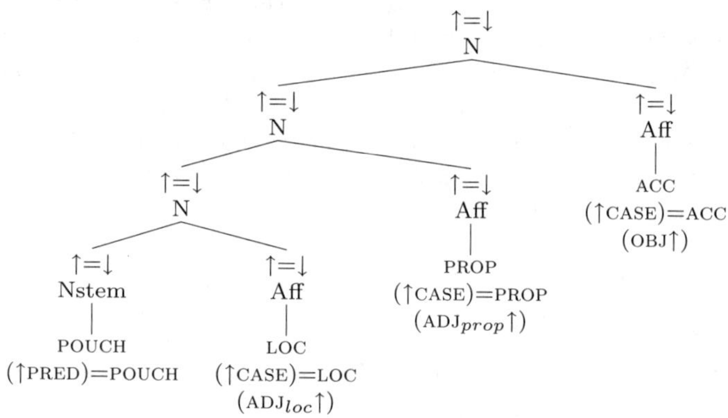

But of course this will not give the desired results because it fails to embed the f-structures in the appopriate manner (and as a consequence it also assigns multiple inconsistent CASE values to the f-structure denoted throughout by ↑). Nordlinger (1998) observes that, informally speaking, each successive affix takes the outer f-structure (call it f_x) described by the previous affix and defines some properties of both it and the higher f-structure which immediately contains f_x. If the process of affixation is constrained to have this syntactic consequence, then the iconic effects exemplified in section 6.2.1 above are accounted for.

This insight is captured in the Principle of Morphological Composition, which composes the information associated with successive affixes. According to the PMC, the f-structure information the affix actually defines depends on the information associated with the preceding morphological element (which could be the root or a more deeply embedded affix). The idea is that context-sensitive substitutions to the f-descriptions in (sub-)lexical entries are carried out: every occurrence of ↑ in the lexical information associated with an affix is substituted with any expression of the form (GF^n ↑) on the preceding morphological element. Nordlinger (1998) formulates this principle as follows:

(14) **Principle of Morphological Composition**: Where x is a string of attributes:

Stem	Aff		Stem	Aff
(GF^n ↑)	((GF^m ↑) x)	⟹	(GF^n ↑)	((GF^m (GF^n ↑)) x)

In the case where the preceding morphological element is annotated simply with outside-in equations, such as (↑ TNS) = PAST, the intention is that substitution of ↑ by ↑ will apply vacuously, while on the other hand if the previous element is annotated (ADJ ↑) then every occurrence of ↑ on the current affix is replaced by (ADJ ↑). In this way, each affix defines information pertaining to a successively larger, containing f-structure. As an example, consider the fate of the sub-lexical entries for the morphemes listed in (15) in the Martuthunira nominal *thara-ngka-marta-a* in (4).

(15)

POUCH-	LOC-	PROP-	ACC
(↑ PRED)='POUCH'	(ADJ$_{loc}$ ↑)	(ADJ$_{prop}$ ↑)	(OBJ ↑)
	(↑ CASE)=LOC	(↑ CASE)=PROP	(↑ CASE)=ACC

As these entries show, the case morphology itself defines the grammatical function of the nominal it marks, the LOCative case signals a locative ADJunct (ADJ$_{loc}$), the PROPrietive case signals a proprietive adjunct, (ADJ$_{prop}$), and the ACCusative case defines an OBJ function. From these entries the derived forms in (16) are output from the process of substitution as formulated in the PMC. This approach permits a maximally general statement of the f-structure information associated with each affix in the lexicon.

(16)

Sub-Lexical Entry	Entry Derived In Context
POUCH (↑ PRED) = 'POUCH'	(↑ PRED) = 'POUCH'
LOC (↑ CASE) = LOC (ADJ$_{loc}$ ↑)	(↑ CASE) =LOC (ADJ$_{loc}$ ↑)
PROP (↑ CASE) = PROP (ADJ$_{prop}$ ↑)	((ADJ$_{loc}$ ↑) CASE) = PROP (ADJ$_{prop}$ (ADJ$_{loc}$ ↑))
ACC (OBJ ↑) (↑ CASE) = ACC	(OBJ (ADJ$_{prop}$ (ADJ$_{loc}$ ↑))) ((ADJ$_{prop}$ (ADJ$_{loc}$ ↑)) CASE)= ACC

With these substitutions to the f-descriptions associated with individual morphs, the sub-lexical tree is as follows:

(17)

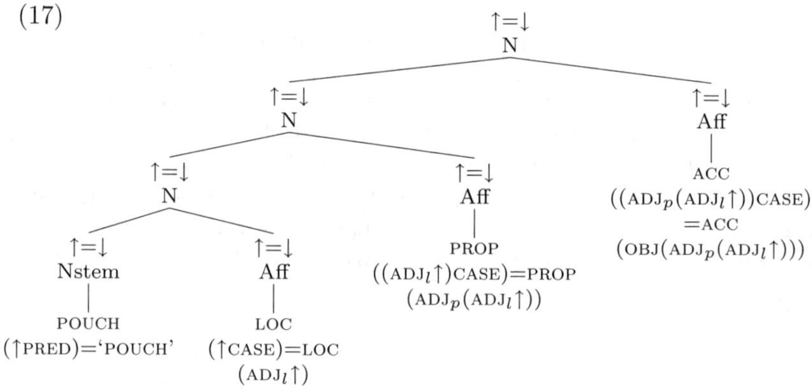

6.2.4 Constructive Stems

The use of inside-out constraints and composition provides us with a simple account of the use of nominals as heads or modifiers in many Australian Aboriginal languages, including Wambaya and Warlpiri. In these languages, nominal roots (that is, without any additional morphology) can themselves introduce syntactic functions, with consequences for the interpretation of the inflectional morphology which builds on those stems, so that nominals can generally function either as NP heads or as modifiers. Thus, consider the Warlpiri and Wambaya examples in (18) and (19) respectively.

(18) Kurdu-jarra-rlu ka-pala maliki wajili-pi-nyi
child-DU-ERG PRES-3.DU.SUBJ dog(ABS) chase-NPST
wita-jarra-rlu
small-DU-ERG
'The two small children are chasing the dog.' (Warlpiri, Austin & Bresnan 1996:225, (13))

(19) Ngajbi ng-a nangi-marnda-rna
see 1.SG.S-PST 3.SG.M.POSS-PL-II(ACC)
alalangmiminya
daughter.PL.II(ACC)[6]
'I saw his daughters.' (Wambaya, Nordlinger 1998:115, (42))

The Warlpiri nominal *wita-jarra-rlu* in (18) is an adjunct which agrees in number and case with the nominal which it modifies. The f-structure corresponding to *wita-jarra-rlu* is shown in (20), in which the ADJ function is projected directly from the nominal stem (Nordlinger 1998), and contributes CASE and NUM features to the f-structure of the nominal which it modifies.

(20) $\begin{bmatrix} \text{CASE} & \text{ERG} \\ \text{NUM} & \text{DU} \\ \text{ADJ} & \begin{bmatrix} \text{PRED} & \text{`SMALL'} \end{bmatrix} \end{bmatrix}$

The information associated with the (sub-)lexical entries is as shown in the first column of (21) and the f-descriptions derived by the operation of the PMC in the second column:

(21)

Sub-Lexical Entry	Entry Derived In Context
WITA (↑ PRED) = 'SMALL' (ADJ ↑)	 (↑ PRED) = 'SMALL' (ADJ ↑)
ERG (↑ CASE) = ERG	 ((ADJ ↑) CASE) = ERG
DU (↑ NUM) = DU	 ((ADJ ↑) NUM) = DU

In fact, the (ADJ ↑) annotation associated with nominal stems such as *wita* is optional. General LFG principles of completeness and coherence will ensure that grammatical f-structures only result if the ADJ function is present for a modifier use and absent when the nominal functions as the NP head.

[6] II in the gloss denotes feminine gender.

Similarly, in (19) the possessive pronominal root is inflected for the case and number of the possessed element, which is the head of the containing f-structure, while the pronominal root itself introduces the POSS function. The structure defined by the fully inflected word *nangi-marnda-rna* is shown in (23).

(22) *nangi*: (POSS $\uparrow$)
(\$\uparrow$ PRED) = 'PRO' (\$\uparrow$ GEND) = 'MASC'
(\$\uparrow$ PER) = '3' (\$\uparrow$ NUM) = 'SG'

(23)
$$\begin{bmatrix} \text{CASE} & \text{ACC} \\ \text{NUM} & \text{PL} \\ \text{POSS} & \begin{bmatrix} \text{PRED} & \text{`PRO'} \\ \text{PER} & 3 \\ \text{GEND} & \text{MASC} \\ \text{NUM} & \text{SG} \end{bmatrix} \end{bmatrix}$$

Notice that once the word formation component is set up to provide the right forms, the constructive morphology approach exemplified here immediately accounts, without further modification, for forms such as this which carry two number and gender values – one for the possessor and one agreeing with that of the possessed element. The Principle of Morphological Composition, in this case in conjunction with the assumption that the stem introduces the POSS function, ensures that the values SG and MASC are in the f-structure of the possessor and the values PL and FEM in the f-structure of the governing nominal 'daughter'.

6.2.5 Evaluating the PMC

The PMC straightforwardly captures the intuition that as they stack, the (case and number) affixes contribute information to the f-structure defined by the morphological structure to which they attach. This places a strong constraint on the relationship between syntax and morphology, imposing a sort of isomorphism: morphological structure and syntactic structure are required to match in the appropriate sense. Because the principle essentially embeds the syntactic information associated with the previous (more deeply embedded) affix into the syntactic information associated with the next (higher) affix, it automatically accounts for the observed iconic behaviour of case stacking.

Despite this, the principle itself is not without problems. In particular, the statement of this principle does not fall within the mathematics which underpins the LFG formalism. As we have seen, the operation of the PMC entails the *substitution of paths* in the f-descriptions associated with affixes. Although the formulation of the principle in (14) might give the impression that these substitutions are local to a sub-tree of depth one, note that this is not actually the case — the substitution is not between sisters in a local subtree. In fact, a crucial aspect of the principle is that the relevant substitutions are really performed at the level of the information lexically associated with the affixes, and not at the level of the derived word. As shown above, the word (and indeed the stem at each level of recursion within the word structure) is annotated $\uparrow = \downarrow$. This is crucial to ensuring that the word itself interacts correctly with the f-descriptions associated with the other nodes in the c-structure tree. What the principle ensures is that the information associated in the lexicon with an affix is modified by substituting for the $\uparrow$ designation on the affix whatever inside-out path is eventually associated with the preceding affix, once any substitutions at that level have been performed. This requires a form of pattern matching, which is not supported within the LFG formalism.

Because the approach to word internal structure in Nordlinger 1998 is basically morphemic, the PMC is formulated with reference to trees which reflect morphemic structure. Once we move away from a morpheme-based morphology, however, we are able to consider different structurings of morphological information which are not tied to exponence, and as a consequence the effect of the principle of morphological composition can be captured directly without the need for any path substitutions. In the rest of this paper, we take as our starting point the recent morphological treatment of the Kayardild case stacking data in Sadler and Nordlinger (to appear) and show how the mapping to syntax can be directly encoded on the basis of these morphological structures.

6.3 The Morphology-Syntax Interface

We noted at the start of this paper that the interface between (inflectional) morphology and syntax has received relatively little attention to date in LFG, the standard view being a lexicalist, incremental one in which f-descriptions are associated with elements of the morphology (for example, affixes or morphological features) and then combined straightforwardly by identifying word-internal instances of $\uparrow$. In very many cases, of course, this is unproblematic, for the simple reason that the information expressed by a word is typically quite local to the f-structure of that word.

Conceptually, the interface between lexical representations and syntactic (f-) descriptions involves two distinct aspects. The first of these is the specification of a mapping between syntactic information and corresponding elements in the morphological domain, that is, morphological features, and lexemes or roots. In very many cases, of course, this mapping is highly transparent, to such an extent that it is often tacitly assumed that the syntax and the morphology involve one and the same set of morphosyntactic properties, but in fact there are good reasons to keep these features distinct. For one thing, there are clearly morphology-internal features (such as conjugation class), which have no place in syntactic representations of any sort, and for another, there are well-known cases of mismatch between morphological and syntactic features, for example where an element is morphologically a member of category A but syntactically a member of category B (see Spencer to appear). The second aspect of the interface between morphology and syntax is the specification of how the syntactic information associated with the morphological "parts" is to be combined. Here too, within an LFG context, simple concatenation of f-descriptions associated with morphological "parts" (with identification of instances of ↑) is generally appropriate. However, as we have seen, this is not the case for the case stacking data, in which the functional information associated with morphological "parts" interacts in a more complex way. In the current section, we show how this interaction can be simply captured in the interface between a realizational morphology and the syntax.

6.3.1 Associating F-descriptions with M-features

In recent work, Sadler and Nordlinger (to appear) provide a morphological account of case stacking within Paradigm Function Morphology (PFM) (Stump 2001). In such a realizational approach, the morphological descriptions are paradigm cells, where a paradigm cell is a pair consisting of a lexeme (or root) and a well-formed feature bundle.[7] For example, the morphological structures associated with fully inflected wordforms in a case stacking language such as Kayardild (which has a modal case function as well as core (adnominal or relational) case functions) are as shown in (24). The structure in (24a) is associated with the word *thabuju-karra-nguni-na* 'brother-GEN-INST-M.ABL' (see (6)), while the nominal *maku-yarr-nurru-naba-walad* 'woman-DU-ASSOC-ABL-MANY(NOM)' (see (8)) is of the more complicated form involving multiple number features, shown schematically in (24b). These examples are given in a notation for specifying paradigm cells in PFM

[7] That is, these structures are the output of morphological (inflectional) analysis, and the input to morphological (inflectional) generation. The rules of (inflectional) morphology relate well-formed paradigm cells to realizations.

(in what follows we will often abbreviate *Core* as *C*).

(24) a. <LEX, {Case$_{Core}$: Z, {Case$_{Core}$: Y, {Case$_{Mod}$: X}}}>

b. <LEX,{Num: A, {Case$_{Core}$: Z, {Case$_{Core}$: Y, {Num: X, {Case$_{Core}$: Z}}}}}>

c. <LEX, {Num: A, {Case$_{Core}$: Z, {Case$_{Core}$: Y, {Case$_{Mod}$: X}}}}}>

Sadler and Nordlinger (to appear) is concerned essentially with morphology-internal matters, rather than with the nature of the interface between morphological structures and f-descriptions, and doesn't address in any detail the issue of how to correctly combine the syntactic information associated with each morphological feature (and the lexemic root). The current paper, on the other hand, takes as its starting point the sorts of structured morphological representations proposed in Sadler and Nordlinger (to appear) and shows how the mapping between morphological stuctures and the syntax can be straightforwardly specified without any extension to the LFG formalism (but with the addition of a minor notational extension), using f-descriptions directly in the morphology-syntax interface.

As noted above, the first step is to specify the syntactic information corresponding to each morphological feature. This is quite trivial, and the syntactic information is precisely that proposed in Nordlinger (1998), although of course in our realizational approach, this information is associated with morphological descriptions or features and not with morphemes. A mapping is specified between morphological A:V pairs and syntactic information, and between roots and syntactic information – this may be thought of as a lexicon or lexical transducer.[8] We show below some examples of (constructive) case, number and nominal stems:

[8]See Kaplan and Newman (1997) and Butt et al (1999) for discussion of a similar "lexicon" of morphological formatives within the XLE computational environment.

(25)

Mfeature	F-description
Case$_C$:Loc	(↑ CASE)=LOC, (ADJ$_{loc}$ ↑)
Case$_C$:Abl	(↑ CASE)=ABL, (ADJ$_{abl}$ ↑)
Case$_C$:Prop	(↑ CASE)=PROP, (ADJ$_{prop}$ ↑)
Case$_C$:Erg	(↑ CASE)=ERG, (SUBJ ↑)
Case$_C$:Nom	(↑ CASE)=NOM, (SUBJ ↑)
Case$_M$:Abl	(↑ TNS)=PAST
Num:Many	(↑ NUM) = MANY
Num:Pl	(↑ NUM) = PL
woman	(↑ PRED) = 'WOMAN'

The second step is to specify how the syntactic information, that is, the f-descriptions, are to combine. The lexical form, that is, in PFM the paradigm cell corresponding to a fully inflected word, can be viewed as a simple tree structure in which each attribute is a preterminal node and each value a terminal node – this is captured in (26) where MF is a metavariable over feature labels Num, Case, and so on. For example, the paradigm cell in (24 a) would define a structure as shown schematically in (27) below.

(26) N → Lex MF*

(27)

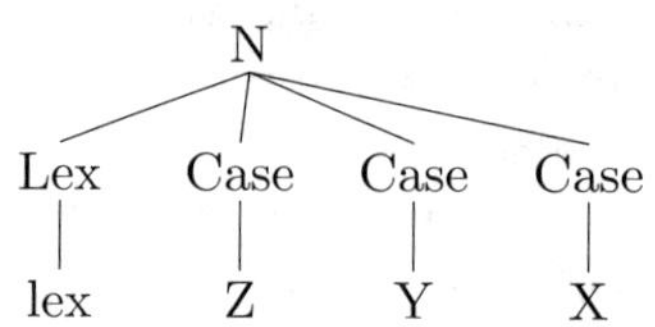

To take an example, we consider the Martuthunira nominal *thara-ngka-marta-a* 'pouch-LOC-PROP-ACC' from example (4). The morphological description is as follows:

(28) <thara, {Case$_C$: Loc, {Case$_C$: Prop, {Case$_C$: Acc}}}>

and the interface tree is represented as in (29) in which morphological feature values are shown as terminal nodes with initial capitalisation.

(29)

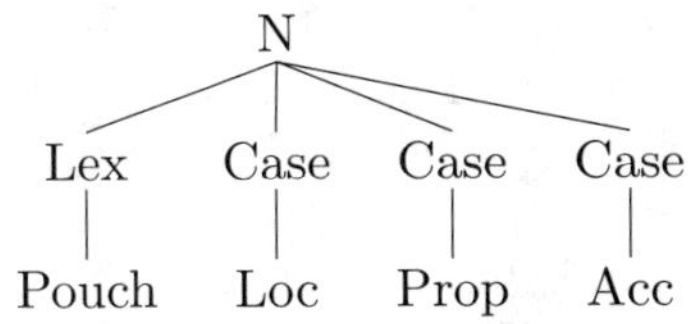

The f-descriptions are associated with the terminal nodes, giving (30):

(30)

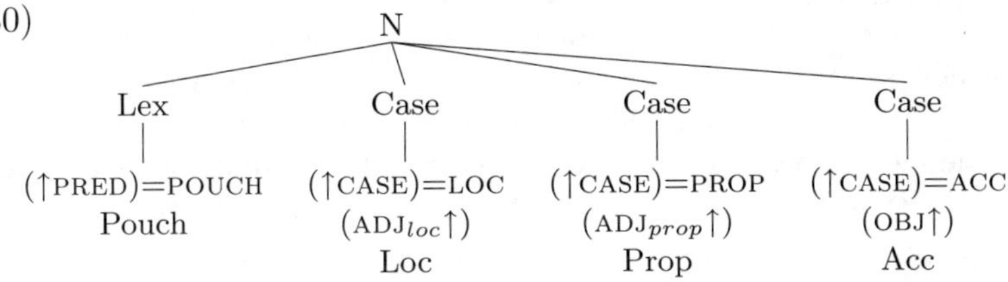

It remains to specify the annotations associated with the pre-terminal tree nodes. The generalization for a language with a constructive case feature, such as Kayardild or Martuthinira, is as follows:

(31) Annotation Principle: For node n, if the immediately preceding left sister node is Case then annotate node n with $\leftarrow_s = (\downarrow \text{GF})$, otherwise annotate with $\uparrow = \downarrow$

The $\leftarrow_s$ appearing here is a notational innovation which we discuss below. Note that the interface grammar does not play a filtering role, rather it is the role of the morphology proper to ensure that only well-formed feature bundles are ever produced, for example by ensuring that Number is never directly embedded under Number, and so forth.

The two operations of the interface, namely lexical look-up and (re-)parsing of the morphological structure, together with the annotation principle, provide the annotated tree-structure shown in (32).

(32)

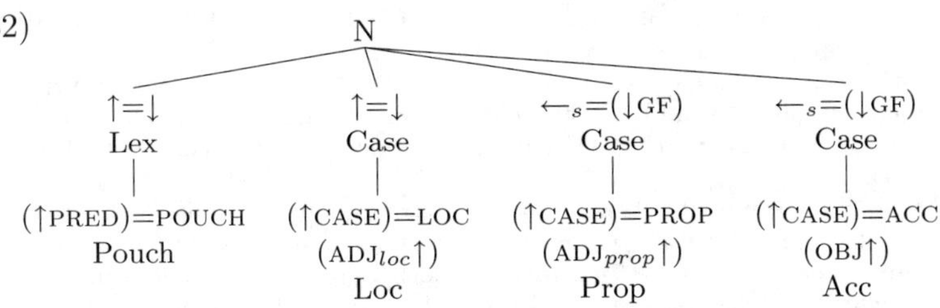

The notational innovation left arrow ($\leftarrow_s$) denotes the f-structure of the immediate *left* sister of the node to which it is attached: that is, while $\uparrow$ denotes the f-structure of the mother node ($\phi(M(*))$) and $\downarrow$ denotes the f-structure of the node to which it is annotated ($\phi(*)$), $\leftarrow_s$ denotes $\phi(LS(*))$, where LS stands for a function which picks out an immediately preceding sister node. Note that $\leftarrow_s$ is distinct from the $\leftarrow$ function used in LFG to refer to the immediately containing f-structure in specifying off-path constraints (Dalrymple 1993),[9] and for this reason we attach an s subscript to the left arrow we use here, $\leftarrow_s$.[10]

6.3.2 Substitution and Simplification

For clarity, we work through the process of constraint simplification and satisfaction for (32) step by step to illustrate what $\leftarrow_s$ does: since this involves multiple Case nodes we label them with subscripts in the tree fragments to improve comprehensibility. The annotations associated with the tree fragment in (33a) define the partial f-structure also shown in (33b).

(33) a.

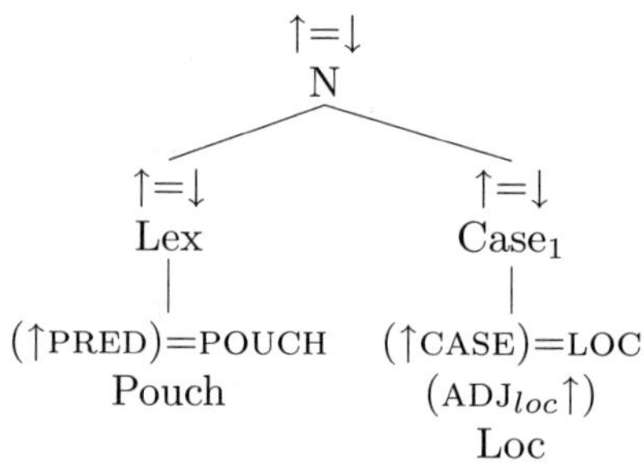

b. $$\left[\text{ADJ}_{loc} \quad {}_{f_1}\!\begin{bmatrix} \text{PRED} & \text{`POUCH'} \\ \text{CASE} & \text{LOC} \end{bmatrix} \right]$$

Continuing through the tree left to right, consider the tree fragment in (34a). The annotation $\leftarrow_s$ on the node Case$_2$ specifies that the f-structure of the sister node (Case$_1$, of which the f-structure is f_1) is the value of some GF in the f-structure (f_2) of the node Case$_2$. Since f_1

[9] Off-path constraints are used especially in the statement of conditions on long distance dependencies and anaphoric dependencies. In this context, $\leftarrow$ associated with an attribute a denotes the f-structure of which a is an attribute (see Dalrymple 2001:151).

[10] It seems very possible that $\leftarrow_s$ will be useful more generally in the description of syntactic phenomena, but we leave this as an open question for future research. A $\leftarrow$ similarly denoting the f-structure of the left adjacent sister node is used in Frank (2003) which is concerned with projection of structures from chunk-based analyses.

is the value of the path ADJ$_{loc}$ (from above), ADJ$_{loc}$ and GF are equated, defining the structure in (34b).

(34) a.

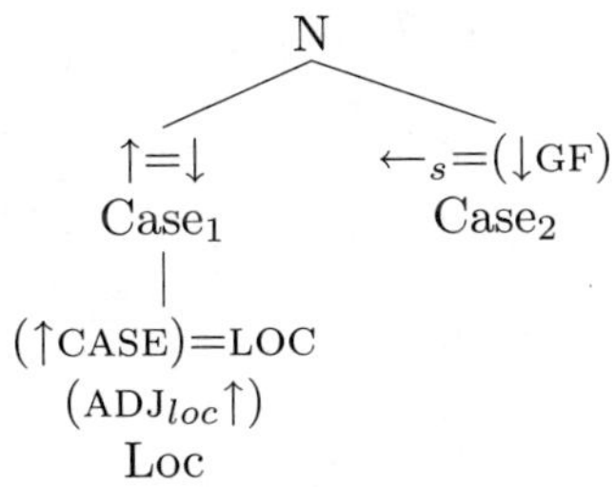

b.

$$f_2\left[\begin{array}{ll}\text{ADJ}_{loc} & f_1\left[\begin{array}{ll}\text{PRED} & \text{`POUCH'}\\ \text{CASE} & \text{LOC}\end{array}\right]\end{array}\right]$$

Substitutions in the rest of the f-descriptions operate in exactly the same fashion. For example, for the next tree fragment, (35a), we know that the f-structure of the Case$_2$ node is f_2. The annotations on the terminal node specify that f_2 is the value of ADJ$_{prop}$ in a larger f-structure and define f_2's own CASE feature as PROP. The annotation $\leftarrow_s$ on the immediate right sister node Case$_3$ specifies that the f-structure of the immediate left sister node (Case$_2$, f-structure f_2) is the value of some GF in the f-structure (f_3) of the node Case$_3$. Since f_2 is the value of the path ADJ$_{prop}$ (from the Case annotations), ADJ$_{prop}$ and GF are equated (35b).

(35) a.

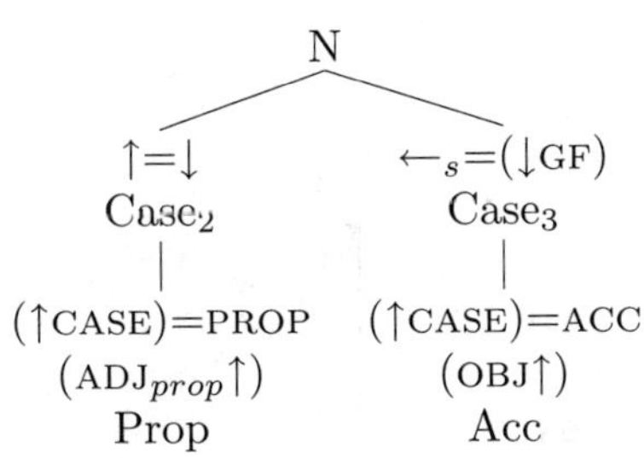

b. Partial f-structure:

$$f_3\left[\begin{array}{ll}\text{ADJ}_{prop} & f_2\left[\begin{array}{ll}\text{CASE} & \text{PROP}\\ \text{ADJ}_{loc} & f_1\left[\begin{array}{ll}\text{PRED} & \text{`POUCH'}\\ \text{CASE} & \text{LOC}\end{array}\right]\end{array}\right]\end{array}\right]$$

The annotations on the terminal node under Case_3 specify that f_3 is the value of OBJ in some larger f-structure and define f_3's own CASE feature as ACC. Thus, the f-descriptions associated with the tree in (32) are satisfied by the following f-structure in the minimal model:

(36)
$$\left[\begin{array}{ll} \text{OBJ} & \left[\begin{array}{ll} \text{CASE} & \text{ACC} \\ \text{ADJ}_{prop} & \left[\begin{array}{ll} \text{CASE} & \text{PROP} \\ \text{ADJ}_{loc} & \left[\begin{array}{ll} \text{PRED} & \text{`POUCH'} \\ \text{CASE} & \text{LOC} \end{array}\right] \end{array}\right] \end{array}\right] \end{array}\right]$$

Turning now to a second example, this time involving the interaction of case and number marking, the morphological description for the Kayardild nominal in (8) is as shown in (37).

(37) <maku, {Num: Du, {Case_C: Assoc, {Case_C: Abl, {Num: Many, {Case_C: Nom}}}}}>

The two operations of the interface, namely lexical look-up and (re-)parsing of the paradigm cell structure, provide the annotated tree-structure (38).

(38)

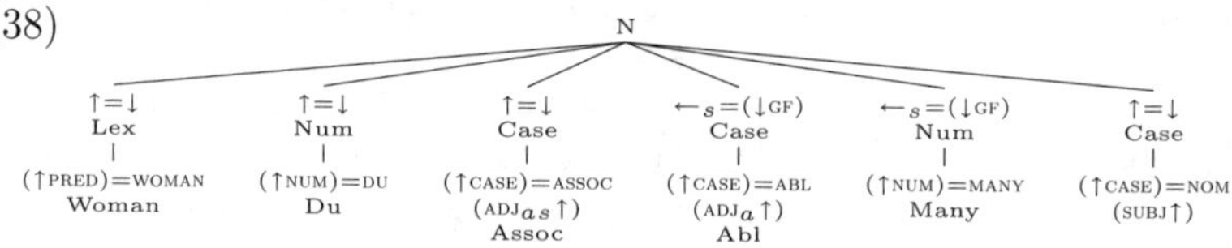

These f-descriptions are satisfied by the structure in (39).

(39)
$$\left[\begin{array}{ll} \text{SUBJ} & \left[\begin{array}{ll} \text{CASE} & \text{NOM} \\ \text{NUM} & \text{MANY} \\ \text{ADJ}_{abl} & \left[\begin{array}{ll} \text{CASE} & \text{ABL} \\ \text{ADJ}_{assoc} & \left[\begin{array}{ll} \text{CASE} & \text{ASSOC} \\ \text{PRED} & \text{`WOMAN'} \\ \text{NUM} & \text{DU} \end{array}\right] \end{array}\right] \end{array}\right] \end{array}\right]$$

6.3.3 Constructive Stems Revisited

We turn now to the treatment of constructive stems. These are the cases, exemplified by (18) and (19), in which the root itself introduces a grammatical function. This is very frequently the ADJ function, as in (18), for there is generally no syntactic distinction in Australian languages between nouns and adjectives, with most nominal elements functioning as either heads or modifiers. As noted above, we follow Nordlinger (1998) in assuming that such nominal roots in the languages we are concerned with optionally introduce an adjunct function. Other examples of constructive stems include Wambaya possessive pronouns, exemplified in (19), which introduce the POSS function. The lexical mappings which we propose treat such stems as optionally introducing a grammatical function, as shown in (40).

(40)

Lexemes	F-description
small:	$\{\{(\uparrow \text{ADJ}) = \downarrow \ \wedge (\downarrow \text{PRED}) = \text{‘SMALL’}\} \vee$
	$\{(\uparrow \text{PRED}) = \text{‘SMALL’}\}\}$
his:	$(\uparrow \text{POSS}) = \downarrow, (\downarrow \text{PRED}) = \text{‘PRO’}$
	$(\downarrow \text{PERS}) = 3, (\downarrow \text{GEN}) = \text{MASC}, (\downarrow \text{NUM}) = \text{SG}$

We illustrate the approach with the Warlpiri modifier *wita-jarra-rlu* ‘small-DU-ERG’ from (18), in which the root constructs an ADJ function and the nominal contributes NUM and CASE features to the f-structure of the head which it modifies. The relevant structures are shown below.

(41) <wita, {Num: Du, {Case$_C$: Erg}}>

(42) a.

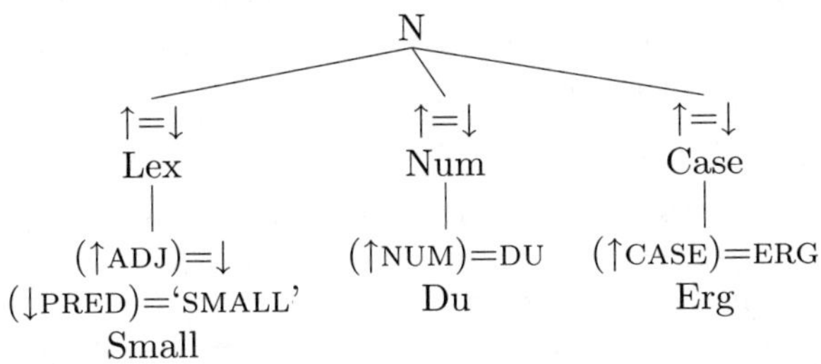

b. $\begin{bmatrix} \text{CASE} & \text{ERG} \\ \text{NUM} & \text{DU} \\ \text{ADJ} & \begin{bmatrix} \text{PRED} & \text{‘SMALL’} \end{bmatrix} \end{bmatrix}$

Notice that the treatment of constructive stems under this proposal differs in one respect from the treatment proposed in Nordlinger (1998). In the earlier account, constructive stems were associated with inside-out descriptions (and thus were treated on a par with constructive case morphology). The difference can be seen by comparing (43a) (from Nordlinger 1998) with (43b) (from the present analysis).

(43) a. *wita*: $(\uparrow \text{PRED}) = \text{‘SMALL’}$
$(\text{ADJ} \uparrow)$

b. *wita*: (↓ PRED) = 'SMALL'
(↑ ADJ) = ↓

Under the proposal made here, therefore, the f-structure projected by the fully inflected word *wita-jarra-rlu* is the f-structure of the head that *wita-* itself modifies.

As an alternative to the current proposal we might instead consider dealing with constructive stems by introducing a morphological feature into the feature bundle with no exponent. For example, for the Warlpiri adjunct *wita-jarra-rlu* we would introduce a Case feature (with no corresponding exponent) at the top of the feature bundle, which would map to an ADJ function, and for the Wambaya possessive pronoun *nangi-marnda-rna* 3.SG.M.POSS-PL-II(ACC) we would introduce a Case feature (with no corresponding exponent) which would map to a POSS function. This approach would certainly reduce the set of constructive roots to instances of constructive inflectional morphology, but it seems otherwise to be incorrect. Firstly, the functional ambiguity of nominals in a language such as Warlpiri is quite systematic and is simply not dependent on morphological case. Secondly, this approach would make the incorrect claim that those languages which have constructive roots necessarily permit case stacking — this claim is incorrect for some languages, including Wambaya. For these reasons, we do not pursue here this alternative approach.[11]

6.3.4 Evaluation

This section has outlined a new proposal for associating f-descriptions with morphological structures. The approach to the morphology-syntax interface involves deriving a simple flat tree structure from the structured morphological representation. The nodes of this morphological structure tree are annotated with f-descriptions in a familiar fashion,

[11] The approach that we take here to constructive stems shows some commonality with the treatment of *derivational* case morphology. It can be established that in some Australian languages some case morphology is derivational rather than inflectional, producing an inflectional stem which defines its own grammatical function (see, for example, Austin 1995, Nordlinger 1998). For example, in Wambaya, which does not permit inflectional case stacking, the cases PROP and PRIV are derivational while other cases are inflectional. In an example such as (11), the derivational morphology produces the root *gijilulunguj*, which is constructive, introducing an ADJ function.

(i)	Yandu	ngi-n	bungmaj-buli-ja	gijilulu-nguj-nuli-ja.
	wait	1.SG.S(PRES)-PROG	old.person-DU-DAT	money-PROP-DU-DAT

I'm waiting for the two old women with money. (Nordlinger 1998:115 (41))

and the resultant equations simplified. The major advantage of this approach over the morpheme-based PMC of Nordlinger (1998) is that, with the exception of a modest notational extension to the language of f-descriptions, it uses the standard LFG formalism with no consequences for the formal power of the language. No pattern matching subsitutions are required because the morphological tree is not based on incremental affixation in morphemic fashion.

From a linguistic point of view, however, the fundamental issue is the extent to which this proposal for the interface captures the basic intuition about constructive morphology. This intuition is the idea that (at least in these languages), morphological and syntactic structures (of the appropriate sorts) are nested or hierarchicalized isomorphically; the syntactic contribution of a particular affix "builds" on that of the (perhaps complex) stem to which it attaches. This intuition is captured in the original PMC formulation by the incremental transformation or substitution into the f-description of a higher piece of morphological structure as a function of the (input from the) f-description of the immediately lower or contained piece of morphological structure/affix. Although not formalized, the substitution is stated in such a manner as to apply invariantly to both constructive and non-constructive morphological features (that is, irrespective of whether or not the f-description contains an inside-out statement). Thus, the syntactic ramifications of a morphosyntactic feature follows purely from the f-descriptions associated with it (namely, whether or not it constructs a grammatical function), and not from the morphosyntactic structure (which remains the same irrespective).

In the current approach, however, a distinction between constructive and non-constructive features is also made in the Annotation Principle (31): the presence of a constructive feature (Case) triggers the $\leftarrow_s =$ ($\downarrow$ GF) annotation on its right sister, while a node following any other category is annotated $\uparrow = \downarrow$. Thus the distinction between constructive and non-constructive features is made twice: in the f-descriptions introduced on terminal and on non-terminal nodes in the mapping structure. While this might be thought to be a disadvantage, it should be noted that the present proposal, which limits the permissible annotations to $\uparrow = \downarrow$ and $\leftarrow_s =$ ($\downarrow$ GF), does rule out anti-iconic relations between morphological features and f-structures, as does Nordlinger's original proposal.[12] Therefore, while the current approach may not have the

[12] It could be argued, however, that in any case a restriction to iconic ordering should be given a functional rather than a grammatical explanation, and therefore should not form a part of the grammar. Whether or not this position is adopted, it remains a fact that the grammar must be able to accommodate the complex

generality of Nordlinger's (1998) PMC it has the same empirical adequacy and, furthermore, is straightforwardly integrated into the standard LFG architecture.

6.4 Conclusion

In most instances, the inflectional features of words define or reflect properties of the very local context — verbs express the tense, aspect and mood features of the clauses which they head, and encode agreement properties of their dependent core arguments, and nouns, adjectives and determiners inflect for properties such as the number, gender and definiteness of the nominal f-structure which they co-define. The phenomenon of case stacking in Australian Aboriginal languages, however, shows that inflectional morphology may express syntactic information pertaining to a much larger context, with words expressing functional information pertaining to f-structures within which their own f-structures are deeply embedded. Furthermore, the association of wider syntactic information with "pieces" of inflectional morphology comes about in a highly structured manner. The importance of this data is that it provides a crucial window onto the nature of the interface between inflectional morphology and functional structure: the f-structure information associated with inflectional morphology must interact in a structured way. For these languages, associating f-descriptions with the sort of morphological structure assumed by a word-syntactic, morphemic model gives the wrong result, because the f-descriptions interact incorrectly. On the other hand, given an approach to inflectional morphology which relates structured property sets to exponents, the correct interaction between f-descriptions associated with morphological features can be obtained by representing morphological structures *in the interface* as relatively flat trees, and associating and resolving f-descriptions associated with tree nodes in the normal fashion, even for languages with complex case stacking morphology of this sort. The present proposal therefore permits us to interface a realizational approach to inflectional morphology with a standard LFG syntax in a straightforward manner.

References

Ackerman, Farrell. 1990. The Morphological Blocking Principle and Oblique Pronominal Incorporation in Hungarian. In K. Dziwirek, P. Farrell, and E. Mejías-Bikandi, eds., *Grammatical Relations: A Cross-Theoretical Perspective*, pages 1–20. Stanford, CA: CSLI Publications.

contributions to relational structure that the case stacking data exemplify.

Andrews, Avery. 1996. Semantic case-stacking and inside-out unification. *Australian Journal of Linguistics* 16:1–55.

Austin, Peter. 1995. Double Case Marking in Kanyara and Mantharta Languages, Western Australia. In F. Plank, ed., *Double Case: Agreement by Suffixaufnahme*, pages 363–79. Oxford: Oxford University Press.

Austin, Peter and Joan Bresnan. 1996. Non-configurationality in Australian Aboriginal langauges. *Natural Language and Linguistic Theory* 14:215–268.

Barron, Julia. 1998. 'have' contraction: explaining 'trace effects' in a theory without movement. *Linguistics* 36:223–251.

Borjars, Kersti, Nigel Vincent, and Carol Chapman. 1997. Paradigms, Periphrasis and Pronominal Inflection: a feature-based account. In G. Booij and J. van Marle, eds., *Yearbook of Morphology 1996*, pages 155–180. Cambridge, MA: Kluwer Academic Publishers.

Bresnan, Joan. 2001. *Lexical Functional Syntax*. Oxford: Blackwell.

Butt, Miriam. 1995. *The Structure of Complex Predicates in Urdu*. Stanford, CA: CSLI Publications.

Butt, Miriam, Tracy Holloway King, Maria-Eugenia Nino, and Frédérique Segond. 1999. *A Grammar Writer's Cookbook*. Stanford, CA: CSLI Publications.

Butt, Miriam, María-Eugenia Niño, and Frédérique Segond. 1996. Multilingual Processing of Auxiliaries in LFG. In D. Gibbon, ed., *Natural Language Processing and Speech Technology*, pages 111–122. Mouton de Gruyter. Also reprinted in this volume.

Culy, Chris. 1990. *The Syntax and Semantics of Internally-headed Relative Clauses*. Ph.D. thesis, Stanford University, Stanford, CA.

Dalrymple, Mary. 1993. *The Syntax of Anaphoric Binding*. Stanford,CA: CSLI Publications.

Dalrymple, Mary. 2001. *Lexical Functional Grammar*, vol. 34 of *Syntax and Semantics*. San Diego: Academic Press.

Dench, Alan. 1995a. *Martuthunira. a language of the Pilbara Region of Western Australia*. Canberra: Pacific Linguistics.

Dench, Alan. 1995b. Suffixaufnahme and Apparent Ellipsis in Martuthunira. In Frans Plank, ed., *Double Case: Agreement by Suffixaufnahme*, pages 380–95. Oxford: Oxford University Press.

Dench, Alan and Nick Evans. 1988. Multiple Case-Marking in Australian Languages. *Australian Journal of Linguistics* 8:1–47.

Evans, Nicholas. 1995a. *A Grammar of Kayardild: With Historical-Comparative Notes on Tangkic*. Berlin: Mouton de Gruyter.

Evans, Nick. 1995b. Multiple Case in Kayardild: Anti-iconic Suffix ordering and the Diachronic Filter. In Frans Plank, ed., *Double Case: Agreement by Suffixaufnahme*, pages 396–428. Oxford: Oxford University Press.

Frank, Anette. 2003. Projecting LFG F-structures from Chunks. In M. Butt and T. H. King, eds., *Proceedings of LFG 2003*. CSLI Publications, Stanford, CA.

Frank, Anette and Annie Zaenen. 2002. Tense in LFG: Syntax and Morphology. In H. Kamp and U. Reyle, eds., *How we say WHEN it happens*, pages 17–53. Niemeyer.

Halvorsen, Per-Kristian and Ronald M. Kaplan. 1988. Projections and Semantic Description in Lexical-Functional Grammar. In *Proceedings of the International Conference on Fifth Generation Computer Systems*, pages 1116–1122. Tokyo.

Kaplan, Ron and Miriam Butt. 2002. The Morphology-Syntax Interface in LFG. Unpublished handout, LFG 2002.

Kaplan, Ron and Paula Newman. 1997. Lexical Resource Reconciliation in the Xerox Linguistic Environment. In D. Estival, A. Lavelli, K. Netter, and F. Pianesi, eds., *Proceedings of the ACL Workshop on Computational Environments for Grammar Development and Linguistic Engineering*, pages 54–61. Madrid.

King, Tracy Holloway. 1995. *Configuring Topic and Focus in Russian*. Stanford: CSLI Publications.

Lee, Hanjung. 1999. The domain of grammatical case in Lexical Functional Grammar. In M. Butt and T. H. King, eds., *Proceedings of the LFG99 Conference*. Stanford, CA: CSLI Publications.

Lee, Hanjung. 2002. A Lexicalist OT Approach to Case. Unpublished ms., UNC.

Nordlinger, Rachel. 1998. *Constructive Case: Evidence from Australian Languages*. Stanford: CSLI.

Nordlinger, Rachel. 2000. Australian Case Systems: Towards a Constructive Solution. In Miriam Butt and Tracy Holloway King, ed., *Argument Realization*, pages 41–72. Stanford: CSLI.

Nordlinger, Rachel and Louisa Sadler. 2000. Tense as a Nominal Category. In M. Butt and T. H. King, eds., *Proceedings of the LFG 2000 Conference*. CSLI Publications.

O'Connor, Rob. 2002. Clitics and Phrasal Affixation in Constructive Morphology. In M. Butt and T. H. King, eds., *Proceedings of the LFG02 Conference*. Stanford, CA: CSLI Publications.

Ørsnes, Bjarne. 2002. Case marking and subject extraction in Danish. In M. Butt and T. H. King, eds., *Proceedings of the LFG02 Conference*. Stanford, CA: CSLI Publications.

Sadler, Louisa. 1997. Clitics and the structure-function mapping. In M. Butt and T. H. King, eds., *Proceedings of LFG97*. CSLI Publications, Stanford.

Sadler, Louisa. 1998. English Auxiliaries as Tense Inflections. *Essex Research Reports in Linguistics* 24:1–16.

Sadler, Louisa and Rachel Nordlinger. to appear. Case Stacking in Realizational Morphology. University of Melbourne and the University of Essex. Under review.

Sadler, Louisa and Andrew Spencer. 2001. Syntax as an exponent of morphological features. In G. Booij and J. van Marle, eds., *Yearbook of Morphology 2000*, pages 71–97. Kluwer Academic Publishers.

Sells, Peter. 2000. Postposing in Japanese. In *Selected Papers from AILA 1999*, pages 427–442. Waseda University Press, Tokyo.

Sells, Peter. this volume. Syntactic Information and its Morphological Expression.

Sharma, Devyani. 1999. Nominal clitics and constructive morphology in Hindi. In M. Butt and T. H. King, eds., *Proceedings of the LFG99 Conference*. Stanford, CA: CSLI Publications.

Simpson, Jane. 1983. *Aspects of Warlpiri Morphology and Syntax*. Ph.D. thesis, Massachusetts Institute of Technology.

Simpson, Jane. 1991. *Warlpiri Morpho-Syntax*. Dordrecht: Kluwer Academic Publishers.

Spencer, Andrew. this volume. Morphology – an overview of central concepts.

Spencer, Andrew. to appear. Paradigm-based Lexicalism: Negation in Japanese. In Farrell Ackerman and Jim Blevins and Gregory Stump, ed., *Paradigms and Periphrases*. Stanford, CA: CSLI Publications.

Stump, Gregory. 2001. *Inflectional Morphology: A Theory of Paradigm Structure*. Cambridge: Cambridge University Press.

7

Syntactic Information and its Morphological Expression

PETER SELLS

7.1 Introduction

In this paper I will look at some instances of apparent mismatch between the actual morphological forms of verbs and the intuitive syntactic and semantic content of those verbs. In the case I will focus on, a piece of the grammatical content in a clause is multiply-marked on verbal forms in the clause. Having established the phenomenon in question, I concentrate mainly on an analysis of representative examples from Swedish, and consider the theoretical implications of the analysis for the relation between syntactic features and the morphological expression of those features.[1]

The view of the relation between syntactic features and their morphological expression that we will come to is a 'realizational' approach, where syntactic features are given in some structure, with principles governing the realized expression of those features in the forms of the

[1]I am grateful to Joan Bresnan for initial discussion of the theoretical approach laid out here. For help in collecting and analyzing the Swedish data, I am indebted to Elisabet Engdahl and Benjamin Lyngfelt. Helge Lødrup helped me understand the complexity of the data presented here, though the analysis falls short of what is required, and Jerry Sadock made other useful suggestions about the phenomenon of multiple exponence. A preliminary version was presented at the Memorial Workshop for Steven Lapointe, at the University of California, Davis, in April 2000, and an expanded version was presented at the September 2000 meeting of the LAGB at the University of Durham. This final version has been improved greatly due to comments from Louisa Sadler and Andrew Spencer.

Projecting Morphology.
Louisa Sadler and Andrew Spencer (Eds.).

language. This contrasts with the 'morphemic' view, where the forms are associated with syntactic features and project them into an agglomerated syntactic structure. I will use the specific formalism of Lexical-Functional Grammar (LFG; Bresnan (1982), Bresnan (2001)) to provide a relatively concrete framework, taking advantage of some features of Optimality-Theoretic LFG (OT-LFG; Bresnan (2000), Kuhn (2001a)), and will show how recent theoretical developments in this approach put the issue of the relation between syntactic features and their morphological expression in a new light.

7.2 Multiple Exponence In Syntax

Swedish, the language I will focus on here, shows various instances of multiple or apparently parasitic marking of inflectional information. I will refer to this as 'multiple exponence'.[2] The first illustration of this is that it is possible to topicalize a finite verb within a finite V2 clause, in which case the supporting verb *göra* ('do') is brought in, also in its finite form, as in (1). Hence, this is an example where the grammatical information that the clause is present tense is apparently expressed twice.

(1) Skriver gör han sällan.
write.Pres do.Pres he seldom
'He seldom WRITES.'

In order for us to have a good understanding of the relationship between syntactic features and their expression, it is important to be somewhat more specific about the verbal inflectional features in Swedish, of which the relevant ones are shown in (1).[3]

[2]The term 'multiple exponence' derives from the work of Matthews (1972) and Matthews (1974), where it is used to refer to a situation where one piece of grammatical information is realized by more than one discontinous segmental part, possibly distinct in form from each other. I follow the work of Niño (1995, 1997) in extending the usage to cases where (essentially) the same segmental material appears on different words in the same clause. My thanks to Andrew Spencer for discussion of the morphologists' view of the term 'multiple exponence'.

[3]For a more thorough overview of the facts, see e.g., Holmes and Hinchliffe (1994, 248ff.).

(2) **Swedish inflectional forms:**

Inflection	*Example* ('read')	*Comment*
Present	*läser*	morphologically finite
Past	*läste*	morphologically finite
Imperative	*läs*	
Infinitive	*läsa*	morphologically unmarked (Base form)
Supine	*läst*	used like the perfect participle in English

All forms except the Imperative can have a Passive in *-s*.

The present and past forms are the only tense inflected forms; there is no future form, for example. There is also no person-number agreement in Swedish (see Holmberg and Platzack (1995)). The imperative and infinitive are distinct forms, and there is reason to believe that the infinitive is really the reflex of the absence of any positively-specified features, and the least marked form in the language—the evidence will emerge below (sections 7.5.3 and 7.5.4). For this reason, I will refer to the traditional infinitive form, as shown in (2), as the 'Base' form. The supine form ends with a *-t*, and it participates with the auxiliary *ha* ('have') in the perfective construction, doing the duty of the perfect participle in English. Swedish also has a form called the 'perfect participle', morphologically distinct from the supine; this participle essentially only has adjectival or adjunct uses, as does the progressive participle.[4] These forms are not listed in (2) as they are not relevant to the issues discussed here.

Additionally, four out of the five forms in (2) have a lexical passive, formed with the suffix *-s*; Swedish also has a phrasal passive involving *blir* ('become'). As an inflectional form, the *-s* passive will figure in the discussion below.

Getting back to the main theme of multiple exponence, Swedish has what has been called the 'parasitic supine'. Here, an embedded base form of the verb can be replaced by the supine form, if there is a higher governing supine form (Wiklund (1998), Wiklund (2001)); the examples in (3) are surface variants, though the parasitic forms are more common in speech than in writing.

(3) a. Han skulle ha kunnat göra det.
he would have be.able.Sup do.Base it
'He would have been able to do it.'

[4]As discussed in Platzack (1989), Swedish is the only (Germanic) language which shows different properties for the form used after *ha* (namely, the supine) and the perfect participle.

b. Han skulle ha kunnat gjort det.
he would have be.able.Sup do.Sup it

In (3), the base complement to the supine form *kunnat* (in a) can itself be in the supine form (the alternative expression in b). This is truly a parasitic construction, for it only occurs in the complement of a supine verb, as seen in the contrast in (4): in the b example, the lack of a higher governing supine form means that the lower form cannot be supine, but rather only the base form.

(4) a. Han har velat läsa/läst den.
he has want.Sup read.Base/read.Sup it
'He wanted to read it.'

b. Han vill läsa/*läst den.
he want.Pres read.Base/*read.Sup it
'He wants to read it.'

Wiklund (2001) presents an analysis of the parasitic supine, using a syntactic derivation with feature copying (from a supine onto an infinitive), under a Distributed Morphology approach: the syntax manipulates abstract grammatical features, and then these are spelled out by overt forms. In this way, the parasitic supine is a kind of surface camouflage: it does not represent the true grammatical featural content of the verbs where its expression is parasitic. Details aside, the important observation from Wiklund's work is that there is a specific domain in which the copying operation that leads to parasitic morphology takes place: she argues that the copying domain is a (supine) verb and its 'restructuring' complement. That is, there must be a very tight syntactic and semantic relation between a supine verb and its base-form complement if the supine features of the higher verb are to be 'copied' onto the lower verb, and in some sense the domain of the copying of information is a single clause. Wiklund argues that restructuring complements are partially underspecified in terms of syntactic features, and the missing pieces of information are filled in from the governing clause.

'Restructuring' is the term proposed in Rizzi (1978) for the process of clause-collapsing or clause-union deriving a monoclausal surface structure from an underlying biclausal structure.[5] In the case of 'want', the standard LFG analysis would have this verb selecting for SUBJ and XCOMP grammatical functions, where the XCOMP would provide a separate f-structure nucleus (e.g., the 'read it' part in the examples in (4)). If 'want' is analyzed instead as a restructuring verb, this means that the

[5]Wurmbrand (2001) offers a recent summary of (transformational) approaches to restructuring.

complement no longer constitutes a separate domain, but rather that the semantic predication in the clause is the single complex predicate 'want-read'. The formal analysis of this is given below in section 7.5.2.

The parasitic supine phenomenon can be considered part of a more general surface 'verb-verb agreement' in Swedish, documented by Anward (1988).[6] Other parasitic morphology can include the spread of the imperative shown in (5) (from Anward) and the apparently upwards copying of passive information in (6) (from Hedlund (1992, 131)).[7] Each of the b forms are common in colloquial varieties.

(5) a. Våga väga dig!
dare.Imp weigh.Base yourself
'Dare to weigh yourself!'

b. Våga väg dig!
dare.Imp weigh.Imp yourself

(6) a. Gräset behöver klippas.
the.grass need.Pres cut.Base.Pass
'The grass needs to be cut.'

b. Gräset behövs klippas.
the.grass need.Pres.Pass cut.Base.Pass

Elisabet Engdahl, p.c., points out that examples like (7) with an impersonal subject are quite common:

(7) Det behöver/behövs forskas mer om
it need.Pres/need.Pres.Pass research.Base.Pass more about
detta.
this
'There needs to be more research on this.'

These examples with passive require further (empirical) research; it is possible that at least some of them do involve passivization of the higher predicate (e.g., 'need'), as such predicates seem to allow transitive basic uses in the Scandinavian languages (as observed in Lødrup (1996)).

Finally, Niño (1995, 1997) has documented a range of similar cases of multiple exponence, with a detailed description and analysis of several

[6]However, the analysis I offer here, namely spreading to the correspondents of a single f-structure nucleus, probably does not cover all of the cases of multiple exponence that Anward documents. Helge Lødrup (p.c.) also observes that there may be examples in Scandinavian involving parasitic supines beyond the domain characterized here by 'restructuring'.

[7]The passive examples seem to have counterparts in Norwegian; see Christensen (1991).

instances from Finnish (simple examples here in (8) and (9)), as well as illustrative examples from other languages, such as the Dagaare serial verb construction in (10).

(8) Äl-kää puhu-ko. Finnish
Neg.Imp-Imp.2.Pl speak-Imp
'Don't (you pl.) speak!'

(9) a. Ei ol-lut sano-ttu
Neg.3.Sg Perf-Ppart.Sg say-Pass.Ppart.Sg
'It has not been said.'

b. Ei ol-ttu sano-ttu Finnish
Neg.3.Sg Perf-Pass.Ppart.Sg say-Pass.Ppart.Sg
'It has not been said.'

(10) Ayuo da zo-ro gɛ-rɛ wuo-ro la Dagaare
Ayou Past run-Prog go-Prog collect-Prog Affirm
haani di-rɛ.
blackberries eat-Prog
'Ayuo was running-going-collecting-eating blackberries (repeatedly).'

Other cases of apparent multiple exponence can be found in Faroese (see Wiklund (2001) and Barnes and Weyhe (1994, 211)) and Lithuanian (see Ambrazas (1997, 284)).

Examples of syntactic multiple exponence are not infrequent, and call for analysis. Returning to a simple parasitic supine example like (3b), the question for us is, how does the same piece of inflectional morphology get to be in several different places in the clause? On a morpheme-based view, somehow the information associated with one morpheme or word must get copied or otherwise spread around onto other words, and this seems quite a strange thing to have happen. I will take up this theoretical problem in the rest of the paper, which is organized as follows. Section 7.3 lays out an existing analysis of multiple exponence in LFG. Sections 7.4 and 7.5 introduce a realizational approach, using ideas from OT. First, section 7.4 presents two kinds of constructional realization, which form the heart of the empirical argument for the realizational approach. Section 7.5 develops an OT-approach to a realizational model.

7.3 Multiple Exponence In LFG

There is an existing account of multiple exponence in LFG, due to Niño (1997). Simply put, the basis of the account is that multiple expressions of the same information can unify, if they are contributing to the same clausal nucleus. More formally, any node annotated '$\uparrow=\downarrow$' contributes its information directly to the clausal f-structure, and there may be many such nodes in a single clause. Let us look at Niño's account of multiple exponence, using the Dagaare example in (10) above. The key to her approach is that different X^0 heads (annotated with $\uparrow=\downarrow$) all contribute to the same f-structure nucleus, and so it follows that in principle, multiple expression of that f-structure information will be possible just in case there are multiple c-structure correspondents of the same nucleus, as is the case with sequences of auxiliary and main verbs, verbs and 'restructured' complements, or serial verb constructions—in other words, with any kind of complex predicate which is monoclausal at f-structure (on these properties, see Alsina (1993, 1997), Butt (1995) and Matsumoto (1996)). Using the $\uparrow=_H\downarrow$ notation from Alsina's work to express the unification of predicates in the Dagaare serial verb construction, Niño gives the LFG analysis in (11), for the example in (10). For my purposes here the notation '$\uparrow=_H\downarrow$' can be considered equivalent to '$\uparrow=\downarrow$'.[8]

[8] The difference between $\uparrow=\downarrow$ and $\uparrow=_H\downarrow$ is that $\uparrow=\downarrow$ represents simple unification, while $\uparrow=_H\downarrow$ represents composition of predicate values, and unification of all other features.

(11) Ayuo da zo-ro gɛ-rɛ wuo-ro la
Ayou Past run-Prog go-Prog collect-Prog Affirm
haani di-rɛ.
blackberries eat-Prog
'Ayuo was running-going-collecting-eating blackberries (repeatedly).'

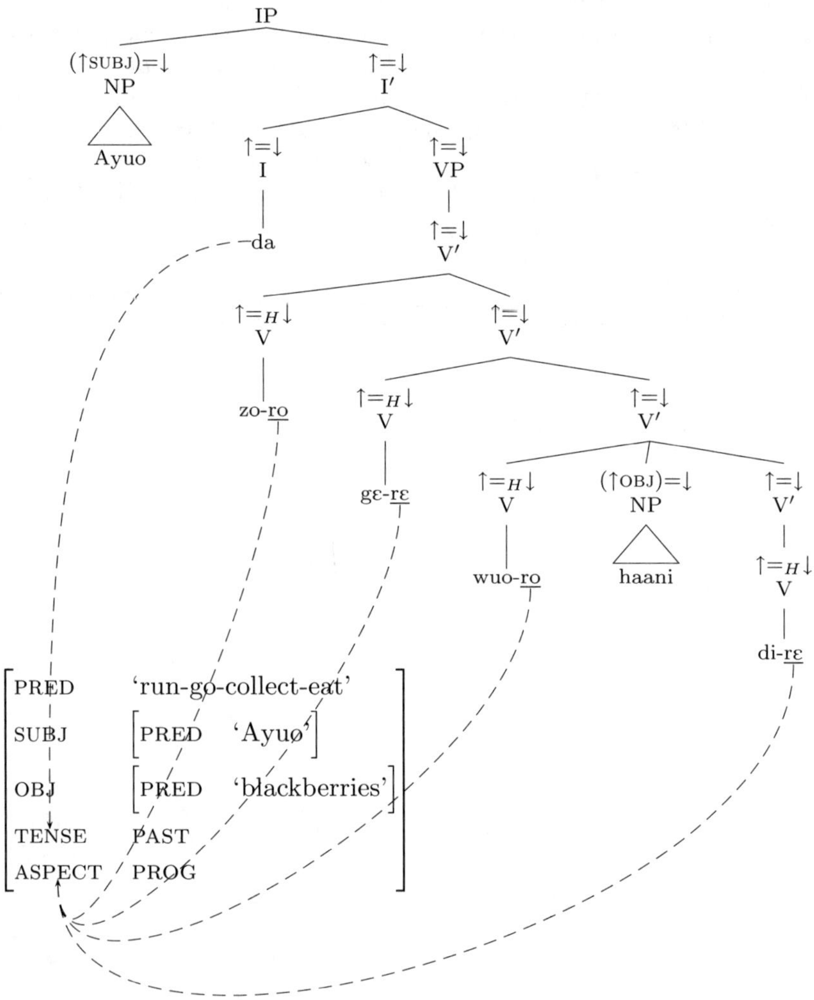

In (11), each V carries the information about progressive aspect, assuming a morphemic entry like that shown in (12).

(12) Dagaare progressive morpheme:
-ro/*-rɛ* Aff (↑ASPECT)=PROG

To aid the reader, the progressive marker is underlined in the c-structure in (11). As all of the Vs contribute to the same nucleus, the information simply unifies, as indicated by the several arrows pointing to the same f-structure attribute-value pair. In contrast, the past tense marker appears just once, but nevertheless corresponds to an f-structure attribute and its value.

An open question on this view is why all verbs are marked this way—for example, the same f-structure would correspond to a c-structure with the aspectual information on just the first and last Vs, or just on every other V. (One possible response here is that each verb needs an inflectional ending, as a morphological requirement, and that any ending other than progressive would fail to unify, if one V has to be marked for progressive. This issue will be taken up below (section 7.5.3).) The problem is more serious for the multiple expression of passive morphology seen above, for the passive morpheme is usually correlated with a change in argument-function linking, but it is far from clear that more than one verb is 'passivized' in such examples as those in (6), (7) and (9b).

7.4 Constructional Expression

The key empirical observations which drive the style of analysis in this paper involve the constructional expression of clausal information, where it is difficult at best to associate the clausal information with just one node in the structure (a node hosting a morpheme with the right properties). In this section, I present two constructions in Swedish grammar which seem to call for a realizational analysis.[9]

7.4.1 Periphrastic Expressions of Tense and Aspect

The first construction type is the familiar case of auxiliary plus participle, expressing tense or aspect; I discuss these cases briefly, followed by the treatment of auxiliary verbs in LFG that I will adopt, and then consider the more formal aspects of auxiliary constructions.

Periphrastic Tense and Aspect

Sadler and Spencer (2001, 85ff.) discuss the Latin example in (13) in the context of developing the model of LFG morphosyntax in which morphological forms are the expression of abstract information (see also

[9]Bresnan (2001, 134ff.) gives a morpheme-based analysis of a situation of split expression of tense in Wambaya, which she terms 'distributed exponence'. This case may also be a candidate for a constructional analysis.

Ackerman and Webelhuth (1998), and especially Ackerman (2000)). These works all fall into the class of realizational approaches to morphology, stated in most depth and detail in Stump (2001).[10]

(13) Clodia laudata est. Latin
Clodia praise.Part.Fem.Nom.Sg be.Pres
'Clodia was/has been praised.'

Similar facts obtain with the supine in Swedish, though I did not remark on them above. The supine form with *har* is ambiguous between a simple past reading and a perfective reading (see, for example, Holmes and Hinchliffe (1994, 279ff.) or Wiklund (1998)), so (14) has either of the two interpretations shown.

(14) Allan har ätit frukost.
Allan have.Pres eat.Sup breakfast
'Allan ate/has eaten breakfast.'

Adverbs and context can favor the simple past or the perfective interpretation, but the grammar provides both.

Sadler and Spencer (hereafter: SS) observe that the Latin example in (13) has a simple past interpretation, but that the syntactic specification TENSE PAST has a morpho-syntactic expression as a present perfective. This is a problem for a morpheme-based accounts, as somehow we have to make 'present' and 'participle' into 'past'.[11] Looking at these issues slightly more broadly, Spencer (2001) argues that periphrastic constructions must be allowed as the exponents of cells in morphological paradigms, alongside morphological (single-word) exponents. Ackerman (2000) and Blevins (2002) make similar arguments. What is crucial here is that the exponent is constructional—it is syntactically complex, but it cannot be said that either part of the construction is directly carrying the relevant f-structure information (see Ackerman and Webelhuth (1998)). So, for the case at hand, SS argue for a constructional realization of the TENSE PAST information: the construction means TENSE PAST, but no parts of the construction contain (parts of) that information.

The LFG Analysis of Auxiliary Verbs

The correct analysis of auxiliary verbs in LFG primarily involves considerations of their argument-taking properties (see Dyvik (1999) for recent discussion). The most straightforward analysis takes auxiliaries

[10] Stump's system of Paradigm Function Morphology is reinterpreted in the context of LFG in Nordlinger and Sadler (2002).

[11] The specific problems for LFG-based approaches are discussed in detail in SS and in Brassil (2001).

to be verbs which select for an XCOMP complement (e.g., Kaplan and Bresnan (1982, 206)); for modal auxiliaries which have both a root and an epistemic use, these two uses can be aligned with either a control or raising analysis, respectively (see e.g., Lødrup (1996)). In this kind of account, each verb (auxiliary or non-auxiliary) corresponds to an f-structure nucleus, and therefore has a contentful PRED value. This also allows morphological form features, which may be in conflict, to be in separate nuclei (e.g., it is not possible to unify the inflectional form features of all the verbs in a sequence like *might have been singing*).

However, it is also possible that auxiliaries are functional co-heads with the verbs that are their complements, once morphological features are taken out of f-structure (see e.g., Frank and Zaenen (2002), Butt et al. (1999)). This also allows some auxiliaries to lack a PRED value, if one is not clearly motivated semantically. For the purposes of this paper, I adopt this view, and assume a definition of 'auxiliary verb' that does not extend to a verb which takes an XCOMP complement (see also Bresnan (2001, Part III), Butt et al. (1999, 60ff.), and Falk (2001, 89)). Specifically, in the system of Andrews and Manning (1999) adopted below, auxiliary verbs can be classified into two types, as in (15).

(15) a. the complement verb is a functional co-head with the auxiliary verb

b. the complement verb is an ARG complement of the auxiliary verb

In either case, both auxiliary and main verb map to the same clause nucleus (see section 7.5.2 below), in distinction to an analysis involving an XCOMP. A complement with the ARG function corresponds to a predicate that is semantically embedded under the predicate that selects for it, while directly sharing the grammatical functions of its dependents with the selecting predicate.

The two types in (15) seem to correspond respectively with the sets of properties of epistemic and root uses of modals in Norwegian (and by extension Swedish) discussed in Lødrup (1996) and Dyvik (1999), as they are effectively the analogues of raising and control within true complex predicates in the system developed by Andrews and Manning (1999).

Auxiliary-Verb Constructions

Directly following the ideas in SS, we can begin to describe the Swedish facts of f-structure attribute-value pairs and their morphological expression. The f-structure information is represented as usual with uppercase letters while the morphological information is indicated by capitalized words, with feature and value separated by a colon. First of all, we have to define a certain construction type; in this case, it is a construction consisting of an auxiliary plus a complement verb, which following Blevins (2002) I list as a form of the LEXEME of the auxiliary, plus an inflectional form feature, which will be the distinguishing property of the VP complement of the auxiliary. The construction in (16) is a general part of the syntax of the language in question (e.g., Swedish), which may be co-opted as the periphrastic exponence of some featural specification.

(16) AVC: Auxiliary-Verb Construction
= Head [LEXEME of auxiliary verb],
Complement (opt. specification of Infl.Form)

Head and Complement map to the same clause nucleus.

The construction is defined here differently from the presentation in SS (cf. their (24), p. 89) to take advantage of some of the non-structural features of LFG. The construction defines two c-structure elements (Head and Complement), where the former is some designated lexeme, and the latter may be required to take a specific inflectional form (e.g., Supine). However, as I treat base forms of verbs below as default forms that have no positive specification (for inflectional features), such as *eat* in *will eat*, it is an option of the construction whether the inflectional form of the complement is specified or not.

As just mentioned, Head and Complement in (16) are c-structure elements, whose participation in the construction is then determined by the requirement that they map to the same f-structure clause nucleus, which means that they share all grammatical function information, and this allows for either type of auxiliary in (15).

The c-structure relation between Head and Complement is deliberately left open in (16) due to the flexibility of phrase structure, as seen in the examples in (17):

(17) a. Jag har kysst henne.
I have.Pres kiss.Sup her
'I have kissed her.'

b. Jag har inte kysst henne.
I have.Pres not kiss.Sup her
'I have not kissed her.'

c. Kysst har jag henne inte. (from Holmberg (1999))
kiss.Sup have.Pres I her not
'I have not KISSED her.'

The structural relation between the form of *HA* and the supine is different in each of these examples, yet all of these represent the relevant construction. In LFG, what unifies them is their f-structure relation, which is the same in each case.[12]

Now the expression of ASPECT PERFECT is intuitively the '*HA* + Supine' construction, which is a sub-type of the AVC given in (16). In other words, the predicate types form an inheritance hierarchy of the kind advocated by Ackerman and Webelhuth (1998). The '*HA*+Supine' construction is defined in (18): it involves *HA* and a Supine form, and it inherits the property of an AVC that the two verbs map to the same clause nucleus, while placing the stronger requirement that the complement is a functional co-head:

(18) 'HA+Supine' = $[_{\text{AVC}}$ H: *HA*, C: [Form:Supine]]
C is a functional co-head

This effectively defines *HA* as an auxiliary of type (15a), *in this construction.*

Next, the realizational part of the grammar shows how f-structure information is expressed as (forms of) words and constructions. The relevant realizational 'rules' are shown informally in (19):

(19) a. '*HA*+Supine' $\Leftarrow$ ASPECT PERF
b. '*HA*[Tense:Present]+Supine' $\Leftarrow$ TENSE PAST (+ ASPECT UNMARKED)
c. Tense:Past $\Leftarrow$ TENSE PAST (+ ASPECT UNMARKED)

(19a) is to be read as indicating that the '*HA*+Supine' construction expresses grammatically perfective information; (19b) indicates that past tense information can also be expressed by the same construction, though the *HA* part must be further restricted to its Present form. (19c) offers a morphological alternative: the use of a straightforwardly Past form of a verb to express grammatical past tense.

One highly relevant fact of Swedish syntax is that it allows '*ha*-deletion' in contexts where *ha* is not necessary for the determination of V2 (e.g., infinitival uses of *ha*, or finite uses in embedded clauses; see den Besten (1983), Platzack (1986), and Holmberg (1986)). Although I will not go into any details here, the important point is that this 'deletion' is possible regardless of whether the construction expresses PERFECT or PAST. Using the terminology of Aronoff (1994), this shows

[12]There is a technical question in LFG as to what the discourse functions are assigned to constituents like verbs which otherwise do not bear a GF but are co-heads, annotated $\uparrow=\downarrow$. Assuming that the initial verb in (17c) is a FOCUS, one possibility is to associate just the PRED information of the verb with that FOCUS; cf. King (1995, 232ff.).

that the '*HA*+Supine' construction is a 'morphomic' form, a pure form that is used to express various grammatical features; and no matter which ones it does express, it still has the same overt properties.[13] Hence, we must define a '*HA*+Supine' construction as in (18) and then further specify how it is used, as in (19).

7.4.2 V2 Clauses

Swedish finite clauses are V2 clauses, a familiar property in all of the modern Germanic languages. The second position in a V2 clause is usually considered to be exclusively a finite verb position, but this is not quite accurate, for the Scandinavian languages at least. For example, the Swedish adverb *kanske* ('maybe') can occupy this position, as in (20) from Holmberg and Platzack (1995, 50) (see also Vikner (1995) and Egerland (1998)). This form is derived historically from a collocation meaning 'can happen', but like *maybe* in English, it is not transparent synchronically. Nevertheless, it can carry the clause-typing function in a V2 clause otherwise associated with a finite verb.

(20) Erik kanske inte har (*inte) rest än.
Eric maybe not have.Pres (*not) go.Sup yet
'Eric maybe has not gone yet.'

Here the placement of negation relative to the finite verb *har* shows that that verb is within VP, rather than occupying a higher inflectional position in I or C. More relevantly for present purposes, (20) shows that the second position is not a position characterized by tense; rather, the second position has some morpho-syntactic marking feature, which is borne by all finite verb forms and *kanske*, and it is the expression of this marking feature in second position which signals a V2 structure. *kanske* can also appear in the second position in a non-subject-initial clause, as in (21), from Egerland (1998).

(21) Det kanske han inte gjorde.
it maybe he not do.Past
'Perhaps he did not do it.'

Additionally, Yes-No interrogatives, which effectively are 'V1' clauses, can have the clause-typing function expressed by the non-verbal form *månne*, and hence, the examples in (22) are basically equivalent.

(22) a. Har Sara varit här?
have.Pres Sara be.Sup here
'Has Sara been here?'

[13] See Sells (2003b) for an account of '*ha*-deletion' building on the analysis developed here.

b. Månne Sara har varit här?
Q Sara have.Pres be.Sup here
'Has Sara been here?'

These facts show that the expression of the clause-type by the element in the second position (or initial position in a Yes-No interrogative) is not determined by the values PRES or PAST of the feature TENSE, which are the only finite values in Swedish. Rather, there is some marking feature, which is present on all finite verbs, *kanske* and *månne*, and it is this feature which must be expressed in a V2 clause. Under the realizational approach, there is no reason not to take this feature to be the (form) feature Finite, with the value +.[14] *kanske* and *månne* can be considered to have lost their specification of the feature Tense, leaving them unable to express TENSE, but to retain the Finite feature from their earlier verbal existence.

Using standard structures in X′ theory (e.g., Chomsky (1986)), it has been assumed that V2 involves an initial specifier position followed by a head, which we now know carries the feature Finite. However, the expression of V2 cannot be characterized simply as a specifier immediately followed by a Finite-bearing element, at least in Swedish. This is because the Finite-bearing element can be pushed into third position by certain scope-bearing adverbials. The example in (23) is taken from Engdahl (1998); part (b) continues the assertion in (a), showing that the scope of 'only' is the constituent consisting of the verb and object.

(23) a. Lisa bara [$_{\text{FOC}}$ läste TIDNINGEN] ...
Lisa only [$_{\text{FOC}}$ read the.newspaper] ...
'Lisa only [$_{\text{FOC}}$ read the newspaper].'

b. hon lagade inte MIDDAGEN.
she prepared not dinner
'She did not [$_{\text{FOC}}$ prepare dinner].'

Egerland (1998) suggests that *bara* can appear in the apparent second position in virtue of its cliticizing onto the verb, so that the second position is really occupied by [*bara*+V]. However, the examples in (23) clearly show that *bara* scopes over a verb plus all of its arguments, at least a VP and probably an I′ (see (24)).[15] These scope considerations

[14] In Sells (2001c) I used μ for the relevant feature name; here I switch to the more transparent 'Finite'. Although it is not relevant to the main points of this paper, there is an issue as to whether the form feature Finite should have a corresponding FINITE attribute in f-structure. For simplicity here, I assume here that it does not, though in Sells (2003b) I develop a detailed argument that there is indeed a FINITE attribute in f-structure.

[15] In Sells (2001c) I argued that subject-initial V2 clauses in Swedish are IPs, rather than adopting the uniform CP approach for all V2 clauses (see e.g., Schwartz

suggest the following structure for (23a), and so in certain cases forced by scope, the finite verb must be in the third position in the clause.

(24)

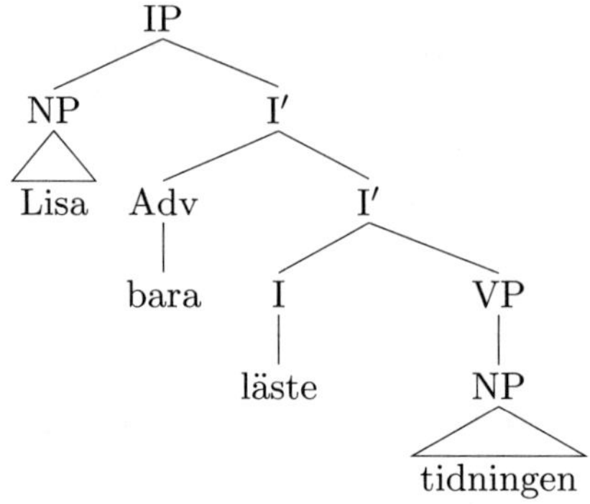

The argument that *bara* is adjoined as in (24) presupposes that the right generalization for the examples in (23) is not "*bara* takes scope over the part of the sentence which follows it" but rather "*bara* takes scope over the c-structure constituent to which it is adjoined". In contrast to (23a), in (25), *bara* scopes only over the following verb.

(25) Lisa bara [$_{\text{FOC}}$ LÄSTE] tidningen ...
Lisa only [$_{\text{FOC}}$ read] the.newspaper ...

While it is possible that intonation alone disambiguates the scope of *bara*, I will suppose that intonation is to some extent read off of phrase structure, and that (25) would have a structure like (24) except that *bara* would be adjoined to I, not I′. In this way, the scope of *bara* is the c-structure constituent to which it is adjoined.

Nothing as such forces the Finite-bearing element to be in second position, though as the head of an X′ projection such as IP or CP, it will naturally be in that position (e.g., (34) below). Adjunction to the intermediate I′ or C′ is extremely restricted, but just in such cases, the Finite-bearing element will actually be in third position, as we have seen. Regardless, this feature of the head will percolate to the whole X′ projection, and so we can express the structure for V2 as in (26a) (see Sells (2001c)). What is key here is the information that the structure carries, not its internal form. We know that we need two crucial pieces of information: there must be some IP or CP bearing the feature Finite:+, which is schematized here as an FP headed by a F^0 element from (26c)); and the FP must dominate an initial category bearing a Grammaticized Discourse Function, which is one of SUBJ, TOPIC, or FOCUS in LFG (see

and Vikner (1996)). However, the choice of category label does not affect the arguments here, which are only about structure.

Bresnan (2001)). These functions are expressed in the specifier positions of IP or CP. The syntactic account of V2 is summarized in (26a–d).

(26) a. The structure for V2:

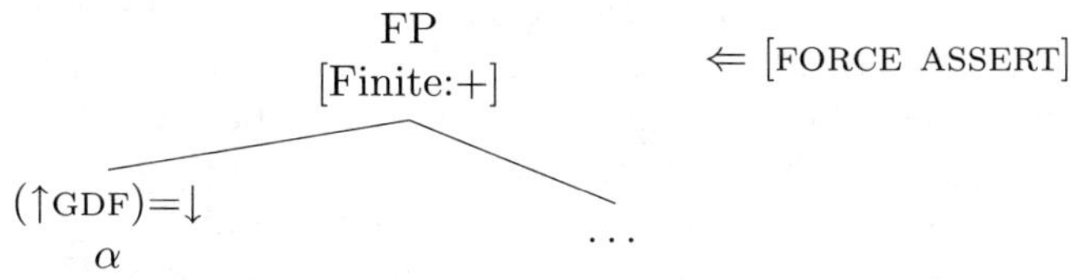

b. FP is either CP or IP.

c. [Finite:+] is carried by all Finite verbs and *kanske*, etc.

d. The GDFs are SUBJ, TOPIC, or FOCUS (which appear in SpecIP or SpecCP).

In stating the structure as in (26a), the assumption is that the Finite marking in (26c) is a c-structure morpho-syntactic feature, shared by every node on the projection of F, as a standard X′ head feature. On the semantic-pragmatic side, this structure entails "Speaker's Assertion" (see Andersson (1985), Wechsler (1991)), and hence I include the f-structure attribute-value specification [FORCE ASSERT] as the syntactic information expressed by (26a) (see also Sells (2003a)).

Crucially, it is the combination of properties in (26a) which expresses V2: neither an initial GDF nor an X′ head which bears Finite express V2 alone. Hence it is only the whole construction which expresses V2. As given, (26a) is not purely about c-structure, for the specifier is annotated (↑GDF)=↓ which is a description of the c-to-f-structure mapping. In certain circumstances, Swedish allows 'topic drop' where the GDF that would be initial in (26a) is implicit from context but is not overtly expressed. The examples in (27) are from Platzack (1998):

(27) a. Vill du ha en kopp kaffe? — Tror inte det, tack.
will you have a cup coffee? think not it, thanks
'Will you have a cup of coffee?' — '(I) think not, thanks.'

b. Hej! Ligger på stranden och skriver detta.
hi! lie on the.beach and write this.

Har badat hala dagen.
have swum every day
'Hi, (I) am lying on the beach writing this. (I) have been in the sea every day.'

It would be possible to postulate a null (structural) topic for such examples, and this is proposed in Platzack (1998). Another analysis could be given simply in terms of the information that the structure is carrying. Note that the examples in (27) can be rooted in an FP bearing Finite—the *tror inte det* part of (27a) is an IP as it has the finite verb *tror* in the I position, preceding negation. What is missing is the subject, which is clearly topical. Hence the same information that is defined by the V2 structure in (26a) is available to the hearer, but the TOPIC/SUBJ is not overt. Nevertheless, this GDF would be represented at the level of f-structure. In other words, if we split out the c- and f-structure information as shown in (28) for the structural part of (26a), repeated here, this would then cover both regular V2 clauses (FPs with an overt specifier expressing the GDF of SUBJ) and the 'topic drop' examples above, where there is no overt specifier.

(28) c-str: + f-str: $\Leftarrow$ [FORCE ASSERT]

$$\begin{array}{c} \text{FP}_1 \\ \text{[Finite:+]} \end{array} \quad f_1 \begin{bmatrix} \text{GDF} & \begin{bmatrix} \ldots & \ldots \end{bmatrix} \\ \ldots & \ldots \end{bmatrix}$$

That is, (28) is satified when there is a GDF in the f-structure corresponding to the root node FP; but it does not require that the GDF be expressed as an overt specifier of FP. If FP is IP, with no overt specifier, we will have examples like those in (27). If FP is CP with no overt specifier, what will be overt is a Finite-bearing element in C, presumably followed by a SUBJ in SpecIP. This will have exactly the overt form of a V1 polarity question (cf. (22a), and so would be difficult for a hearer to interpret as a topic-dropped declarative. For this reason, I would assume that the canonical example of topic-drop involve IPs, not CPs, though not for any formal syntactic reason.

The fact that Finite needs to be marked, possibly independently of tense, sheds light on examples like (1), repeated here, which have a focussed finite verb in first position and the finite supporting verb *gör* ('do') in the second position.

(1) Skriver gör han sällan.
write.Pres do.Pres he seldom
'He seldom WRITES.'

From a standard perspective, it is rather puzzling here that there are two expressions of present tense (and putting *skriver* into its base form *skriva* would be ungrammatical), but on the more complex view of features proposed here, it is *skriver* that is expressing TENSE PRES, but not marking Finite, as it is not in second position, and the function of *gör* is precisely to mark Finite. I take up the analysis of this example again in section 7.5.5 below.

7.5 Multiple Exponence In OT-LFG

As we saw in section 7.3, due to the unification-based nature of LFG, multiple exponence can happen because it is a possibility allowed by the c-to-f-structure relationship. I will use the key insight of the fact of multiple correspondence from Niño's work, in the somewhat different account that follows.

Recently, LFG has been combined with Optimality Theory, with many promising and enlightening results (see, for example, Bresnan (2000), Kuhn (2001a), and Sells (2001b)). Initially, though, moving to OT-LFG seems initially to be a retrograde step, with regard to multiple exponence: if the c-structure is an expression of the f-structure information, multiple exponence appear to be a massive violation of faithfulness, as the same piece of INPUT information is realized multiple times. The family of faithfulness constraints includes MAX constraints (which require that every element of the INPUT has a correspondent in the OUTPUT: "no deletion"), and DEP constraints (which require that every element of the OUTPUT has a correspondent in the INPUT: "no insertion"). If we take the example of ASPECT PROG from (11), that piece of INPUT information is expressed not once, but four times, and this appears to be a violation of DEP.

What I would like to suggest here is that if we take the lead of recent formal developments in LFG and OT-LFG, in particular the work of Kuhn (2001b, 2001a), we can show that what seemed to be a problem is in fact a virtue, for there are actually multiple correspondents for certain pieces of INPUT information, and, therefore, faithfulness constraints would require expression of that INPUT information on each of the correspondents.

7.5.1 The OT-LFG System

The bare outline of OT-LFG is that the INPUT is an underspecified f-structure representing essential semantic and grammatical information, and each candidate is a pair of an f-structure and a corresponding c-structure (see Bresnan (2000)). For any given language, the OUTPUT for a given INPUT is the candidate that fares best with regard to a ranked set of evaluation constraints. Faithfulness constraints hold between the INPUT and the f-structure part of the OUTPUT, and structural markedness constraints hold of the c-structure part of the OUTPUT. This model is elaborated by Kuhn (2001b, 2001a). The overall architecture with respect to a simple example like *Anna will meet Manny* is shown in (29).

(29)

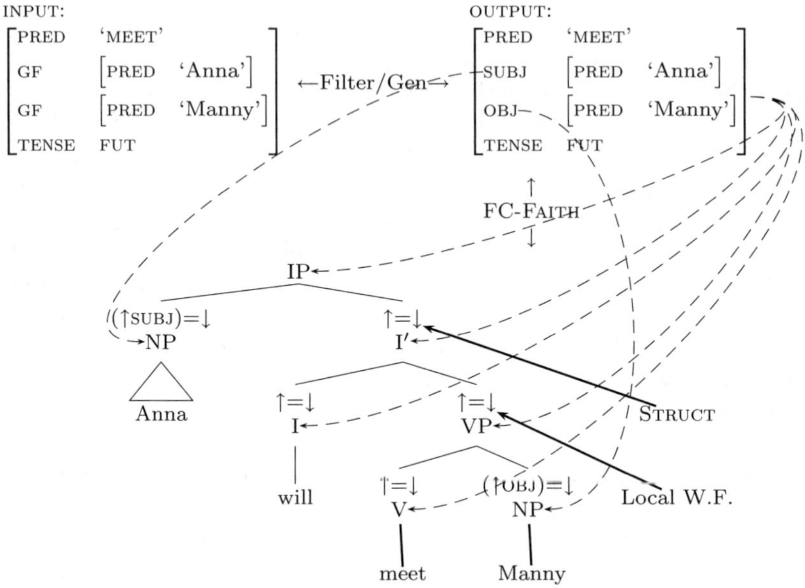

(29) shows that c-structure, which is the overt linguistic expression, is subject not only to Struct constraints, but also to Local Well-Formedness constraints (see section 7.5.3 below).

Starting with the INPUT, it is an underspecified f-structure. The OUTPUT is a pair of an f-structure and a corresponding c-structure. In Kuhn's model, the f-structure part of the OUTPUT must be subsumed by the INPUT: that is, the OUTPUT may contain more information than the INPUT, but it cannot contain less, nor can it contain information that contradicts the INPUT. These are the relations indicated by 'Filter/Gen'.[16]

The OUTPUT itself has faithfulness relations between its two parts: roughly, semantic faithfulness must hold from the c-structure to the f-structure (Dep constraints), and expressive faithfulness must hold from the f-structure to the c-structure (Max constraints). These are the relations that constitute Fc-Faith (called Io-Faith in Kuhn's work). Additionally, following Frank and Zaenen (2002) and Sadler and Spencer (2001), I take it that morphological expression is projected from f-

[16] In Kuhn's approach, context is also part of the INPUT, though I ignore its role here. As can be seen from (29), Filter/Gen must mediate the mapping to grammatical functions such as SUBJ and OBJ; voice is not represented in the INPUT, but is derived via OT constraints. As argued in Aissen (1999) and Sells (2001a), following the work of Legendre et al. (1993), context (discourse prominence) plays an important role in determining voice in the OUTPUT.

structure information: there are principles of morphological expression of the f-structure attributes and values. This is a crucial part of the proposal here, and can be seen in the dotted lines in (29). For the f-structure nucleus, there are corresponding nodes IP, I′, I, VP and V, as each is annotated $\uparrow=\downarrow$ in the c-structure. These are the co-heads, and they are, in principle, the nodes which should express the information of the main nucleus.

Thinking about morphological expression of syntactic features, the effect of the ideas mentioned above is to turn around the dotted assocation lines in (11), so that now they run from the f-structure to the (leaves of the) c-structure, as in (29). Now, as noted above, there are several co-heads in the c-structure, and each is in correspondence via $\uparrow=\downarrow$ with the same f-structure. That is to say, for the f-structure clause nucleus, there are many corresponding pieces of c-structure which are correspondents in virtue of being co-heads, and several of those are co-heads with direct morphological expression (i.e., any X^0 node annotated $\uparrow=\downarrow$ (or $\uparrow=_H\downarrow$)). Faithfulness constraints can therefore force expression of the INPUT information for each morphological correspondent. Simply put, this leads to the conclusion that multiple exponence should be the norm; other constraints will come in to control exactly how many times each feature is expressed. What is noteworthy about this approach is that the possibility of multiple exponence arises without any special constraints or copying procedures, and in fact, copying or spreading is not really capturing the right insight: under the approach here, each piece of information is spelled out on its correspondent a maximum of one time; it just happens that some pieces of information have many correspondents.

The way that MAX and DEP constraints work can be illustrated using a familiar case, namely that of '*do*-insertion' in English, as in (30a). Following the analysis of *do* proposed in Grimshaw (1997), and updated in the OT-LFG setting by Bresnan (2000) and Kuhn (2001b, 2001a), the PRED information will be as shown in (30b); but this information is not represented in the f-structure when *do* is used as a dummy verb. In other words, the dummy use of *do* is unfaithful to the PRED information: semantically-based information associated with the word in c-structure is not matched in the f-structure. The information fails to flow from c-structure to f-structure, which is a DEP violation in Kuhn's proposal. On the other hand, the morphological inflection on *did* can and will express the TENSE PAST information in the INPUT, by (19c) above, repeated here. Intuitively, this information (correctly) flows from f-structure to c-structure, as satisfaction of a MAX constraint.

(30) a. Manny did not sleep.

b. *did* V, (↑PRED)='do ⟨x⟩'

(19) c. Tense:Past ⇐ TENSE PAST (+ ASPECT UNMARKED)

(30b) actually represents a mixture of the morphological and realizational approaches, but I will continue to use such informal representations as they are more transparent with regard to the points under discussion. Strictly, on the realizational approach, the PRED information in (30b) is contributed by the lexeme *DO*, of which *did* happens to be the exponent of Tense:Past; and by (19c), that is the expression of TENSE PAST.

7.5.2 C-structure–F-structure relations

Let us first consider a little more carefully how the relevant grammatical information should be represented. To do this, I will show a representation for a complex predicate in the system of Andrews and Manning (1999), which is flexible enough to allow multiple predicates to be c-structure co-heads, as desired.[17] Andrews and Manning (1999, 14) partition the information in syntactic structures into five types:

(31) a. κ: X′ categories such as N, V, etc.

b. β: the BAR attribute in X′-theory.

c. ρ: grammatical relations (GFs in LFG).

d. α: argument-structure attributes (below, represented as LCS and TERMS).

e. μ: morphosyntactic features.

Andrews and Manning (AM) argue that a complex predicate is a structure in which two separate argument structures stand in some structured relation to each other (one embedded inside the other, in the examples I discuss here) while the grammatical function information of the expression of their arguments is merged into a single f-structure nucleus. Roughly speaking, this means that the semantics is biclausal while the syntax is monoclausal. AM restrict the ↑=↓ mechanism of standard LFG to each of the five information-types in (31), which will allow selective inheritance of some particular type of information. For example, in a standard X′ structure, the mother node inherits the κ information from the structure's head, but not the β information.

The inheritance of different types of f-structure information is governed by structure-function annotations, as is standard in LFG. Direct inheritance into the f-structure is represented as '=$\{x\}$', for any

[17] Other representations for complex predicates, such as those given in Butt (1995) or Alsina (1997), would be alternatives here.

choice(s) of x from the relevant Greek letters in (31). Hence $\uparrow=\downarrow$ in standard LFG would correspond to '$=\{\rho, \alpha, \mu\}$', which covers all of the information types represented at f-structure.

The representational system provides semantic and syntactic parts for complex predicates, allowing them to have semantic embedding without necessarily having an embedded structure syntactically; even though these feature structures encode more information than traditional LFG f-structures, for simplicity I will continue to refer to them as f-structures. For our purposes here, the crucial information is in the α and ρ partitions. I will deal with the μ-type information in a different way from Andrews and Manning (1999), due to the realizational approach that I adopt.

To see an example of how the system will work, let us take (32), a Swedish example with a parasitic supine:

(32) Han har velat läst den.
he have.Pres want.Sup read.Sup it
'He wanted to read it.'

Limiting ourselves first to just one piece of information in the f-structure of this example, namely that of ASPECT PERF, we know that that must involve the expression of *HA*, and a Supine form (from section 7.4.1). Now, on the assumption that the three verbs in (32) form a complex predicate, in the way described above in section 7.3, a single f-structure clause nucleus will be in the same mapping relation to all of them, via the chain of nodes annotated $\uparrow=\downarrow$ in the c-structure. So we need to ask the question, *which* of the X^0 correspondents of the f-structure nucleus actually do express the relevant information?

We begin with the f-structure, because in the OT approach we can start with what needs to be expressed, and then consider candidate expressions (c-structures) of that information. The f-structure of (32) is shown in (33); instead of a PRED attribute, the verb 'want' has a Lexical Conceptual Structure (LCS) with two semantic arguments, U and V. The nucleus also has two TERM arguments (core GFs), U and W, where U is the subject. These express the argument-structure properties of 'want'.[18] The V argument of 'want' is not associated with a GF (such as XCOMP), but is a separate predication under the ARG attribute, which is α information in this system (but not ρ information). The embedded predicate is 'read', which has arguments U and W, and TERMs U and W. The pronoun 'it' is the object of the complex predicate "want-read". I have added the notations on the left to indicate how the different parts

[18]This is quite like the account of argument structure in HPSG; see for example Manning et al. (1999) or Manning and Sag (1998).

of this structure are expressed under a realizational approach.

(33)

Expression	F-structure	
A FORM OF *VILJA*	LCS	[*want*(U,V)]
	TERMS	⟨U,W⟩
A FORM OF *LÄSA*	ARG	[LCS [*read*(U,W)] TERMS ⟨U,W⟩]$_V$
han	SUBJ	[PRED 'he']^U
den	OBJ	[PRED 'it']^W
A PRESENT FORM	TENSE	PRES
HA + A SUPINE FORM	ASPECT	PERF
(See (26a) above)	FORCE	ASSERT

The semantic predicate 'want' must be expressed by a form of the lexeme *VILJA*; 'read' is expressed by a form of *LÄSA*. The expression of the pronouns is straightforward. The grammatical features of TENSE and ASPECT require the forms shown, and the expression of V2 is as in (26) above.

The c-structure of (32) is shown in (34). Structurally, it is unsurprising, but the annotations are of interest.

(34)

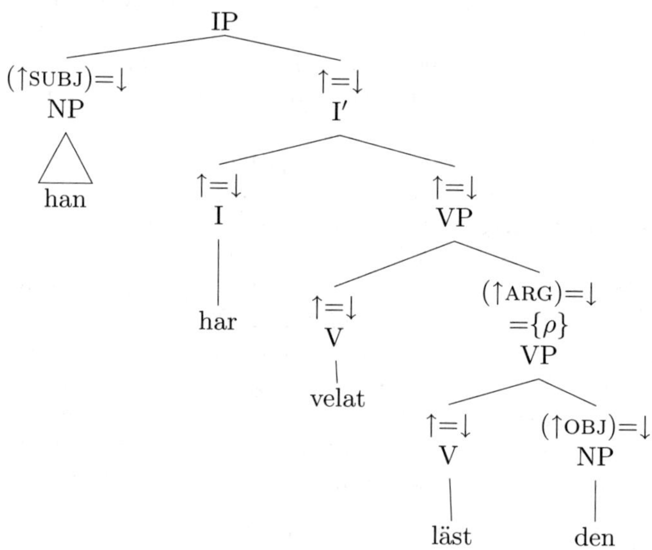

The standard annotation $\uparrow=\downarrow$ means here that information of all types is mapped from a given node to the f-structure nucleus: for example, both α and ρ information associated with I, I′, and the higher V and VP map directly to the outer nucleus in (33). As only these two types of information are relevant here, $\uparrow=\downarrow$ in standard LFG is equivalent to $=\{\alpha\}$, $=\{\rho\}$ in the notation of Andrews and Manning.

For the lower VP in (34), only its ρ information is directly inherited, while its argument-structure properties appear as the value of an ARG attribute in the outer nucleus. In other words, the annotations in (34) are just like standard LFG annotations, with the exception that only the ρ (GF) information from the lower VP is directly mapped to the f-structure nucleus, while the α information (which is the LCS and TERMS information of 'read') is mapped as the value of an ARG attribute.

Note that *har* in (34) is treated as a co-head with its sister VP, which is only possible if *har* lacks an LCS (or lacks a PRED, in standard LFG), for the head of the VP complement *velat* certainly has an LCS. This use of *HA* without any LCS value is parallel to the account of *DO* given above in (30), derived by forcing a faithfulness violation, and is required by the *HA*+Supine construction as given in (18).

Intuitively (33) expresses the grammatical information of a clause, and the c-structure of that clause is (34). With regard to the realization of inflectional features, I am following the idea that each of the verbal heads in (34) could be involved in the realization of clausal inflectional features. To make this clear, I will define a notion of 'correspondent' for the f-to-c-structure mapping:

(35) Correspondent
For an f-structure f, a c-structure correspondent of f is any node whose ρ information maps to f.

Practically, what this means for the whole f-structure in (33), each node in (34) annotated $\uparrow=\downarrow$ or $=\{\rho\}$ is a correspondent of it, so there are potentially multiple correspondents. Given the lexicalist basis of LFG, only X^0 correspondents are relevant (they are the overt manifestations of form), so there are three correspondents for the outer f-structure in (33). Consequently, the realizational approach to expressing ASPECT PERF requires that the f-structure containing that information should have a correspondent that is a form of the lexeme *HA*, and the f-structure should have a correspondent in the Supine form. In fact, there must be two separate correspondents, for the *HA*+Supine construction in (18) (actually, the AVC in (16)) calls for two constituents.

Now in standard LFG, slightly revised for the Andrews and Manning format, we might propose the lexical entry for *har* with the morphological properties and defining constraints shown in (36).

(36) *har* V, ((↑FORCE)=ASSERT)
(↑TENSE)=PRES
((↑LCS)=[*have*(X,Y)])

The first line shows *har* with the clause specification FORCE ASSERT, which must be optional as the finite form *har* may appear in both V2 clauses which have assertive force and non-V2 clauses, which do not. The second line provides the f-structure attribute TENSE with the value PRES. The final line of (36) of the entry indicates that the *have* relation is the value of the LCS attribute. This is also optional, for when *har* is used an auxiliary, it cannot have any LCS information, as it is a co-head with the main verb.

The hypothetical entry in (36) is problematic in two respects: first, the optionality in the specifications, which are necessary for the cases when *har* is not used in the way that the positive descriptions dictate. Second and more serious, the treatment of assertive force is wrong: (36) should not specify FORCE ASSERT itself, because *har* by itself does not determine a V2 clause. This is another manifestation of the by-now familiar problem for morpheme-based approaches posed by constructional expressions.

Let us compare the failed attempt in (36) with a realizational approach to *HA*, in which we have a different array for *har*, as shown in (37):

(37) *har* V, Finite:+
Tense:Pres
HA: (↑LCS)=[*have*(X,Y)]

Here, I have rather distorted the realizational model to make it look more parallel to the morphological one; what *har* really is of course is just one of the inflectional forms of *HA*. Hence *HA* provides the LCS information shown in (37), and the other inflectional information is just the set of realizational features for this specific form. The Finite feature is correctly treated as a morphological feature: a purely formal feature that is involved in the expression of the clause type information (cf. (26a)). *HA* only projects its semantic (LCS) information from c- to f-structure, and its other properties are expressive: it can express TENSE, and in construction with a supine, it can express ASPECT. Note that the view we now have of the grammar does not say that these attributes must be expressed by *har*, only that they may be. This builds in a kind of optionality into the way the system works; on the morpheme-based view, such optionality must be explicitly stated, as in the treatment of the FORCE attribute in (36).

Along the same lines, *läst* will have the 'entry' in (38).

(38) *läst* V, Form:Supine
LÄSA: (↑LCS)=[*read*(U,V)]

Finally, for comparison, *läsa* will have the 'entry' in (39).

(39) *läst* V, *LÄSA*: (↑LCS)=[*read*(U,V)]

This is just the default form of the lexeme: in the realizational model, the Base form of a verb corresponds to taking the lexeme and doing nothing to it.

7.5.3 General OT-Based Constraints on Expression

Returning to the theme of multiple exponence, the intuition that I am pursuing is that because the f-structure (33) has multiple correspondents, as defined in (35), a realization rule that says that ASPECT PERF is realized (in part) as a Supine form will find several different potential c-structure expressions, leading to multiple exponence. However, if this is so, then why do we not find examples where all clause-level information, including TENSE, FORCE, ASPECT, etc., is multiply expressed? Why is multiple exponence not the normal case? In (32), a Supine form appears twice, not three times, and a Present form appears only once, on the verb in INFL. Moreover, the *HA* part of the expression of ASPECT PERF only appears once, even though there are two Supine forms.

The reason why multiple exponence is not so common is that, as in any OT analysis, there are several different types of constraint which place conflicting requirements on expression, and it is the relative ranking of constraints which determines surface form, or rather, which determines from a set of surface forms which one is the best, as an expression of the INPUT information. Let us look at some general considerations and then move to more specific instances for the examples at hand. In (40) I list several different types of constraint that the overall analysis will have.

(40) **Types of Constraint on Morphological Expression**

a. c-structural form selection, e.g., the form of some verb's complement is a Supine form.
b. f-structural selection, e.g., *vilja* takes an ARG complement, as opposed to an XCOMP (see section 7.4.1 above).
c. projection from f-structure to morphological features in the exponents in c-structure, e.g., Tense:Past ⇐ TENSE PAST.
d. structural markedness in morphology, e.g., avoidance of structure as expressed by *Affix, *Inflection, etc. (see Sells (1998),

Aissen (1999)).

e. positional markedness in syntax, e.g., a Supine form never appears in INFL.

f. local well-formedness of morphology, e.g., every participle in Finnish is marked for person (cf. (9)).

The structural markedness (STRUCT) constraints in morphology have been alluded to above and are familiar: structural constraints on output forms which disfavor certain kinds of structure. In the basic conception of OT, STRUCTural markedness constraints disfavor overt expression, while FAITHfulness constraints (specifically, the MAX constraints) favor overt expression. The simplest kind of morphological markedness constraint such as *Affix or *Inflection will of course disfavor multiple exponence, as it disfavors any kind of morphological expression at all. I use $^*\text{STRUCT}_V$ to represent the relevant markedness constraint for the data under consideration: in the realizational model, it really means 'use the least inflected form of V'. This would have the consequence that a Base form is preferable to a Supine.

Hence there is a tension with any positive requirements of form selection in the c-structure, such as the Supine when it appears with *HA*. Interestingly, the *have*- and *be*-type auxiliaries always seem to select for more specified forms in their uses as parts of periphrastic exponents. These positive specifications of features are therefore candidates for multiple expression just in case there are multiple correspondents.

We might also normally say that a modal verb like *vilja* in Swedish or *can* in English selects for a particular morphological form on its complement—a bare or base form. In fact, though, there is no reason to suppose that the base form has any (morphological) features, but rather it is the form with the absence of any specification. In realizational approaches, the base form is that exponent which is derived by no change from the form of the lexeme itself. Consequently, in general, this is the form that should get 'overwritten' in cases of multiple exponence, as no other element is positively selecting for its form.

There may also be local well-formedness conditions operating in the morphology, as in (40f). This is again a very familiar aspect of morphology; for example, in Korean (see Cho and Sells (1995), Yoon (1995)), each verb may just be a morphological stem which requires some kind of suffix in order to be morpho(-phono)logically well-formed. Hence, by requiring some morphological expression, such constraints may indirectly favor multiple exponence. This could also be the case with Dagaare verbs, as noted above at the end of section 7.3. In Finnish, it seems that participles used in the clause necessarily inflect for person, again leading to the potential for multiple exponence (see (9)). However, in Swedish, uninflected forms (base forms) are clearly acceptable as they stand, so multiple exponence cannot be driven by the need for inflection.

A different kind of constraint from (40) is selection in the f-structure, which bounds the conditions for multiple exponence. If a verb has a PRED feature and selects for a particular kind of GF complement, the two verbs cannot be contributing to the same nucleus; this arises, for example if the complement expresses the XCOMP complement of the main verb. In such cases, there can be no multiple exponence, as by definition, the two verbs do not correspond to the same nucleus.[19] However, if the predicate takes an ARG complement, this is effectively a complex predicate, and there are more c-structure correspondents of the same f-structure.

OT also recognizes the existence of positional markedness constraints: a certain kind of element is not necessarily marked per se, but is marked in a certain position. For example, the Swedish Supine is never realized on a verb in I; hence the Supine can only possibly appear on verbs inside a VP. Additionally, finite forms are always the leftmost verbs, even in embedded clauses where there is no I node, and it is generally the case that if any verb has a Tense form, it is the leftmost verb (see (43d) below).

Finally, the realization constraints in (40c) are the kinds of constraints presented above in (19): certain syntactic features of an f-structure can be expressed by certain morpho-syntactic expressions. These constraints therefore belong to the OT family of MAX constraints, though their more precise interpretation is discussed immediately below.

This has been a rather brief overview of the different types of constraint that on overall OT analysis will have. In the final subsection of the paper, I introduce more specific versions of these general types, as part of my account of the option of multiple exponence with regard to the Supine in Swedish.

7.5.4 Parasitic Morphology

Going back to the expression of the f-structure in (33), the two structures in (41) illustrate the case of the parasitic supine and the normal base form complement, respectively. For compactness I subscript the relevant morphological features on each c-structure head and its projection. The insight from Wiklund (2001) is that it is the lack of fea-

[19]The restriction to the same clause may not be general enough to cover all cases of multiple exponence; see footnote 6.

ture specification on the base form which allows the supine features to 'spread' onto it. We know that there are competing kinds of constraint; in favor of realization is the MAX constraint for ASPECT PERF which will somehow prefer a '*HA*+Supine' form of every X^0 correspondent in the c-structure; and against inflectional realization is the markedness constraint $*\text{STRUCT}_V$ which prefers a base form of every verb. Essentially, then, allowing reranking of these two constraints will give the two observed surface forms, as in (41)–(42) below. For simplicity, I use standard LFG notation for the annotations.

(41)

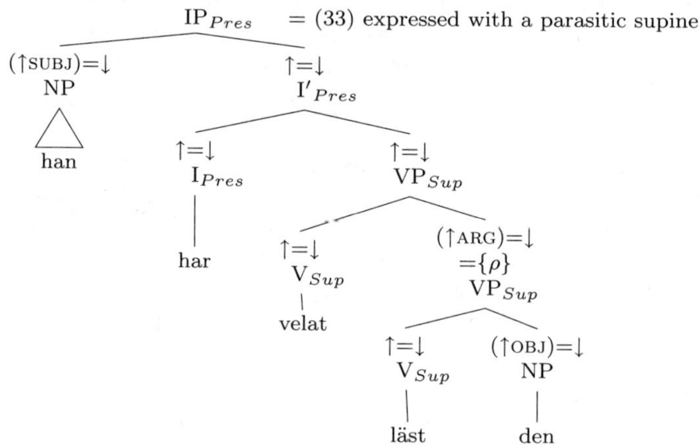

(42)

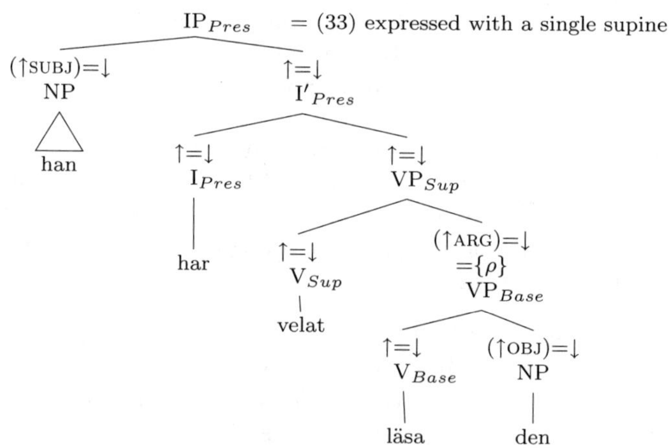

The overall form of the c-structure is determined by properties of Swedish X′-theory (see Sells (2001c)), as are the structure-function annotations. The semantic embedding in (32) requires that the exponents of *HA* and *VILJA* are true co-heads, while the exponent of *LÄSA* is an

ARG complement. This much is taken as given in (41)–(42). The analysis will use the constraints in (43), which can relate (33) and the structures in (41)–(42) when appropriately ranked.

(43) a. MAX(ATTRIB): each attribute A has an exponent in the c-structure.
(intuitively, every grammatical feature is expressed somewhere)

b. IDENT-IO(ATTRIB): each attribute A and its value is expressed on A's correspondent.
(intuitively, every grammatical feature is expressed with the correct value, on each correspondent; this prefers 'feature spreading' everywhere)

c. *STRUCT$_V$: avoid inflected morphological structure on V.

d. TENSE-LEFT: the correspondent of TENSE is as left/high in the structure as possible.
(this prefers the expression of TENSE on just one verb)

As OT regulates correspondences between different structures, we assume that there are many c-structures which could stand in an expressive relation to an f-structure, and look at how each constraint filters down the set of available structures. In the case at hand, we are considering what c-structures can be expressions of (33), and the formal parts of the analysis here determine and constrain those correspondences. Following Bresnan (2000) and Kuhn (2001a), I assume that MAX constraint is satisfied with the correct expression of both attribute and value on some correspondent (i.e., when any one of the realizational principles is satisfied). A stronger requirement comes from IDENT-IO constraints, which I interpret as requiring a form expressing the right attribute and value on each correspondent (cf. Kager (1999, 205ff.)).

A further assumption is that constructional exponents satisfy these faithfulness constraints by being interpreted as sets of properties that the c-structure or c-structure/f-structure pair has. In the case of the expression of ASPECT PERF, IDENT-IO essentially looks for pairs of { form of *HA*, Form:Supine }, for as many pairs of correspondents as there are. So a c-structure with one *HA* and two Supines in it satisfies IDENT-IO more than a structure with just one Supine (two pairs vs. one). In each case, of course, there will be other pairs of correspondents that do not have the correct properties and which violate the constraint, but these will effectively 'cancel out'.

A Supine form where a Base form would be otherwise expected is a relatively innocuous change, and this is why multiple exponence for inflectional material is possible. However, multiple exponence never seems to involve 'extra' lexemes: we never see multiple forms of *HA*, and, as noted above, while Swedish allows multiple exponence of the morphological passive form as seen in (6) and (7), such multiplication never happens with the periphrastic passive construction that the language has. The reason for this lack of multiple exponence with constructions, at least with auxiliary-verb constructions, is that the use of each auxiliary verb is unfaithful to its LCS or PRED information, and the constraints which regulate semantic faithfulness are always very highly ranked. Consequently, we expect to see evidence of multiple exponence only in the morphological domain.[20]

In order to see how the pieces of the analysis account for the Swedish data involving supines, we can now consider the local effects of the different constraints, summarized below in (44). In cases where constraints conflict, the constraint ranking will determine which one takes preference.

(44) a. The c-structure must have realizations of the lexemes *HA, VILJA, LÄSA*; the last two are needed by faithfulness (MAX) constraints with respect to LCS information; and *HA* is required by the expression of ASPECT PERF.

b. TENSE-LEFT assures only *har* is finite: *har vilja läsa* (Pres-Base-Base) fares better than *har vill läsa* (Pres-Pres-Base), for *vill* violates the constraint while *vilja* does not.

c. V2 (as in (26)) ensures that *har* appears in INFL, to provide the Finite feature.

d. Assuming that the first verb is *har*, then *vilja läsa* (Base-Base) fully satisfies $*\text{STRUCT}_V$, but violates IDENT-IO (ASPECT) twice, as neither of these verb forms is Supine, and, crucially, the sequence violates MAX (ASPECT), as there is no exponent of ASPECT at all.

e. Assuming that the first verb is *har*, then *velat läst* (Sup-Sup) satisfies MAX (ASPECT) and satisfies IDENT-IO (ASP) as much as possible, but violates $*\text{STRUCT}_V$ twice.

f. Assuming that the first verb is *har*, then *velat läsa* (Sup-Base) satisfies MAX (ASPECT) but violates IDENT-IO (ASPECT) and $*\text{STRUCT}_V$ once each.

[20] This prediction only follows on the assumption that auxiliary verbs have LCS values which go unused (violating faithfulness), and therefore is another reason to prefer the account of apparent optionality resulting from constraint conflict in OT rather than the simple direct statement of optionality as in (36).

g. Assuming that the first verb is *har*, then *vilja läst* (Base-Sup) violates MAX (ASPECT) and IDENT-IO (ASPECT)

The effect of MAX constraints is to ensure that each piece of grammatical information in the INPUT is present somewhere in the OUTPUT. While IDENT constraints will favor multiple exponence, other markedness constraints like $*\text{STRUCT}_V$ and alignment constraints like TENSE-LEFT will limit expression to just one element. Hence, the constraint rankings in (45) will guarantee different c-structural expressions, as described after each ranking. There is no crucial evidence for the relative ranking of TENSE-LEFT.

(45) a. MAX(ATTR) $\gg$ IDENT-IO(ASP) $\gg$ $*\text{STRUCT}_V$
yields a Supine form on as many V co-heads as possible.

b. MAX(ATTR) $\gg$ $*\text{STRUCT}_V$ $\gg$ IDENT-IO(ASP)
yields a Supine form on just one V co-head.

The MAX constraint is satified by a pair of X^0 elements in the syntax, one of which is the Supine form; the IDENT constraint prefers as many such pairs as possible, and hence the ranking in (45a) leads to multiple exponence (with respect to the expression of ASPECT). As stated, the account predicts that when there is just one Supine form, but more than one verb other than *HA* which corresponds to the same f-structure as *HA*, it does not matter which of those other verbs is in the Supine form. In other words, alongside *har velat läsa* (Pres-Sup-Base), the account as given predicts *har vilja läst* (Pres-Base-Sup) to be equally available. This is because the auxiliary-verb construction was very loosely defined as in (16), on account of the flexibility of the c-structure relation of the parts, as illustrated by (17).

What is missing from the account is so far is a slightly tighter notion of 'construction', which expresses the idea that the parts of the construction should be local to each other. However, as the examples in (17) show, this must be an OT constraint itself, as the parts should be local to each other unless there is some reason for them to be separated (e.g., due to information-structure properties). I leave this as an open problem for future work.

Finally, the editors of this volume raise the issue of the status of example (46b), in contrast to (46a):

(46) a. Han skulle ha velat läst boken.
He should.Pres have.Base want.Sup read.Sup the.book
'He should have wanted to read the book.'

b.* Han skulle haft velat läst boken.
He should.Pres have.Sup want.Sup read.Sup the.book

The question is why the parasitic supine cannot spread upwards to *HA*, as in the b example. There are two reasons why the example is unacceptable. The first is due to the 'pair' interpretation I gave to the *HA*+Supine construction above: there is no other verb *HA* which can form a pair with the Supine *haft*, so the presence of the Supine inflection in *haft* serves no realizational function at all.

The second reason is semantically-based. Dyvik (1999) observes that while modal auxiliary verbs generally have epistemic and root uses, a modal verb in the Supine form only has a root use. In the analysis here, a root use would correspond to a verb with an LCS value that takes an ARG complement. Thus, it seems that the Supine form is correlated with a non-trivial semantics (LCS), while by assumption *HA* in the *HA*+Supine construction is vacuous with regard to LCS properties.

7.5.5 Multiple Expressions of Tense

The very first example in this paper has two finite verbs in it; a similar example is given in (47):

(47) Sjunger gör han gärna.
sing.Pres do.Pres he readily

The main verb here is in the initial (focus) position, and the TENSE information of the clause is expressed both on it, and on the supporting verb *gör*; hence this is another kind of multiple exponence. By the TENSE-LEFT constraint, we would otherwise expect only one tensed verb, for while *sjunger* does not violate the constraint, *gör* does. In this case, the need to satisfy other constraints renders this an unimportant violation. In order to be in a structural focus position, some form of *SJUNGA* must be in the initial position, and if this is the Tense:Present form, then TENSE-LEFT will also be satisfied. However, this is a main clause, and therefore some form with Finite:+ must be in the head of the highest projection, in second position, due to (26a), and this is the function of *gör*. Unlike dummy uses of *do* in English, which typically are motivated to express TENSE, the use of *gör* here is only to mark Finite.

Now, if this is the right account of the supporting verb in second position, we might ask why (48) is not possible:

(48)* Sjunger gjorde han gärna.
sing.Pres do.Past he readily

In contrast to (47), (48) is ungrammatical. Yet if it is true, as I have argued, that the first verb is the 'true' expression of TENSE, and the second verb is there just to carry the Finite feature, it is not clear why (48) should be ungrammatical. In the analysis I have developed, there are at least two reasons why (48) is grammatical. First, the 'spreading' effects of IDENT-IO(TENSE), which prefers tense to be expressed on every correspondent, are usually overriden by the outranking TENSE-LEFT. But in this example, a TENSE-LEFT violation is unavoidable because a Finite form is necessary in the second position, as part of the expression of V2. In a sense, what we see here is 'The Emergence of the Unmarked' with respect to multiple exponence: it happens because there is no higher-ranking constraint to forbid it.

Additionally, *gjorde* in (48) represents a DEP violation—if it is an inflected form, some attribute of the f-structure or some other verb's selection should be dictating that inflectional form, but there is no such attribute or selection in the clausal information of (48) (by assumption, this is a present tense example).

7.6 Conclusion

In this paper I have developed the foundation of an approach to morphological expression in OT-LFG. The key aspects of the approach are found in its constructional and realizational nature, and in the fact that a clausal nucleus in f-structure has several correspondents in c-structure. This last property leads to multiple exponence, without the need for add-on spreading or copying operations, which is a crucial advantage of the approach advocated here. I have used the OT approach primarily to allow optionality of multiple exponence, though of course much wider typological predictions would be made by a fuller account involving the full range of constraints as outlined in (40).

References

Ackerman, Farrell. 2000. Syntactic expression as morphological exponence. In Proceedings of CLS 2000. Ms. University of California San Diego.

Ackerman, Farrell and Gert Webelhuth. 1998. *A Theory of Predicates*. Stanford, CA: CSLI Publications.

Aissen, Judith. 1999. Markedness and subject choice in Optimality Theory. *Natural Language and Linguistic Theory* 17:673–711.

Alsina, Alex. 1993. *Predicate Composition: A Theory of Syntactic Function Alternations*. Ph.D. thesis, Stanford University.

Alsina, Alex. 1997. Causatives in Bantu and Romance. In A. Alsina, J. Bresnan, and P. Sells, eds., *Complex Predicates*, pages 203–246. Stanford, CA: CSLI Publications.

Ambrazas, Vytautas. 1997. *Lithuanian Grammar*. Vilnius: Institute of the Lithuanian Language.

Andersson, Lars-Gunnar. 1985. *Form and Function of Subordinate Clauses*. Gothenburg University: Department of Linguistics.

Andrews, Avery and Chris Manning. 1999. *Complex Predicates and Information Spreading in LFG*. Stanford, CA: CSLI Publications.

Anward, Jan. 1988. Verb-verb agreement in Swedish. In D. Fekete and Z. Laubitz, eds., *McGill Working Papers in Linguistics: Special Issue on Comparative Germanic Syntax*, pages 1–35. Montréal: Department of Linguistics, McGill University.

Aronoff, Mark. 1994. *Morphology By Itself*. Cambridge, MA: MIT Press.

Barnes, Michael P. and Eivind Weyhe. 1994. Faroese. In E. König and J. van der Auwera, eds., *The Germanic Languages*, pages 190–218. London & New York: Routledge.

Blevins, James P. 2002. Periphrasis as syntactic exponence. Ms. RCEAL, Cambridge.

Brassil, Dan. 2001. Periphrasis, standard lexicalism and realizational lexicalism. Unpublished ms. UC San Diego.

Bresnan, Joan, ed. 1982. *The Mental Representation of Grammatical Relations*. Cambridge, MA: MIT Press.

Bresnan, Joan. 2000. Optimal syntax. In J. Dekkers, F. van der Leeuw, and J. van de Weijer, eds., *Optimality Theory: Phonology, Syntax and Acquisition*, pages 334–385. Oxford: Oxford University Press.

Bresnan, Joan. 2001. *Lexical-Functional Syntax*. Oxford: Blackwell.

Butt, Miriam. 1995. *The Structure of Complex Predicates in Urdu*. Stanford, CA: CSLI Publications.

Butt, Miriam, Tracy Holloway King, María-Eugenia Niño, and Frédérique Segond. 1999. *A Grammar Writer's Cookbook*. Stanford, CA: CSLI Publications.

Cho, Young-mee Yu and Peter Sells. 1995. A lexical account of inflectional suffixes in Korean. *Journal of East Asian Linguistics* 4:119–174.

Chomsky, Noam. 1986. *Barriers*. Cambridge, MA: MIT Press.

Christensen, Kirsti Koch. 1991. Complex passives reanalyzed. *Working Papers in Scandinavian Syntax* 48:45–75.

den Besten, Hans. 1983. On the interaction of root transformations and lexical deletive rules. In W. Abraham, ed., *On The Formal Syntax Of The Westgermania*, pages 47–131. Amsterdam/Philadelphia: John Benjamins.

Dyvik, Helge. 1999. The universality of f-structure: Discovery or stipulation? The case of modals. In M. Butt and T. King, eds., *Proceedings of the LFG99 Conference*. Stanford, CA: CSLI Publications.

Egerland, Verner. 1998. On verb-second violations in Swedish and the hierarchical ordering of adverbs. *Working Papers in Scandinavian Syntax* 61:1–22.

Engdahl, Elisabet. 1998. Inte bara V2 ('Not just V2'). Handout, ms. Gothenburg University.

Falk, Yehuda. 2001. *Lexical-Functional Grammar: An Introduction to Parallel Constraint-Based Syntax*. Stanford, CA: CSLI Publications.

Frank, Anette and Annie Zaenen. 2002. Tense in LFG: Syntax and morphology. In H. Kamp and U. Reyle, eds., *How We Say WHEN It Happens: Contributions to the Theory of Temporal Reference in Natural Language*. Tübingen: Max Niemeyer Verlag. Also reprinted in this volume.

Grimshaw, Jane. 1997. Projection, heads, and optimality. *Linguistic Inquiry* 28:373–422.

Hedlund, Cecilia. 1992. *On Participles*. Stockholm: University of Stockholm, Department of Linguistics.

Holmberg, Anders. 1986. *Word Order and Syntactic Features in the Scandinavian Languages and English*. Stockholm: University of Stockholm, Department of Linguistics.

Holmberg, Anders. 1999. Remarks on Holmberg's generalization. *Studia Linguistica* 53:1–39.

Holmberg, Anders and Christer Platzack. 1995. *The Role of Inflection in Scandinavian Syntax*. New York: Oxford University Press.

Holmes, Philip and Ian Hinchliffe. 1994. *Swedish: A Comprehensive Grammar*. London & New York: Routledge.

Kager, René. 1999. *Optimality Theory*. Cambridge: Cambridge University Press.

Kaplan, Ronald M. and Joan Bresnan. 1982. Lexical-Functional Grammar: A formal system for grammatical representation. In J. Bresnan, ed., *The Mental Representation of Grammatical Relations*, pages 173–281. Cambridge, MA: MIT Press.

King, Tracy Holloway. 1995. *Configuring Topic and Focus in Russian*. Stanford, CA: Dissertations in Linguistics, CSLI Publications.

Kuhn, Jonas. 2001a. *Formal and Computational Aspects of Optimality-Theoretic Syntax*. Ph.D. thesis, Institut für maschinelle Sprachverarbeitung, Universität Stuttgart.

Kuhn, Jonas. 2001b. Generation and parsing in Optimality Theoretic syntax: Issues in the formalization of OT-LFG. In P. Sells, ed., *Formal and Empirical Issues in Optimality Theoretic Syntax*, pages 313–366. Stanford, CA: CSLI Publications.

Legendre, Géraldine, Paul Raymond, and Paul Smolensky. 1993. An Optimality-Theoretic typology of case and grammatical voice systems. In J. Guenter, B. Kaiser, and C. Zoll, eds., *Proceedings of the 19th Annual Meeting of the Berkeley Linguistics Society*, pages 464–478. University of California, Berkeley: Dept. of Linguistics.

Lødrup, Helge. 1996. Properties of Norwegian auxiliaries. In K. Ottósson et al., ed., *Proceedings of The Ninth International Conference of Nordic and General Linguistics*, pages 216–228. Oslo: Novus.

Manning, Christopher and Ivan Sag. 1998. Dissociations between argument structure and grammatical relations. In G. Webelhuth, J.-P. Koenig, and A. Kathol, eds., *Lexical and Constructional Aspects of Linguistic Explanation*, pages 63–78. Stanford, CA: CSLI Publications.

Manning, Christopher, Ivan Sag, and Masayo Iida. 1999. The lexical integrity of Japanese causatives. In R. Levine and G. Green, eds., *Studies in Contemporary Phrase Structure Grammar*, pages 39–79. Cambridge: Cambridge University Press.

Matsumoto, Yo. 1996. *Complex Predicates in Japanese: A Syntactic and Semantic Study of the Notion 'Word'*. Stanford, CA: CSLI Publications.

Matthews, Peter. H. 1972. *Inflectional Morphology*. Cambridge: Cambridge University Press.

Matthews, Peter. H. 1974. *Morphology*. Cambridge: Cambridge University Press.

Niño, María-Eugenia. 1995. A morphologically based approach to split inflection in Finnish. Unpublished ms. Stanford University.

Niño, María-Eugenia. 1997. The multiple expression of inflectional information and grammatical architecture. In F. Corblin, D. Godard, and J.-M. Marandin, eds., *Empirical Issues in Formal Syntax and Semantics*, pages 127–147. Bern: Peter Lang.

Nordlinger, Rachel and Louisa Sadler. 2002. Revisiting morphological composition. Paper presented at LFG2002, Athens.

Platzack, Christer. 1986. COMP, INFL, and Germanic word order. In L. Hellan and K. Koch Christensen, eds., *Topics in Scandinavian Syntax*, pages 185–234. Dordrecht: Reidel.

Platzack, Christer. 1989. The Swedish supine: An active verb form or the non-agreeing form of the Past Participle? In D. Jaspers et al., ed., *Sentential Complementation and the Lexicon: Studies in Honour of Wim de Geest*, pages 305–319. Dordrecht: Foris Publications.

Platzack, Christer. 1998. *Svenskans inre grammatik – det minimalistiska programmet*. Lund: Studentlitteratur.

Rizzi, Luigi. 1978. A restructuring rule in Italian syntax. In S. J. Keyser, ed., *Recent Tranformational Studies in European Languages*, pages 113–158. Cambridge, MA: MIT Press.

Sadler, Louisa and Andrew Spencer. 2001. Syntax as an exponent of morphological features. In G. Booij and J. van Marle, eds., *Yearbook of Morphology 2000*, pages 71–96. Dordrecht: Kluwer Academic Publishers.

Schwartz, Bonnie and Sten Vikner. 1996. The verb always leaves IP in V2 clauses. In A. Belletti and L. Rizzi, eds., *Parameters and Functional Heads: Essays in Comparative Syntax*, pages 11–62. Oxford & New York: Oxford University Press.

Sells, Peter. 1998. Optimality and economy in Japanese and Korean morphosyntax. In N. Akatsuka et al., ed., *Japanese/Korean Linguistics*, vol. 7, pages 499–514. CSLI, Stanford Linguistics Association.

Sells, Peter. 2001a. Form and function in the typology of grammatical voice systems. In G. Legendre, J. Grimshaw, and S. Vikner, eds., *Optimality-Theoretic Syntax*, pages 355–391. Cambridge, MA: MIT Press.

Sells, Peter, ed. 2001b. *Formal and Empirical Issues in Optimality Theoretic Syntax*. Stanford, CA: CSLI Publications.

Sells, Peter. 2001c. *Structure, Alignment and Optimality in Swedish*. Stanford, CA: CSLI Publications.

Sells, Peter. 2003a. Finiteness in non-transformational syntactic frameworks. Ms. Stanford University. To appear in Frans Plank and Irina Nikoleva (eds.) *Finiteness: All Over the Clause.*

Sells, Peter. 2003b. Morphological and constructional expression and recoverability of verbal features. Ms. Stanford University. To appear in C. Orhan Orgun and Peter Sells (eds.) *Morphology and the Web of Grammar: Essays in Memory of Steven G. Lapointe.* Stanford, CA, CSLI Publications.

Spencer, Andrew. 2001. The paradigm-based model of morphosyntax. *Transactions of the Philological Society* 99:279–313.

Stump, Gregory. 2001. *Inflectional Morphology: A Paradigm Structure Approach*. Cambridge: Cambridge University Press.

Vikner, Sten. 1995. *Verb Movement and Expletive Subjects in the Germanic Languages*. New York: Oxford University Press.

Wechsler, Stephen. 1991. Verb second and illocutionary force. In K. Leffel and D. Bouchard, eds., *Views on Phrase Structure*, pages 177–191. Dordrecht: Kluwer Academic Publishers.

Wiklund, Anna-Lena. 1998. Morphosyntactic parasites as underspecified heads: on the Double Supine Construction. Licentiate Thesis, University of Umeå.

Wiklund, Anna-Lena. 2001. Dressing up for Vocabulary Insertion: the Parasitic Supine. *Natural Language and Linguistic Theory* 19:199–228.

Wurmbrand, Susanne. 2001. *Infinitives: Restructuring and Clause Structure*. Berlin/New York: Mouton de Gruyter.

Yoon, James Hye-Suk. 1995. Nominal, verbal, and cross-categorial affixation in Korean. *Journal of East Asian Linguistics* 4:325–356.

Subject Index

Language Index